DIVORCE: A PSYCHOSOCIAL STUDY

For Andrew

Divorce: A Psychosocial Study

SHELLEY DAY SCLATER
University of East London

Ashgate

Aldershot • Brookfield USA • Singapore • Sydney

© Shelley Day Sclater 1999

Published by
Ashgate Publishing Ltd
Gower House
Croft Road
Aldershot
Hants GU11 3HR
England

Ashgate Publishing Company
Old Post Road
Brookfield
Vermont 05036
USA

Ashgate website: http://www.ashgate.com

British Library Cataloguing in Publication Data
Sclater, Shelley Day
    Divorce : a psychosocial study
    1.Divorce - Psychological aspects 2.Divorced people -
    Psychology
    I.Title
    306.8'9

Library of Congress Catalog Card Number: 99-66642

ISBN 1 84014 900 0

Printed and bound by Athenaeum Press, Ltd.,
Gateshead, Tyne & Wear.

Contents

Acknowledgements

My profound thanks go to the women and men who participated in my project, and without whom none of my work would have been possible. I would also like to thank those solicitors, mediators and newspapers who assisted with the recruitment of the participants. For reasons of confidentiality, I will not say their names, but they know who they are.

I have had a great deal of help and an immense amount of encouragement from friends, family and colleagues during the period of this research and the writing of this book. I would like to thank them all. Special thanks go to Margaret O'Brien, Martin Richards and Mavis Maclean for support and encouragement in the early stages when this project and book were only a dream.

I am grateful to the University of East London for providing funding to enable me to carry out the pilot stages of the work, and to my colleagues and students there for their willing tolerance of my preoccupations. The project was funded by the ESRC (Award number R000236323) and I am grateful for their support.

Jackie Brown at the Lord Chancellor's Department, and Marian Roberts at National Family Mediation showed an interest in the project at a crucial stage. Julie Jessop, as my Research Assistant, worked over and beyond the call of duty in doing most of the interviews and covering some of my teaching. She has also worked on the analysis of the quantitative data and kept up to date with the literature on the psychology of divorce (which she reviews in chapter 3).

My thanks also go to my colleagues at the Centre for Family Research, Cambridge, where I spent a sabbatical term as a visiting scholar, analysing data and discussing my ideas; particular thanks to Nina Hallowell, Ginny Morrow and Martin Richards. Many of the ideas in chapter 1 were discussed and worked through with Christine Piper and I am grateful for her inspiration and support. Christine Piper and Lorraine Radford gave useful comments on a draft of chapter 2. My ideas for chapter 4 have had a particularly long gestation; for feedback and support I am particularly grateful to Molly Andrews, Phil Bradbury, Nina Hallowell, Wendy Hollway, Mike Michael, Barry Richards and Candida Yates.

Joanne Brown and Candida Yates were an immense help to me in working through the psychoanalytic ideas which inform my analysis of the narrative interview data, and I would like to say a special thank you to them. Stephanie Macek gave me considerable help with locating bibliographical material.

Poppy Sclater worked long hours for me doing database searches and working on the bibliography. Andrew Sclater has provided invaluable editorial assistance in the final stages of the production of this book. Thanks also to my son Nico for his cheerful tolerance of my absences and preoccupations.

Other colleagues and friends have provided comments, support or inspiration at crucial stages; thanks to Andrew Bainham, Richard Collier, Gwynn Davis, Felicity Kaganas, Ros Minsky, Sian Morgan, Bren Neale, Heather Price, Jeremy Roche and Corinne Squire.

My thanks also go to Avalon Associates of Chelmsford for final checking, formatting and preparation of camera ready copy.

The responsibility for all errors and omissions, though, remains my own. Finally, I am grateful to the Office for National Statistics for permission to use ONS material in chapter 1.

Shelley Day Sclater

Whilst this book was in press, it was announced that the present Government does not intend to implement the provisions of Part 11 of the Family Law Act 1996 in 2000 as originally envisaged (LCD press release No. 159/99). Preliminary results from the Pilot Studies were disappointing and further results are unlikely to be available until 2000. At that time, it is understood that the Government will assess whether further research is needed before the Act can be implemented.

Foreword

Martin Richards

The rising divorce rate over the past century has stimulated a rapidly growing body of research. Much of this has focussed on children and how they may be affected, and on the legal process and particularly the ways in which disputes may be resolved. However, the central actors in the process, the separating husband and wife, have received much less attention from researchers. We have noted their numbers, their patterns of remarriage or other post divorce relationships, the arrangements they may make for their children, their financial circumstances and their disputes, but very little has been said about their feelings and emotional experience. The study which is the centrepiece of this book concerns the adults' experience of divorce. Shelley Day Sclater takes a psychosocial approach, letting divorcing adults tell their own stories of their experiences and feelings. The scene is set with perspective views of earlier research on our changing divorce laws, dispute resolution processes and the psychology of divorce - the latter contributed by her research assistant, Julie Jessop. She then analyses her informants' stories, describing how divorce strikes at the roots of their identity and destroys old certainties. But not all is negative, certainly the divorcing spouses describe emotional pain and raw feelings of anger, but there is also the development of survival strategies with new strengths and autonomies. And, most importantly, there is always a very wide diversity of divorce experience.

This book, which I am confident will become a landmark text, challenges some of the most widely held assumptions about divorce - that divorce is simply damaging for those most closely involved, that the angry and negative feelings should be pushed aside or regarded purely as inconvenient pathology. Rather, Dr. Day Sclater argues very convincingly that in the process of divorce and, particularly, dispute resolution, we need to find ways of integrating and accepting the negative and destructive emotions that almost everyone feels when a marriage relationship ends. As she puts it, 'the coping strategies which many people adopt to enable them to weather the emotional storms of divorce often involve a "splitting" at a psychological level, a defence strategy which places husband and wife on the opposite sides of a divide and which provides a psychological basis for conflict and bitterness.' It is a message which poses a serious and unsettling challenge to those professionals who manage divorce dispute resolution, solicitors, court welfare officers and, perhaps, most directly, divorce mediators.

In recent years, mediators have been much taken up with organisational issues about training, quality assurance and provision while less attention has been paid to the practice itself. The arguments in this book are particularly challenging to the currently prominent labour dispute resolution approach to mediation which leaves little or no space for the expression or recognition of clients' feelings, in contrast to the more therapeutically informed approaches.

Shelley Day Sclater has all the qualifications to provide a challenging insight into the divorce process. After training as a research psychologist she became a solicitor and had a successful practice specialising in family law before she returned to academic research and teaching. And her book could hardly be more timely, coming as it does as we are in the middle of a huge flurry of action research and development in the run up to the implementation of the Family Law Act. It has been my privilege to watch the research grow from the first set of ideas to its conclusions in this book. It is now for the community of divorce practitioners and researchers to take up the challenges it offers.

Professor Martin Richards
Professor of Family Research
University of Cambridge

1 Introduction: Changing Families, Changing Law

The Family Law Act 1996 introduced a new scheme for divorce, abolishing fault-based provisions and envisaging that party-controlled mediation, rather than adversarial negotiation or litigation, will become the norm for resolving divorce disputes. The legislation aims to encourage more 'civilised' divorce, and to reduce the costs, both financial and emotional, seen to be associated with the traditional adversarial process. The reform is underpinned by a conviction that the adversarial process itself encourages acrimony and conflict (which is seen as particularly damaging to children); mediation, it is thought, will provide the means to reduce conflict and promote co-operation and harmony (see Lord Chancellor's Department, 1993, 1995). This book reports the findings from a qualitative project[1] which present a challenge to those assumptions.

The focus in this research was on adults' experiences of divorce. In a series of in-depth interviews, we listened to the stories of divorcing women and men and our findings revealed that some degree of conflict is crucially linked to the emotional trauma of divorce; it is not just an artefact of the adversarial system, and we suggest that it is not likely to be waved easily away by the magic wand of mediation. We suggest that conflict in divorce is to be expected; there is considerable emotional work involved in reaching and in implementing compromise agreements. Other researchers (see Fisher, 1994) have drawn a useful distinction between 'conflict' in divorce, which dispute resolution practices cannot address, and 'disputes', which can be resolved. Our findings suggest, however, that the two are linked in complex ways; the psychological basis for 'conflict' is likely to be present in all divorces, both shaping and being shaped by the formation and resolution of disputes.

In this work, we aimed to develop an interdisciplinary approach and integrative framework in which the sociological and political context of divorce could be considered alongside its deeper, personal, emotional and 'hidden' aspects; and in which psychological insights were used to inform sociological theory, and *vice-versa*. Our findings challenge the negative images of divorce as damaging which abound in our culture, images which have emerged from a broad psychological literature in the traditional paradigm[2] and which have been sustained by dominant ideologies. In departing from that paradigm, we have found a wide diversity in divorce experiences, expressed in a range of stories which tell, at once, of the pain but also of the hope that divorce entails.

Our key argument is that divorce can be a difficult and emotionally painful process, but it should not be regarded as a 'pathological' one. The emotions that accompany divorce are readily explicable in terms of an ordinary human reaction to the experience of separation and the breakdown of a significant intimate relationship. In psychological terms, divorce is about coming to terms with 'loss', but our findings show that it is about much else besides. It is also a positive process of the reconstruction of identity, and the pursuit of autonomy as a new and valued goal.

We argue that the 'survival strategies' which divorcing people commonly adopt reflect both of these aspects of divorce and involve attempts at resolving the tensions between them. Importantly, too, divorcing people usually have quite mixed feelings, as their psychological coping strategies are put to work in what are often very difficult material circumstances. Furthermore, divorcing people are not immune to dominant ideologies; but the idea, for example, that 'conflict' is harmful to children and should be avoided, clashes with many people's very raw feelings of anger and their need to reassert themselves in the face of perceived betrayals and injustices. In psychological terms, conflict can be seen as an integral part of the psychology of divorce and is not just an artefact of the adversarial process, as it is so often portrayed. Negative and destructive feelings are natural, and may need to be expressed during dispute resolution. We argue that if we are to achieve a truly 'civilised' divorce, we need to find ways of integrating, accepting and owning negative and destructive emotions, instead of relegating them to the realms of the pathological.

An emphasis on the positive aspects of divorce, however, should not result in adults' experiences and feelings being trivialised. Divorcing parents are commonly exposed to exhortations to put their own feelings aside 'for the sake of the children'. 'You are the adults and you have to stay in control if you want your kids to be OK' (Magnus, 1997, quoting family therapist and author Janet Riebstein) is a popular sentiment. This is the central premise of the dominant 'welfare discourse' in divorce, and there are powerful moral prescriptions involved here. Crucially, however, we may be trivialising the feelings of adults too much; there is a danger that prioritising the welfare of children does not sufficiently acknowledge adults' own vulnerabilities, and that this very step that we take, ostensibly to protect the interests of children, can result in children becoming a repository for the unbearable vulnerabilities with which we, as adults, cannot cope.[3] Our findings, therefore, represent a challenge to reformers, policy-makers, mediators and lawyers; the voices of ordinary people, speaking about their divorce experiences, reveal the distance between the ideals of the professionals and the realities of life on the ground.

Our work was carried out in the wake of the passing of the Family Law Act 1996. An inevitable question arose: why *these* reforms, and *why now?* We begin our discussion by putting contemporary divorce and legal reform in context. We highlight, for example, the profound and dramatic changes that have taken place in 'the family' and in patterns of intimacy over the last five decades, and we discuss the social anxieties that have accompanied those changes, and the ways in which family law has sought to manage them. We discuss the psychological correlates of those changes, which both reflect and underpin the social policy response.

This book is about the psychology of divorce, at both an individual and a social level. The discussion is centred upon our own research work, but the stories which our participants told us also provide a point from which we link up with wider theoretical explorations in sociology, psychology and psychoanalysis. We think that we have something important to say to a range of professionals in divorce, to students and academics interested in the fields of sociology, psychology and law, and to divorcing people themselves.

The Context of Divorce and Divorce Reform: Changing Family Patterns

Surely no-one gets married with divorce in mind. Yet, current statistics tell us that two out of every five marriages will end this way (Haskey, 1996a). At a time in our history when governments of different political persuasions, a variety of pressure groups, as well as a large section of the mass media, are prone to assert the crucial importance of 'family values', we are confronted on a daily basis with images of family breakdown as negative and damaging, for individuals and society alike. A wide range of current social problems, from unruly children in schools, through teenage pregnancies, to crime, all seem to touch base at the level of 'the family', appearing to testify to family 'breakdown' as *the* epidemic of our age. It seems that widespread anxieties, which at times verge on moral panic, are provoked by the idea that 'the family' is 'in decline'.[4]

There can be no doubt that family patterns, household structures and intimate relationships are indeed changing, but do we need to regard such changes as representing a 'decline of the family'? More important, perhaps, is to explain *why* we are prone to regard such changes in disastrous terms. 'Family' is a potent signifier at both a social and individual level; it has been constructed in a range of political and academic discourses as the linchpin of social stability and, crucially, it has profound psychological meanings for all of us. In short, we have an emotional investment as individuals and as a society in a notion of 'family' as comforting, stable and enduring.[5]

The Decline of the Family?

'The family' is increasingly a site of tension, as rapid social change seems to undermine its very foundations. Demographic trends, such as the high divorce rate, a declining marriage rate, increasing cohabitation, increasing numbers of children born outside marriage (see, for example, Kiernan and Wicks, 1990; Coote *et al.*, 1994), and so on, cannot be contested, yet such evidence can be interpreted in different ways, and demographic statistics alone do not present the full picture. Alongside these changes in family patterns, traditional beliefs about the family show a remarkable persistence as indicated in surveys of social attitudes (see, for example, Scott *et al.*, 1993; Scott, 1998). It seems that there is a gap between what people believe and what they do in relation to 'the family'. The picture is further complicated if we consider that there are widely divergent interpretations of the demographic evidence, giving rise to different ideas about what, if anything, the state should do about it.[6]

One view is that the 'relationship revolution' (Elliott, 1996; Stacey, 1996), the increasing separation of sex and marriage, and of marriage and parenthood, which characterise our 'divorcing society' (Giddens, 1992), are testimony to the 'decline of the family'. Morgan (1996, pp. 1-2), for example, has stated that marriage and the family are under threat such that 'the loss of the framework of society itself...civilisation is at stake'. An alternative view is that the demographic evidence reveals family patterns and structures to be merely changing, along an historical trajectory that has its roots in the long distant past. Elliott (1986, 1996) reminds us, for example, that historical change is neither uniform nor straightforward, and that many continuities persist alongside changes.

These two views about what is happening to 'the family' lead to very different ideas about what law can or should do. Those who take the view that 'the family' is in decline look to the state for a response which will restore the *status quo* or at least provide some support for 'traditional' family structures and values in a society which seems to be fast losing touch with its own moral sense. As Abbott and Wallace (1992) point out, such thinking tends to characterise 'new right' thinking and social policy.[7] Those who take the view that 'the family' is merely changing look to the state to provide laws and policies which acknowledge the reality of such changes and which accord legitimacy to a wide diversity of family forms.

Importantly, however, both points of view are based on an implicit belief that the state can and should *do* something, and a conviction that law and policy can have some influential effect on the behaviours and attitudes of citizens. Such beliefs are perhaps naive, as almost certainly there is no simple one-to-one correspondence between policies and outcomes, and the relations among laws, values and behaviour remain matters of some dispute (see, for example, Lamb and Sagi, 1983; Fox Harding, 1996). Perhaps it is best to begin by looking for ourselves at some of the demographic data.

Changing Family and Household Structures: The Demographic Evidence

Governments routinely collect information in statistical form about family patterns and household structures. The *General Household Survey* appears annually; the Office for National Statistics publishes regular reviews of the data collected; and commentaries on statistical trends are published in *Population Trends*. Looking at this range of evidence, there can be no doubt that marriage is becoming less popular,[8] whilst divorce is now very common. A recent review of the marriage and divorce statistics (Office for National Statistics, 1997) reveals that between 1984 and 1994, the marriage rate[9] fell from 14.0 to 11.3, whilst the divorce rate[10] rose from 12.0 to 13.7 (see Tables 1.1 and 1.2).[11] The tables show that most marriages are first marriages for both parties, but that a significant proportion, about one third, are remarriages for one or both parties. Since 1972, there has been a decline of some 11% in the percentage of marriages which are first marriages (see Table 1.3).[12] The median age at marriage has continued to rise for all groups. There is a marked gender difference in remarriage rates, with widowers and divorced men twice as likely to remarry than widows and divorced women (Babb, 1995).

Table 1.1   Marriages and divorces, 1984-94; numbers

Marriages

Year	Total	First marriage, both parties	First marriage, one party only	Remarriage, both parties
1984	349,186	244.015	67,798	57,373
1985	346,389	221,927	67,531	56,931
1986	347,924	220,372	68,976	58,576
1987	351,761	226,308	69,092	56,361
1988	348,492	219,791	69,419	59,282
1989	346,697	218,904	69,185	58,608
1990	331,150	209,043	67,013	55,094
1991	306,756	192,238	63,159	51,359
1992	311, 564	191,732	66,296	53,536
1993	299,197	181,956	64,551	52,690
1994	291,069	174,200	64,009	52,860

Divorces
Decrees made absolute

Year	Total	First marriage, both parties	One party previously divorced	Both parties previously divorced
1984	144,501	122,453	20,115	9,740
1985	160,300	121,601	24,405	12,293
1986	153,903	116,677	24,106	11,533
1987	151,007	114,111	23,766	11,665
1988	152,633	114,661	24,451	12,105
1989	150,872	112,343	24,765	12,455
1990	153,386	113,898	25,378	12,848
1991	158,745	117,232	26,806	13,487
1992	160,385	117,565	27,679	13,956
1993	165,018	119,911	29,173	14,773
1994	158,175	114,174	28,641	14,265

Over a quarter of all couples who married in the late 1970s and early 1980s had divorced by the end of 1994 and it has been predicated that two out of five marriages will end in divorce (Haskey, 1996a). There are gender differences in divorce, with 72% of petitions being presented by wives. Most (54%) of divorces granted to wives are on the basis of allegations of unreasonable behaviour, whilst most (37%) of those granted to husbands are on the basis of adultery (Haskey, 1996b). Four out of five couples obtain the *decree nisi* within one year of filing the petition, with a median interval of 7 months (Haskey, 1996b). Fifty-six per cent of divorces involve children (Haskey, 1996b). It has been estimated that 28% of children will live through a parental divorce before they reach 16 (Craig, 1997). One in 15 families with dependent children is a step-family (Haskey, 1994) and 6% of children living in families with dependent children are step-children (Craig, 1997).

Table 1.2   Marriages and divorces, 1984-94; rates

Year	Marriages*	Divorces**
1984	14.0	12.0
1985	13.9	13.4
1986	13.9	12.9
1987	14.0	12.7
1988	13.8	12.8
1989	13.7	12.7
1990	13.1	13.0
1991	12.0	13.4
1992	12.2	13.7
1993	11.6	14.2
1994	11.3	13.7

*   persons marrying per 1,000 population of all ages
**   persons divorcing per 1,000 married population

Table 1.3   Marriage by previous marital status, 1972-92

Year	Total marriages (000s)	% first for both	% first for one	% second or subsequent
1972	426	73	15	11
1978	368	65	19	16
1982	342	64	19	16
1988	348	63	20	17
1991	307	63	21	17
1992	312	62	21	17

In 1992, 18% of unmarried people were cohabiting (Babb, 1995). By 1993 the figure was 20% (Haskey, 1995). In 1994, the proportion of couples under the age of 60 who were cohabiting was 13% compared to 6% in 1986 (Craig, 1997). The percentage of families which were cohabiting couples increased from 5% in 1986 to 11% in 1994 whilst over the same period the percentage of married couple families declined from 83% to 71% (Haskey, 1996c). There is some uncertainty as to whether cohabitation represents a substitute for marriage, a prelude to it, or something else altogether. That 6 out of 10 couples who marry gave identical addresses (Haskey, 1997) indicates that, for a significant proportion of people, cohabitation is a stage in the courtship, a prelude to marriage, but this is not so for everyone. It should also be noted that cohabitation rates vary by geographical area and by ethnic group (see Table 1.4).[13] For example, cohabitation is uncommon in the Indian, Bangladeshi and Pakistani communities.[14]

Table 1.4   Ethnic group of head of household by family type with dependent children, 1991, Great Britain (expressed in proportions per thousand)

Family Type	White	Black Caribbean	Black African	Black Other	Indian	Pakistani	Bangladeshi	Chinese
Married	218	138	246	190	497	583	636	385
Cohabiting	17	35	20	44	5	5	4	5
Lone parent	50	202	206	242	44	73	83	53

Over the course of this century we have seen a decline in household size, from 4.6 to 2.5 persons (Haskey, 1996c) and a consequent increase in numbers of households. Between 1981 and 1994, the number of households in Great Britain increased by 21% compared with an increase of only 10% in the proportion of the population aged 25 and over (Craig, 1997). This increase is accounted for in part by an increase in lone parenthood (Murphy and Berrington, 1993). In 1991, one in five families was a lone parent family, compared to one in twelve in 1971. There are about 14 times as many lone mothers as lone fathers (Haskey, 1996c). Lone parenthood results from, in most cases, broken relationships, but there are gender differences; lone mothers become so either because of relationship breakdown or out of a choice to parent alone, whereas the latter option is not so available to fathers. After 1986, births to never-

married, non-cohabiting women grew at a faster pace than lone
motherhood through relationship breakdown. Approximately one in 5
children now lives in a lone parent family, and lone mother families
account for one in twelve families with dependent children, a proportion
which has doubled in the last eight years. Never married lone mothers
outnumbered divorced lone mothers for the first time in 1991 (Haskey,
1996c). It should be noted, however, that lone parenthood varies by ethnic
group (see Table 1.4).[15] For example, lone parenthood is common in the
Black communities, and is more common than married parenthood in the
African-Caribbean community. This is in marked contrast to the situation
which prevails across the Asian communities (see Haskey, 1996c).[16]

The increase in the number of households also reflects changes in
household composition, with more people, including elderly people, living
alone. 'Traditional' families, consisting of a married couple and their
dependent children living in their own home, have declined considerably in
the last thirty years; they formed 3 in 10 households in 1961, but only 2 in
10 in 1994 (Haskey, 1996c). However, households are also smaller
because women are having fewer children and are having them later in life.
For women born in the mid-1930s, the average number of children was
2.45. This has fallen steadily to 2.0 for women born in 1955. In the latest
projections, it is assumed that the rate will fall to 1.8 for women born after
1975, which is some 14% below the replacement level at which the
number of births and deaths would be in balance (Craig, 1997). Not only
are larger families becoming less common, but an increasing number of
women are remaining childless (Haskey, 1996c).

In 1984, 17% of births occurred outside marriage. By 1993 this had
risen to 32% (Babb, 1995), and to 34% in 1995 (Craig, 1997), increasing
twofold over 11 years. However, most such births are registered by both
parents who are living together at the same address (Babb and Bethune,
1995). Over the same period, births within marriage fell (Craig, 1997).

This range of statistics presents a complex picture of changing
family patterns, and illustrates a number of ways in which lifestyles have
altered over recent years.[17] Particularly important are the rise in divorce,
the decline in marriage, the steady rise in cohabitation and the sharp
increase in births outside marriage. There is not likely to be any single or
straightforward explanation for this range of changes, although some have
suggested that common threads are a growth in individualism and an
increasing exercise of choice (see, for example, Haskey, 1996c). In order
to provide a more complete picture, it is useful to consider evidence of
changing attitudes and mentalities.

Changing Family Patterns: Attitudes and Mentalities

The *British Social Attitudes Survey*, published yearly, sometimes reports on attitudes to family and kinship. In 1985, for example, the report included a section on 'sex roles and gender issues' (Witherspoon, 1985), which discussed attitudes in relation to, amongst other things, gender roles in the family. The survey found that a sizeable minority of about a third of people, maintain traditionalist views about gender roles, although there was some evidence that egalitarian attitudes were more widespread than they had been at the time of the *Women and Employment Survey* in 1980. For example, 32% of women agreed with the statement 'A husband's job is to earn the money; a wife's job is to look after the home and family'. The survey also revealed some discrepancies between what people believe about women and work (where attitudes are more likely to be egalitarian) and what they believe about domestic divisions of labour (where more traditional attitudes are likely to prevail).

The 1987 survey (Ashford, 1987) found that more than two thirds of the respondents supported the notion that 'as a society, we ought to do more to safeguard the institution of marriage', and that only 6% disagreed. Three quarters of the people felt that 'most people nowadays take marriage too lightly', with only 10% disagreeing. As in previous surveys, this one found that older respondents were more likely to hold traditional attitudes than younger ones. Faithfulness in marriage was as highly valued as it had been five years earlier. Further, the domestic arrangements (gendered divisions of labour) preferred by the great majority of respondents were conventional, particularly for families with children at school, and Ashford points out that the notion that partners should play symmetrical or equal roles 'is still rather alien' (p. 128).

However, the survey revealed a gulf between what people would ideally like to happen, in terms of divisions of labour, and what they actually do. For example, 70% of those from households with full-time working wives believed that mothers of young children should stay at home. Sixty-one per cent of respondents thought that 'to grow up happily, children need a home with both their own father and mother', despite the increasing prevalence of divorce. Ashford concludes that, 'in their attitudes towards marriage and other family matters, the British emerge as highly and consistently conventional. The ideal household consists of a breadwinner father, a homemaker mother and two children' (p. 140). Divorce, however, is seen to be justified when personal relations between the spouses are poor, and the vision of an ideal marriage is one of sharing and companionship. As Ashford points out, there are clear discrepancies between ideals and realities, between what people say they believe in and what they actually do.

The 1989 report (Harding, 1989) considers whether the evidence supports the sounding of a 'death knell' for 'the family' or whether marriage and the family are passing through a period of change, as roles become less likely to be prescribed and more likely to be negotiated. His data reveal considerable ambivalences about changing family patterns, and he sees families as being put under increasing strain as they seek to reconcile traditional prescriptions with individual preferences.

In 1992, Kiernan found that 33% of people (35% men, 31% women) agreed that 'a husband's job is to earn the money; a wife's job is to look after the home and family'. These findings are consistent with those of Witherspoon (1985) discussed above. Kiernan found no strong evidence that men and women were becoming more likely to reject the traditional model of domestic labour. She also found that even in dual-earner households, where women were employed full time outside the home, women were mainly responsible for general domestic duties in 67% of households. In only 16% of households were these duties shared equally. Thus the 1992 data support the idea that traditional gendered patterns of labour in the family are remarkably persistent, despite the fact that increasing numbers of women are going out to work.

The authors of the 1993 survey (Scott *et al.*, 1993) consider their data in the light of the prevalent notion that the traditional nuclear family is fast becoming an endangered species. They found no data to support this, but found some evidence that traditional attitudes are beginning to change, particularly amongst younger people. They emphasise the increasing range of choices open to people about their domestic arrangements, although these remain constrained by social and economic circumstances. However, they argue, 'it would be premature to mourn the loss of traditional family values in Britain' (p. 23), although there are some signs of strain and change. Women, in particular, are less likely to see marriage as a recipe for happiness, and more likely to favour divorce if the marriage goes wrong. Support for traditional gender roles is eroding, particularly among women and younger people. The authors conclude that 'traditional' family values continue to co-exist in some degree of tension with values of individual autonomy and gender equality, allowing people's options to become more a matter of choice and less a matter of expectation and duty.

The 1996 report (McGlone *et al.*, 1996) states that:

In spite of its many detractors, family life in Britain continues to thrive. Most people are in regular contact with their immediate family who remain of primary importance in their lives. The family is still the dominant source of support and care for most people (p. 70).

Scott (1998) reports that the only major change in attitudes over the last three decades has been in relation to pre-marital sex; fidelity is still regarded as important across all cohorts.

We have seen, therefore, that despite the widespread demographic changes in family patterns and household structures, families continue to retain their central significance for most people, and that traditional values show a remarkable persistence. Traditional beliefs are likely to exist alongside more modern or progressive attitudes, rather than having been extinguished altogether by newer ideas. Let us now consider how these ambiguities were manifested in the making of the Family Law Act 1996. These issues touch upon the broader question of what it is that family law *is doing* in respect of the social changes we have discussed above.[18]

The Making of the Family Law Act, 1996

As Day Sclater and Piper (1999) argue, there are two possible interpretations of the demographic and attitudinal evidence we have been examining. One view is that family law is addressing the 'crisis in the family' by attempting to engineer social change in a desired direction, namely the reinstatement of the traditional nuclear family. This is the view taken by the feminist sociologist, Carol Smart (1995, 1997). An alternative view is that family law is acknowledging the reality of social change, and is attempting to keep pace with it by assisting in the construction of a new post-divorce family form. Let us consider these arguments in a little more detail.

Smart (1995, 1997) sees recent family law as trying to manage the tensions brought about by changing family patterns and relationships, and she links these changes, and the responses of family law, with the changing patterns and expectations of intimacy discussed by sociologists Giddens (1992) and Beck (1992). Smart argues that recent legislative changes in the area of family law represent efforts to reinstate the so-called traditional nuclear family, as though the widespread demographic changes we have discussed had either not occurred, or could be ignored or even reversed. The 'transformation in intimacy' which Giddens (1992) identifies, he argues is closely tied with an ascendant individualism and the ideology of 'choice' of the kind which emerged in the *British Social Attitudes Surveys* which we have discussed. The individual is seen as pursuing rights to autonomy and personal fulfilment, in accordance with the ideals of 'companionate' intimate relationships (Finch and Summerfield, 1991). Thus, where one relationship fails to satisfy, Giddens argues that the individual in late modernity increasingly feels free to move on and to try another; so develops the pattern of 'serial monogamy', involving an increasing. separation of marriage, sexuality and parenthood.

Smart, however, takes issue with Giddens for side-stepping the issue of children.[19] She points out that people with children, particularly mothers, cannot and do not easily move from one relationship to another in pursuit of individualist goals, however much they might want to. She sees family law as important among the forces that constrain individuals, particularly custodial parents, in this way. Smart goes on to argue that family law, in its particular interpretation of the principle of the 'child's best interests', may be seen as attempting to stem the tide of social change by forging a continuing link between the child's parents when the parents themselves have no desire other than to end their relationship. There is, of course, a sense in which the provisions of the Children Act and the Child Support Act signify an acknowledgement by the state that marriage and parenthood are no longer tied together,[20] but in invoking fathers as necessary financial and/or emotional providers, there is also a sense in which the security of older family structures is being re-invoked. Thus, Smart argues that family law is in the business of reasserting old ideals. Crucial in these developments has been an image of the child as damaged and pathologised by parental separation, or as the 'victim' of divorce (Piper, 1996), an image that has been in evidence in both academic research and legal practice, and which also featured prominently in the debates leading up to the passing of the Family Law Act 1996.[21]

As Day Sclater and Piper (1999) suggest, an alternative view to that proposed by Smart is that family law is not so much attempting to reverse social change as it is attempting to constrain and contain changes that are regarded as threatening. These attempts to contain the problem do implicitly acknowledge the social evolution of 'the family' and, importantly, they address the profound social anxieties which such developments bring. The difference is a subtle but an important one.[22] Thus, the alternative view to that proposed by Smart sees family law as currently in the business of reconstructing a *new* kind of post-divorce family.

In this light, the Family Law Act can be read as a statute which 'normalises' divorce as simply another event in the life-cycle of 'the family'; here, divorce no longer signifies either the 'breakdown of families' or the 'decline of the family', but instead simply represents an opportunity for reorganisation. In the face of the high divorce rate, the Family Law Act can be seen as paving the way for a new family form to emerge. This is a family that is constructed within the discourses and practices of welfare, that coheres around a child positioned as vulnerable and as in need of state protection. Crucial here is the concept of 'parental responsibility' which first found legislative expression in the Children Act 1989. Particular meanings are allotted to this concept within the welfare discourse. As Kaganas (1999) argues, family law currently constructs children as 'at risk' of 'harm' if their parents are not 'responsible', if they cannot manage their divorce without conflict and acrimony, and if they fail to appreciate the child's 'needs' for a 'quality' relationship with the non-residential parent.

Analysis of the Parliamentary debates leading up to the Family Law Act supports this view that family law is currently reconstructing a new kind of post-divorce family.[23] These debates were heated, and intensely polarised; there were those who argued that the proposed reforms undermined marriage and the family and those who argued that, on the contrary, the new law would support those sacred institutions. In July 1996, a compromise was reached, and the Act was given the Royal Assent.

Crucially, the image that emerges from the Act in its final form is that of divorce as a 'transition' in the family life cycle; the nuclear family, riven by divorce, becomes what Ahrons (1994) calls a 'bi-nuclear' family. This shift, arguably, is a move in the direction of normalising divorce and, far from signifying problems in 'the family', divorce instead marks out the possibility of a solution to the 'crisis in the family'. McIsaac (1995), for example, sees the practice of divorce dispute resolution by mediation as consistent with the emergence of a 'new family system' for our post-industrial age. For him, this new form resembles the 'old extended family'. It is brought into being by a discourse which represents divorce as 'a reorganisation of the family, not an end of the family' and it depends upon a concept of 'not being divorced "from" someone, but being divorced "to" them' (McIsaac, 1995, p. ix).

In a sense, this amounts to a denial that there is any kind of 'crisis' in 'the family' at all; the concept of 'family' is simply being broadened so as to incorporate families who have been torn asunder by divorce. In this way, the Family Law Act 1996 may be seen as responding to social and demographic change and as attempting to contain the anxieties so engendered by offering new discourses which reconstruct the post-divorce family in a new non-threatening form. New discourses are being created, and older ones adapted, to facilitate social change in a desired direction.

This argument that discourse can effect social change is not new, but is one that has been advanced by Norman Fairclough. Fairclough (1989) argued that 'ideology is the prime means of manufacturing consent' (p. 4), by which he meant that social and political power was exercised, not through coercion, but through the 'manufacture' of consent, with language playing a central part in the process. Fairclough (1992) argued that, far from language being a transparent medium by which information was conveyed, language was a political system, organised in historically specific discourses, which served social functions. For him changes in language increasingly include 'attempts to engineer the direction of [social] change' (p. 6). Thus, in being reworded, activities and relationships are also being fundamentally transformed. Fairclough alerts us to the increasing salience of language and discourse for social and cultural transformations; for him, the engineering of semantic change is part of an attempt to effect cultural change. On this view, the Family Law Act can be seen as an attempt to address the contemporary 'crisis in the family', and as a way of containing the 'problem' of divorce and the complex emotions associated with it, at both social and individual levels.

It may be that fears about the 'decline of the family' are as old as history itself, as moralists in different ages have expressed concerns over what Goode (1993) calls 'the classical family of Western nostalgia'[24] but, as we have seen, there can be little doubt that family structures are continuing along a trajectory of historical change. However, it is worth remembering that the demographic and attitudinal data are as remarkable for their continuities as for their changes (Elliott, 1986, 1996). Undoubtedly we are witnessing an increasing separation of marriage, sex and reproduction,[25] and these issues continue to cause concern, often fuelled by media rhetoric. This may be explained by the fact that, traditionally, 'the family' has been regarded as being of vital importance for individual development and psychological health, and as central to social stability and cohesion (Parsons, 1955). It is also the case that, at both a social and personal level, 'the family' is a potent signifier with a profound emotional pull. Small wonder, then that, when rapid social change appears to undermine its very foundation, anxieties and anger surface. As we have seen, it was in this context that the recent reform of the divorce law took place.

Divorce: The New Law

In July 1996, the Family Law Act received the Royal Assent after a troubled passage through Parliament, and only after a number of amendments had been incorporated into the Bill. For the purposes of our discussion, the most significant changes in the divorce law brought about by the Act are the abolition of 'fault' as a basis for divorce and the encouragement of more widespread use of mediation as the preferred dispute resolution procedure.

In the English-speaking jurisdictions (Britain, USA, Canada, Australia and New Zealand), as well as in most Western European and Scandinavian countries, the trend over the last three decades has been towards 'no fault' divorce. Closely linked to this development have been measures designed to ensure the gender-neutrality of family law, particularly as regards parenting and financial settlements, and measures to diminish or alter the adversarial nature of the legal divorce process. In some countries, such as Australia and New Zealand, these issues have been addressed by the establishment of Family Courts; in other places there has been a consolidation of the family jurisdiction, and the incorporation of welfare-based ideologies and practices into or alongside the legal process (see, for example., Dingwall and Eekelaar, 1986; King, 1991; Sales *et al.*, 1992). In Britain, the desire to remove 'fault' from divorce culminated in the Divorce Reform Act of 1969, but such was the nature of the debates which attended the passing of this legislation that, in fact, 'fault' was retained, if not in the 'ground' for divorce (which became 'irretrievable breakdown') then at least in the 'facts' that were required to 'prove' it. However, matrimonial fault has been abolished once and for all in the Family Law Act, 1996.

In 1988 the Law Commission in their consultation paper *Looking to the Future*[26] had taken the view that the retention of 'fault' in divorce was not helpful, particularly for children, insofar as it was seen to encourage acrimony and recrimination between the adults involved, and they pointed to the desirability of calm and sensible negotiations about the future needs of the parties and their children. Their 1990 report, *Family Law: The Ground for Divorce*[27] (which included a draft Bill that was effectively ignored by government at the time) formed the basis of John Major's government's attempt to introduce more 'civilised' divorce in 1993. The consultation paper (Lord Chancellor's Department, 1993) advocated a 'no fault' basis for divorce; divorce would follow a waiting period during which time the couple would be expected to consider the consequences of their decision to divorce, and to make plans for the future. It was envisaged that couples would avail themselves of mediation services during this period, with the aim that the involvement of lawyers would be curtailed, resulting in a reduction in both the financial and emotional costs of divorce. The White Paper which followed (Lord Chancellor's Department, 1995) put forward concrete proposals for divorce reform which were then embodied in a Bill[28] which began its passage through the House of Lords. In March 1996, an amended version[29] entered the Commons.

It was, however, the abolition of 'fault' in divorce which caused the most consternation in the debates leading up to the passing of the Act. It was the basis from which the Bill's proponents were able to argue that they were providing a remedy for the evil of 'quickie' divorces, and thus supporting marriage and 'the family'. At the same time, the removal of 'fault' provided the grounds upon which the Bill's opponents were able to allege that the reforms would have the opposite effect, that of undermining marriage and 'the family'.

No-fault divorce, however, has not been without its critics, as the Parliamentary debates leading up to both the 1969 Act and the 1996 Act bear testimony. Further, the focus on the removal of 'fault' has arguably led to too blinkered an approach being taken to broader inequities. In the USA, where the 'divorce revolution' (Weitzman, 1985) took place some years ahead of Britain, a number of problematic issues have now emerged.[30] For example, the divorce reforms which are now well-established in the USA, Canada, Australia and New Zealand, have consistently failed to address the issue of poverty which accompanies divorce for many, especially women and children (Weitzman, 1985; Maclean, 1991). The reforms have also failed adequately to address issues of diversity among divorcing couples, particularly that which arises in connection with ethnicity (Day Sclater, 1995a).[31] Issues of equality have also arisen in relation to gender (Bottomley, 1985; Fineman, 1991; 1995) and the heated debate on gender and mediation continues in all English-speaking jurisdictions.[32] Sugarman and Kay (1990) conclude that divorce reform is at a 'cross-roads', and the papers in their edited volume all point to the conclusion that the divorce debate continues and that there is, as yet, no consensus on the best way forward.

Part and parcel of this removal of 'fault' has been an apparent 'rolling back' of the state from the private sphere of 'the family' (Eekelaar, 1991; Hoggett, 1992). However, although overt state intervention into 'the family' may appear to be receding, it remains the case that the governance of citizens *through* the family[33] (Donzelot, 1980; Rose, 1987, 1990; Parton,

1992) may have now achieved unprecedented heights, through the employment and deployment of discourses whose effect is to reconstruct family relationships in particular ways.[34] The current emphasis on mediation can be regarded as an expression of the ascendancy of these new discourses to dominance.

The Development of Conciliation/Mediation [35]

In Britain, the first mediation services were set up in the late 1970s.[36] Many see the Finer Report[37] as being the impetus for conciliatory approaches.[38] The early schemes focused on child-related issues and developed on something of an *ad hoc* basis, in response to local initiatives, some connected to local county courts and others operating independently. According to Parkinson (1986), who was closely involved in these new developments, the new conciliation movement reflected 6 main concerns: (1) to provide an alternative to the adversarial system which was seen as exacerbating conflict and hostility; (2) to protect children; (3) to give people more control over their own affairs; (4) to achieve greater administrative efficiency; (5) to reduce public expenditure, particularly on Legal Aid and (6) to stem the rising tide of divorce. Pioneering work began at the Bristol County Court in 1977, where an in-court conciliation scheme, which addressed disputes relating to children on divorce, was set up. The Registrar[39] and the Court Welfare Officers took up new roles as conciliators and attempted to encourage the parties and their solicitors to reach negotiated agreements. In 1979, this was extended into an independent private scheme in Bristol, which complemented the work of the local court.[40]

By 1983, the Interdepartmental Committee on Conciliation[41] reported that there had been an enormous growth of interest in conciliation, and that over 50 schemes had by then been established.[42] Most were in-court schemes, an outgrowth of the divorce court welfare service, which were established on the initiative of local courts and had no statutory basis. The development of these schemes was supported by the occasional Practice Direction from the Family Division.[43] In the private voluntary sector, the National Family Conciliation Council (NFCC), a national 'umbrella' organisation, had achieved charitable status, and had begun work on a formula for affiliation and the establishment of a training programme. The NFCC held its first AGM in 1983, and shortly afterwards received Nuffield funding to assist development work. The NFCC subsequently changed its name to National Family Mediation and Conciliation Service (NAFMCS) and, later again, to National Family Mediation (NFM). Its journal *Family Mediation* was established in 1993.

In 1985, the *Report of the Matrimonial Causes Procedure Committee*, chaired by Mrs Justice Booth DBE, expressed support for conciliation, but few of its recommendations were ever implemented (Bird and Cretney, 1996; Bishop *et al.*, 1996). Whilst Government committees and the Law Commission continued to debate a range of possible amendments to statute law, conciliation/mediation services in the private voluntary sector continued to develop across the country, drawing inspiration from developments abroad.

In 1985, the Lord Chancellor's Department established the Conciliation Project Unit (CPU) at the University of Newcastle with a brief to evaluate the effectiveness and efficiency of family conciliation. The CPU report was published in 1989[44] and concluded that mediation, as an alternative dispute resolution procedure, had clear potential. However, the voluntary schemes seemed to be more effective than those annexed to the courts and staffed by the probation service. In addition, the exclusive focus on child-related issues of the schemes evaluated was seen to create an unrealistically narrow focus. The developments in the voluntary sector were further assisted in 1990 when the Joseph Rowntree Foundation helped fund the development of five pilot projects at mediation services based in Brighton, Bristol, Cambridge, Coventry and Newcastle. These projects went beyond the usual children's issues remit, and the services instead began to offer mediation on all issues associated with divorce (comprehensive mediation). Again, the Newcastle team was engaged to evaluate the five projects, and their report was published in 1994.[45]

By the end of the 1980s, alternative dispute resolution in divorce was well established, particularly in America, and mediation research, like that of the 'effects of divorce' on children, was burgeoning. Singer (1992) reported that more than half the states in the USA had mediation programmes available in their courts, and that some courts were mandating mediation, particularly in disputed children cases, in an effort to provide a less adversarial setting for dealing with the consequences of marital breakdowns. However, as in Britain, the take-up of mediation, where it was not mandated by the court, was low,[46] and it was acknowledged that:

> while many people would be receptive to mediating their separation agreement, an extensive, professional, and carefully planned marketing program is needed before the process will gain widespread acceptance (Hauser-Dann, 1988, p. 15).

During the 1980s a large number of books on mediation were published in the USA.[47] In the UK, Lisa Parkinson's[48] *Conciliation in Separation and Divorce* appeared and by this time Gwynn Davis had already begun publishing articles from his research on mediation.[49] In 1990 there appeared a collection of papers, edited by Thelma Fisher, Director NFCC, *Family Conciliation Within the UK*. In this early work, mediation tends to be hailed as a 'constructive' way of dealing with marital breakdown, with which the traditional legal process is unfavourably compared. In many cases, these books were written by practising mediators. By and large, these publications unashamedly employed rhetorical strategies aimed at convincing the reader that mediation was to be preferred over traditional dispute settlement procedures and stressing the detrimental effects of 'conflict' for children of divorce.[50] Importantly, however, these volumes also began to counter the emerging criticisms of mediation, particularly objections raised by members of the legal profession. Significantly, too, some reviewers made such critical observations as: 'there is relatively little attention given to the theoretical foundations of mediation' and that 'there is no evidence provided for the effectiveness of marital mediation' nor is there much 'discussion of the effects of self selection or of techniques for extending mediation to couples other than the relatively well-educated, middle-aged, middle-class couples who now constitute the bulk of the clientele' (see Wood, 1981, p. 245).

According to Carbonneau, the drawbacks of mediation include the possibility that some couples are not suited to resolve their disputes in a self-determined manner. He pointed out that mediation seemed to apply with particular effectiveness to marital disputes involving middle and upper-class couples who are skilled at verbal communication and who are in roughly equal bargaining positions (Carbonneau, 1986, p. 1127). In an overview of mediation research, Pearson and Thoennes (1985) also pointed out that those who chose mediation tended to come from the higher socio-economic groups,[51] and exhibit better spousal communication patterns, than those who rejected it.

We shall be discussing the dispute resolution research literature in more detail in chapter 2, and simply make the point at this stage that, despite the early identification of some of the limitations of mediation (Day Sclater, 1995a), conciliatory approaches have increasingly come to predominate in dispute resolution practice, not always with the desired results (see, for example, Bailey-Harris *et al.*, 1998). With the benefit of hindsight, the many claims which have been made for the efficacy and desirability of mediation may seem premature, although they can certainly be seen as consistent with the expression of the now dominant discourses which seek to address the contemporary crisis in the family.[52] One aspect of these discourses is the reliance on welfarism[53] and the increasing calls for the involvement of mental health professionals in divorce. Is this development a genuine response to perceived human need, or is it just one more manifestation of the proliferation of what Lasch (1980) has called the 'therapeutic state', another way of what Rose (1990) calls 'governing the soul' or Donzelot (1980) refers to as the 'policing' of families?[54]

The Welfare Discourse

In Britain, counsellors are now sometimes attached to solicitors' practices, and are available, for both adults and children, in some Family and Divorce Centres. In the USA, Zibbell (1995) has explicitly argued for the involvement of mental health professionals as arbitrators in post-divorce child-oriented conflicts. Others (for example, Johnston and Campbell, 1988) practice 'therapeutic' forms of mediation, although this model has not yet found favour in Britain. In Australia, family court 'counsellors' occupy something of an anomalous position mid-way between therapeutic counsellors and mediators of disputes.[55]

In line with the links between these demographic changes and state responses to public concerns, 'children' have become the objects of a new welfare discourse (King and Piper, 1995), and it is ostensibly to the needs of children[56] that mediation is designed to address itself (Piper, 1993). In short, it is around a child who is rendered vulnerable and pathologised by divorce[57] that a new family form coheres, and mediation becomes part of the solution to the 'crisis in the family' (Day Sclater, 1996b; Day Sclater and Piper, 1999).[58] As Carbonneau (1986) points out:

> Under the mediation alternative, divorce need not become a dismantling of the family under the aegis of legal principles and procedures. Rather, divorce could lead to an *effective restructuring of the family unit* in the light of the new personal reality between the spouses (Carbonneau, 1986, p. 1170), (italics added).

This, then, would seem to be the underlying promise which alternative dispute resolution procedures in divorce hold. In the context of a rising divorce rate and changing family structures, the shift from adversarial dispute resolution to mediation in divorce makes good sense.

The Family Law Act is very much a product of its time; it both reflects old and produces new dominant familial discourses which, like the Children Act, will almost certainly produce shifts in thinking, feeling and behaviour. Whether these shifts will be in the desired direction cannot be predicted. Recent work by researchers at the University of Bristol (Bailey-Harris *et al.*, 1998) indicates that the implementation of the private law provisions of the Children Act 1989 (and contrary to what was envisaged by the Act's proponents) has been accompanied by an increase in child related disputes, and that procedural delays are increasing, possibly as a result of the settlement-orientation of contemporary practice. In relation to the Family Law Act, the findings of our study on the nature and manifestation of psychological issues in divorce similarly indicate that the achievement of harmony may yet elude us.

Outline of the Book

This book discusses the psychological aspects of the divorce process and considers their implications for dispute resolution. In chapter 2 we review the research on divorce dispute resolution; our aim is to critically examine the dominant discourses[59] in the light of research evidence about what solicitors and mediators do, or can do. We reach two main conclusions: first, that the rhetoric which portrays the adversarial process as anathema to dispute resolution over-simplifies the complexity of the divorce process and overlooks the evidence that bi-partisan negotiation most often results in agreed settlements. Secondly, that the status of mediation as the preferred dispute resolution procedure is attributable to the dominance of discourses of welfare and harmony, as the research evidence on which this view is based is, at best, equivocal.

Chapter 3 reviews the research on the psychology of divorce. We critically examine the traditional paradigm upon which most research on the psychological 'effects' of divorce has been based, and conclude that it has been beset by a number of conceptual and methodological difficulties which have contributed to the prevalent view of divorce-as-pathology. Chapter 4 presents an alternative theoretical and methodological framework which we find more conducive to a nuanced understanding of the experiences and psychological processes of divorce. In this chapter, we outline our own 'psychosocial' approach to divorce and emphasise the importance of making explicit the theoretical background to our methodology.

Chapters 5 and 6 present the findings from this empirical study. In chapter 5 we discuss our quantitative data about symptoms and feelings, and supplement this with broader insights gleaned from the qualitative data collected through in-depth interviews and case studies. Chapter 6 focuses on people's narrative accounts of divorce, and discusses the connections between the form and content of the narratives and psychological coping strategies. Chapter 7 concludes by discussing the complexities and ambivalences of divorce as, at once, an emotionally traumatic yet also a positive and constructive process. We examine the ways in which it might be possible to 'accentuate the positive' in divorce and consider the barriers to achieving an idealised 'harmonious' divorce.

Notes

[1]   The research was supported by the ESRC (award number R000236323) and fieldwork was carried out between April 1996 and June 1997. Shelley Day Sclater was the award holder and Julie Jessop the research assistant on the project.

[2]   This literature is reviewed by Julie Jessop in Chapter 3. A critique of the traditional paradigm in psychological research, and details of the theoretical and methodological framework in which our research was conducted, are given in Chapter 4.

[3]   This point is discussed in detail in Day Sclater (1998d). See also Day Sclater and Piper (1999).

[4]   These anxieties are not peculiar to Britain. For a parallel in the United States, see Popenoe (1993).

[5]   As Langellier and Peterson (1993) argue, family stories are 'under our skin' as well as out in the world as discursive practices and ways of 'doing' family (p. 73).

[6]   For a full discussion of 'what family law is for', see Hale (1997).

[7]   Such ideas, however, are also in evidence in the recent consultation paper *Supporting Families* issued by the Blair ('New' Labour) government.

[8]   Marriage, however, remains popular, although its meanings are changing. See Mansfield and Collard (1988); Clulow and Mattinson (1995); Stacey (1996).

[9]   Persons marrying per 1000 population of all ages.

[10]   Persons divorcing per 1000 married population.

[11]   Tables adapted from Office for National Statistics (1997), p. 1.

[12]   Table adapted from Babb (1995), p. 8.

[13]   Table adapted from Haskey (1996c), p. 19.

[14]   See Heath and Dale (1994).

[15]   Table adapted from Haskey (1996c), p. 19.

[16]   See also Heath and Dale (1994).

[17]   See Kiernan (1998) for a broader discussion of European trends.

[18]   For a brief discussion of the historical development of family law, see Hale (1997) and Day Sclater, Bainham and Richards (1999).

[19]   For a critical discussion of Smart's contribution, see James and Richards (1999).

[20]   For a fuller discussion of this point, see Maclean and Richards (1999).

[21]   See Day Sclater and Piper (1999) for a full discussion.

22   There is some tension between these two positions in the recent consultation paper *Supporting Families* issued by Tony Blair's government (HM Government, 1998). The Right Honourable Mrs Justice Hale sees the history of family law in terms of managing the tensions between preserving the 'privacy' of families and the need for state intervention to protect the vulnerable, and in terms of striking a balance between offering prescriptions and responding to the realities of family life and social change (Hale, 1997).

23   See Day Sclater and Piper (1999).

24   Coontz (1992) makes a similar point.

25   See Scott (1998).

26   Law Commission, No 170.

27   Law Commission, No 192.

28   HL Bill 1 1995.

29   Bill 82.

30   For a comprehensive discussion of these issues, see the papers in Sugarman and Kay (eds) (1990).

31   For a review of current literature on family mediation and ethnicity, see Irving and Benjamin (1995). See also Schuz (1996) and Shah-Kazemi (1996). On the broader issue of the family and cultural diversity, see, for example, Hutter (1991); Gelles (1995).

32   This debate is discussed in greater detail in chapter 2.

33   A process which has been referred to as 'familialisation'; see Rose (1989).

34   See, for example, Collier (1995) on the discursive construction of the 'family man' in relation to law, and O'Donovan (1994) and Smart (1989a) for feminist perspectives on these developments.

35   In the USA, mediation was formally founded in 1975; see Coogler (1978).

36   For discussions of the historical developments see, for example, Fisher (1990, 2nd edn. 1992). See also Parkinson (1986); Eekelaar and Dingwall (1988); Bowen (1987); Ahier (1986); Forster (1982); Ogus *et al.* (1989).

37   The Finer Report on *One Parent Families* (1974).

38   This committee discussed the development of conciliation in the wider context of a major reform of family law; the setting up of a new and comprehensive family court system was envisaged, but was never implemented.

39   Now referred to as the District Judge.

40   The work in Bristol has been extensively investigated by Gwynn Davis and his colleagues; see, for example, Davis (1988); Dingwall (1988).

41   Lord Chancellor's Department (1983).

42   Davis and Roberts (1988) studied one such scheme in South-East London. Other schemes in Cleveland, Humberside and in Scotland were researched in the mid-1980s. The National Family Conciliation Council, in 1985, undertook a survey of ten independent conciliation services. The results of these studies are summarised in Ogus *et al.* (1989).

43   See, for example, Parkinson (1986), chapter 4.

44   Ogus, Walker and Jones-Lee (1989).

45   Walker. McCarthy and Corlyon (1994). See also Joseph Rowntree Foundation, *Social Policy Research Findings*, No. 48, 1994. The findings of this evaluation study are discussed in chapter 2.

46   See also Pearson and Thoennes (1985) on this point.

47 See, for example, Coogler (1978) (reviewed by Wood, 1981); Irving (1981) and Haynes (1981) (both reviewed by Herman, 1982); Kressel (1985), Haynes (1981) and Lemmon (1985) (all reviewed by Hall, 1987); Friedman (1993) (anonymously reviewed in the 1993 *Negotiation Journal*, vol. 9, p. 381); Irving and Benjamin (1987).

48 Lisa Parkinson was one of the founders of mediation in Britain.

49 See also M. Roberts (1988/1997).

50 For an overview of research into the effects of divorce on children, which highlights the shift from a 'loss' model to one based on 'conflict', see Day Sclater (1996a). See Rodgers and Pryor (1998) for a recent comprehensive review of the British studies.

51 In the early British studies, Davis (1988) reports a tendency among mediation clientele towards the 'middle class' but excluding the most privileged members of our society. The very poor are also under-represented (Davis, 1988, p. 61).

52 It is perhaps also significant that much of the early mediation literature was written by mediators themselves. Some of the academics writing in the area are practising mediators themselves or they co-author with practitioners (see, for example, Folberg and Milne, 1988). Irving and Benjamin (1995) state that, 'early research in mediation was, in part, intended to sell mediation to policy makers, for whom it was still novel and untested' (p. 425). Astor (1995) points out that writing about mediation frequently falls into one of two categories; the rhetorical or the practical. Critical scholarship, supported by sound empirical work, has been rather more rare than it ought to be in this area. See also the British debate between a practitioner and two academics in the *Journal of Social Welfare and Family Law* 1992-95, discussed in chapter 2.

53 See Murch (1980); Freeman (1984).

54 Making a similar point, Dingwall (1988) expresses concern about the unacknowledged power of mediators, and the potential for abuse of that power.

55 See Bordow and Gibson (1994).

56 As Davis points out, 'it is equally plausible to regard the practice of the new mediators as underpinned by their strongly 'pro-child' and 'pro-family' values. This is not simply a matter of seeking to identify and promote children's interests; it reflects a vision of *the whole family as needing help*. This is consistent with the view...that, following separation, the family is still a family - and should be treated as such' (Davis, 1988, pp. 57-58, emphasis in original). Davis does point out, however, that these values are not confined to mediators; they are social values that many in the legal profession also increasingly endorse.

57 See Piper (1996) who argues that the child is positioned as a 'victim' of divorce by the Family Law Act 1996. See also King and Piper (1995).

58 Bottomley argues that, 'the unifying feature of all the arguments in favour of conciliation is a symbolic one: conciliation has become the site for a reaffirmation of familial ideology. What is being presented and celebrated is the image of a caring, liberal and egalitarian society which only intervenes in the private domain of the family with good cause and great sensitivity' (Bottomley, 1985, p. 185).

59 For a fuller critical discussion of the dominant divorce discourses, see the papers in Day Sclater and Piper (eds) (1999).

2   Divorce Dispute Resolution: A Review of the Literature

Conciliation may be defined as a structured process in which both parties to a dispute meet voluntarily with one or more impartial third parties (conciliators) who help them to explore possibilities of reaching agreement, without having the power to impose a settlement on them or the responsibility to advise either party individually (Parkinson, 1986, p. 52).

By mediation, I refer to a mode of intervention in which an impartial third party, the mediator, assists the disputants to reach consensual joint decisions on the issues over which they disagree. The mediator has no power to impose a decision. The location of authority is with the parties (Roberts, 1990, p. 89).[1]

In this chapter, we critically review the literature on divorce dispute resolution. As we shall see, much of the available work on mediation has been carried out in the USA and such findings are not unproblematically applicable to the British situation.

In a lengthy article, Carbonneau (1986) considered a number of alternatives to divorce litigation. He began by examining the traditional adjudicatory approach and cited the now commonplace criticisms: that it renders divorce expensive and difficult, it substantially increases the length of the divorce process,[2] that it exacerbates conflict between spouses, and that the logic of law is estranged from human reality. However, for him, the advantages of litigation (for example, allowing the spouses to voice their disagreements in a 'contained' setting, and reinforcing the institution of marriage) were far outweighed by its disadvantages, and he argued that the complexities of divorce disputes call for a 'choice of remedies' (pp. 1124-5). It was, however, a focus on 'parenting' which seemed to underlie the need for alternative dispute resolution procedures; as Carbonneau put it: 'Self-determination in divorce might also enhance the parties' capacity to engage in parenting after divorce' (p. 1125).

Next, Carbonneau discussed arbitration, but as divorce actions are fundamentally different from labour and commercial disputes, to which arbitration has most successfully been applied, this form of dispute resolution he regarded as only of limited utility in divorce. Mediation was Carbonneau's preferred option; he saw it as a 'humane framework' for resolving difficulties associated with divorce (Carbonneau, 1986, p. 1167). Its advantages, he argued, are that it redistributes decision-making authority, and it emphasises individual rationality and responsibility. He stated that mediation 'shields' children from the trauma of litigation, and allows the parents themselves to determine what is in the best interests of their children (p. 1169). Another advantage of mediation was stated to be its ability to 'teach parents to communicate on more business-like terms, and to compromise' (p. 1169). Finally, he argued that mediation would reduce the possibility of relitigation, because parties are more likely to adhere to an agreement that they have reached of their own accord:

> [A]lthough the mediator provides pace and guidance, the spouses retain ultimate control over the process.[3] The fact that the final result is the product of personal involvement, and largely self-determined, facilitate initial and continuing compliance with the mediated agreement (Carbonneau, 1986, p. 1169).

Research on Litigation and the Role of Solicitors

Much of the impetus behind the move towards mediation as the favoured dispute resolution practice lies in a conception of the traditional formal legal process as dissatisfying to clients and as inimical to the welfare of children, primarily because of its adversarial nature[4] which is said to exacerbate bitterness and conflict.[5] This starting point appeared in the White Paper which preceded the Family Law Act 1996 as follows:

> The need to cite evidence in support of an alleged fact has the effect of *forcing couples to take up hostile positions* from the very beginning, which may quickly become entrenched. Allegations alienate and humiliate the respondent to such an extent that the marriage is seemingly irretrievable. While children are inevitably affected when their parents separate, research shows that it is conflict between the parents which has been linked to greater social and behavioural problems among children rather than separation and divorce itself (Lord Chancellor's Department, 1995, para. 2.11) (emphasis added).

Litigation and arms length negotiation can heighten conflict, reduce communication and exacerbate the stress and hostility arising from marriage breakdown (Lord Chancellor's Department, 1995, para. 2.20).

Research[6] has shown that children suffer and are damaged as a result of *conflict* between their parents, whether the parents are living together or apart. Consultees considered that the current system encourages conflict, by providing an incentive to seek a quick divorce on the basis of allegations of fault (Lord Chancellor's Department, 1995, para. 2.22) (emphasis in original).

Two important assumptions are being made here: first, a clear dividing line is being drawn between the legal process and 'alternative' dispute resolution procedures. However, as will be discussed below, research has shown such an assumption to be problematic. As Ingleby (1992, p. 18) points out, 'no conceptually satisfactory dividing line can be drawn between the processes of negotiation and litigation.' Secondly, the involvement in, and commitment to, negotiated settlements by solicitors is being ignored. The fact is that most cases reach negotiated settlements, through bipartisan solicitor-led negotiations.[7] The rhetoric which portrays the adversarial process as an unnecessary evil also begs the question, however, as to the nature of the research findings upon which such an assumption is based. There has never been a randomised controlled trial[8] in which litigious divorces are compared with mediated ones, in terms of either process or outcome, and possibly the ethical problems involved in such research would be likely to preclude it ever being done. In this section, we shall present a summary of the main research findings from studies that have examined the traditional legal process.

Carbonneau (1986) reviews American research on public perceptions of the judicial process. He makes the now commonplace assertion that 'fairly high numbers of clients are dissatisfied with the legal process of divorce' (p. 1150); 45% from a study in Georgia seems a typical figure.[9] It is difficult to say much, however, about the sources of such dissatisfaction. Do they, for example, reside in clients' personal unhappiness with their situation, or in their unrealistic expectations of what the legal process can do for them? Or is public dissatisfaction an inevitable outcome of the adversarial process *per se*? There are many elements in the divorce process, and it is difficult to discern what precisely it is that clients seem to be dissatisfied with. It remains a fact, as Galanter and Cahill (1994) point out, that most cases settle, and do not require judicial determination.[10] This is a useful corrective to the naive, though prevalent, tendency to regard the legal process as inimical to reaching negotiated agreements. If most cases do settle, what then accounts for public dissatisfaction with the legal process?

In Britain, there have been three main studies on the legal process of divorce,[11] and a major American study has also recently been published.[12] In the early British[13] work, Davis (1988) considers the question of where the responsibility for acrimony in divorce actually lies. Can it be explained in terms of the parties' emotional needs to work out their feelings of anger and rejection, is it accounted for by solicitors' aggressive conduct of divorce proceedings, or does it lie in the nature of the adversarial process itself? As Davis points out, there is no easy answer to this question. The difficulties are compounded by the finding that 57% of those interviewed in the study reported that their solicitor had tried to keep the divorce 'as friendly as possible' (Davis, 1988, p. 110), and the finding that most family law solicitors and barristers recognise that divorce is characterised by ambivalence and is a complex interplay of separate and mutual interests, which have to be sensitively handled and carefully balanced. These complexities, taken together, may account for client dissatisfactions with the legal process, but perhaps the rhetoric that the adversarial nature of the process exacerbates conflict also has an influence. As Davis (1988) found, solicitors can, and often do, manage to be both partisan and conciliatory,[14] but it is a difficult balance to achieve in the emotional context of divorce. This is a balance which facilitates the client's feeling of security, and a confidence that her or his 'rights' are being protected, at the same time as it acknowledges frustrations and anxieties, as the formal legal process serves as a buffer between potentially warring parties.

Davis's study also sheds some light upon what it is that clients are dissatisfied with in the legal process. The prevalent view is that dissatisfaction arises because solicitors are perceived as being too litigious, and too willing to engage in acrimony. However, Davis found that clients were often dissatisfied because of the perceived willingness of their lawyers to make too many concessions that departed from their own sense of justice in the case.[15] Thus, many solicitors were criticised for being 'too accommodating' to the demands of the other side. This problem arises because, although a solicitor is retained first and foremost to protect the client's interests, it is not always clear what those interests are. Often, they may not be what the client thinks they are, particularly if the client wants no more than to 'stand up and fight' (Davis, 1988, p. 115).

Ingleby (1992) raises the question of whether clients are disadvantaged by the non-adversarial approaches of their solicitors, but finds that it is not easy to give a conclusive answer. There is a multiplicity of factors that influence both the process and the outcome of any given case and there is great variation even in outcomes that are judicially determined because of the wide discretion available to trial judges. In some cases, there may be a tension between the solicitor's perceived commitment to the client and her or his commitment to a non-adversarial approach, but this is by no means inevitable. In any event, each individual case involves a number of different aspects and dimensions, and any tensions in commitment will not necessarily equally affect all aspects of the case. Moreover, as Ingleby (1992) points out, the application of legal rules by solicitors or judges can do nothing to address such structural and substantive inequalities as may exist between the parties and which cause them concern.

What is clear from Davis's study is that solicitors approach their work using many different styles. Just as there is no single 'mediation',[16] so there is no single adversarial approach that can unequivocally be said to produce or to exacerbate conflict. Rather, lawyers seem to recognise the complexities involved, and try hard to achieve the delicate balances that have to be made. Ingleby (1992) makes the important point that even individual solicitors vary their approach to different aspects of their clients' cases. A solicitor will not necessarily employ a straightforwardly litigious or unproblematically conciliatory attitude throughout the negotiation process. Rather, they will switch techniques as the progress of the case demands; it is useful here to draw a distinction between 'negotiation' over the whole case and 'bargaining' over specific issues in it (Ingleby, 1992, p. 163). The evidence produced by Davis (1988) and Ingleby (1992) is clearly at odds with the rhetoric which denounces the 'evils' of the adversarial system (Davis, 1988, p. 125) and this work challenges the prevalent assumption that British solicitors necessarily behave in an adversarial manner.

Even the influence of the formal law does not guarantee the adversarial nature of the negotiation process. Whilst solicitors undoubtedly conduct their bargaining 'in the shadow of the law' (Mnookin and Kornhauser, 1979), the actual influence of the formal law on both the process and the outcome of bipartisan negotiations is dependent upon the resolution of the 'tensions' between the norms of solicitor-solicitor conduct and the formal law (Ingleby, 1992, p. 164). For example, depending on the particular facts of a case, the solicitors involved might agree that the case can be adequately resolved without the necessity to raise or to investigate certain issues such as 'conduct'.

Ingleby's work (1992)[17] points to conclusions similar to those from Davis's (1988) study. Ingleby examined solicitors' activities in the resolution of matrimonial disputes in order to derive some understanding of out-of-court processes. He identifies disparities between the formal law and practical realities, and it is in this disparity that he locates the 'inevitability of conflict' (Ingleby, 1992, p. 7). One aspect of this is 'the various inequalities between the disputants' (p. 7). Ingleby studied three such areas of inequality: emotional, physical and financial. Crucially, he regarded these not as fixed, but as dynamic processes which interact in significant ways with dispute resolution. Davis *et al.* (1994) identified four such areas of inequality that contribute to conflicts within the divorce process: the ability to tolerate a postponed resolution; the ability to manipulate or conceal resources; having (or being free of) responsibility for the care of young children, and the energy and 'grasp' of the respective legal advisers. Further, these authors suggest that the 'settlement culture' is one reason why significant inequalities between the parties are not always redressed by the legal process (Davis *et al.*, 1994, p. 259).

The work of Davis *et al.* (1994) permits further insights into the complexities of the legal resolution of divorce disputes, and sheds further light onto the range of possible reasons for clients' dissatisfactions with the legal process. This work makes it clear that any characterisation of the legal process as necessarily engendering 'conflict and bitterness' is a gross over-simplification, and it supports the earlier work, previously discussed, that the majority of solicitors seek to achieve negotiated settlements in as amicable a way as possible. Nevertheless, conflicts and tensions do occur, but they are not necessarily negative, and can be productive of satisfying outcomes.

One source of such tension is the discrepancy between the parties' views of what constitutes 'justice' in their particular case.[18] The parties' views are often divergent, with each other and in relation to the issues that the formal law permits to be raised. Psychological factors enter into this, and the work of Davis *et al.* (1994) shows the tenacity with which some divorcing people hold on to 'mythical' ideas about the appropriate outcome for their case, a tenacity which can only be explained by a deep psychological investment. These myths interact in complex ways with both the formal law and the provisions of the welfare state. One particularly prevalent belief is 'conduct' should have a bearing on outcome, whereas the formal law permits conduct to be taken into account in only very limited circumstances.[19]

The parties' assumptions concerning the relevance of marital conduct are almost invariably denied within the legal framework...the result is effectively to bury a major component of the parties' perception of the justice of their case (Davis *et al.*, 1994, p. 54).

This single issue could account for a large part of the dissatisfaction that many people feel at the conclusion of their case. But, crucially, each party is likely to have a very different perception of the 'wrong' they have suffered at the hands of the other during the marriage. Davis *et al.* give numerous examples of cases in which the man's sense of justice was far removed from that of his wife, but also at odds with the basis upon which the court would eventually decide the case. This situation is frustrating and may account for the deep resentment that some people feel about the way their cases are handled within the legal process.

The findings of Davis *et al.* (1994) concerning the approach of British lawyers, contrasts with that of Felstiner and Sarat (1988) and Sarat and Felstiner (1995) in the USA. The main dimension of difference seems to be a willingness on the part of the most effective British practitioners to give unequivocal advice, with a clear expectation that the advice will be followed. This contributes to what Davis *et al.* refer to as a 'picture of reasonable certainty' (p. 258) which contrasts with the way in which US lawyers present the legal process to their clients. They tend to present the process as arbitrary and unjust, to be redeemed only by the lawyer's specialist knowledge and insider status. British lawyers also give the impression that the values of fairness which they espouse involve a sense of obligation to the whole family, and particularly to the children, so that the partisanship they exhibit is circumscribed by these broader values.

Sarat and Felstiner's work (1995) also identifies discrepancies between the legal process and the real world lives of people that it regulates. These authors are concerned with questions of power and meaning in the legal process. They attribute the dissatisfactions, felt both by lawyers and their clients, to problems inherent in the negotiation of meaning and power in the legal process. As in the British work, these authors identify as salient the tensions between the demands of the legal process, and people's own perceived realities; the task of the lawyer is to resolve these tensions. Again, a particularly problematic area is the way in which people's expectations and their sense of justice are closely tied to their perceptions of what went wrong with the marriage; divorce narratives are commonly ones of blame and responsibility.[20] Most lawyers resist participating in their clients' constructions of accounts of the failed marriage, and instead try to focus the client's mind on issues of legal relevance and on negotiatory tactics.[21] Thus, from the start, clients and their lawyers are using different languages, working within different frameworks of meaning, as clients work with a 'vocabulary of blame' (Sarat and Felstiner, 1995, p. 38), which the lawyer may challenge, but the tensions frequently remain unresolved. The authors point out that lawyers' refusals to engage with the efforts of their clients to give meaning to the past often results in clients feeling that their lawyer does not truly understand them (p. 51).

In summary, to lawyers, the adversarial system is a way of acknowledging the fact of separate and competing interests; it does not have to imply aggression or ill-feeling, and it can be consistent with a conciliatory approach. Research shows that settlement without adjudication is the goal of the vast majority of divorce lawyers, both here and in the USA and that, in the overwhelming majority of cases, this is achieved. But it is not without its tensions and contradictions; these are inevitable in the negotiation process. Most lawyers attempt to address these in constructive ways, in the framework of the formal law, by balancing delicate personal issues with the requirements of the legal process.

The more recent move towards 'no fault' divorce, and the privileging of the interests of children[22] and/or those of 'the family' as a whole, seriously alters this implicit function of divorce dispute resolution as a process of balancing separate and competing interests. As Davis (1988) points out, it is only on the basis of a perception of competing interests that divorce retains its identity as a legal process. Once this is removed, there is no reason why divorce should not become a solely administrative procedure, or be dealt with by, for example, mental health professionals or child welfare experts (Davis, 1988, p. 120).

Inter-Professional Relationships in Divorce

> There is a growing consensus that conciliation is a means of dispute resolution independent of the legal process and clearly distinguished from social work, counselling and family therapy (Roberts, 1990, p. 89).

In this section, we will be looking at inter-professional tensions in the management of divorce cases. A central question relates to whether mediation belongs in the domain of law and lawyers or in that of therapy and mental health professionals. As will become apparent, this is not an easy question to answer, despite the fact that there have been many calls in

Britain for mediation to be 'independent' of the legal process, on the one hand, and clearly distinguished from counselling or therapy, on the other.[23]

First, however, it is important to put the recent changes in the ways of dealing with divorce in context. Bastard and Cardia-Voneche (1995)[24] argue that the many changes that are taking place in family life have an impact on the professionals who work with families, both on their interventions and on their relationships with each other. It is their contention that there is a correlation between the changing character of the divorce professional and the changing social situations with which they deal. Thus, the evolution of 'the family', that of the law, and changes in professional practices are interlinked in complex ways. As in Britain, mediation in France is a new form of quasi-professional involvement in divorce dispute resolution, with the new mediators being drawn from social work and mental health professions;[25] a new profession is developing. Like any other profession-in-the-making, mediators are presently concerned to establish boundaries and defend a claim to professional territory which is distinctly theirs (Dingwall and Greatbatch 1993, 1995), and much of the rhetoric which surrounds mediation may perhaps best be understood in this context. To this we might also observe an increasing tendency for individualised therapeutic approaches to be used to address social problems (Rose, 1990).

It is difficult, however, strictly to separate mediation from the adversarial process, both conceptually and in practice. According to Davis (1988), the solicitor is more than just a partisan, although her or his multiplicity of roles (advice giver, negotiator, personal counsellor, and so on) remains largely unacknowledged. As has been stated, however, bipartisan negotiation is not a unitary process, and each individual solicitor is likely to apply different approaches to different aspects of the case.[26] Thus, the adversarial process of divorce dispute resolution is never straightforwardly 'litigation' as much popular rhetoric would imply. In addition, it is important to note, as Davis (1988) does, that in recent years the boundaries of the adversarial process have become increasingly blurred.

Morrison (1987) indicates that the boundary between the adversarial process and mediation is a difficult one to draw; both lawyers and non-lawyers serve as divorce mediators.[27] [28] Whether mediation constitutes the practice of law is an impossible question definitively to answer. Morrison's own conclusion, that mediation by non-lawyers should not be considered to be the practice of law, whist mediation by lawyers should, is obviously unsatisfactory. Moreover, it begs the question of what it is, then, that mediators are doing.

McEwen *et al.* (1994)[29] challenge the assumption that divorce mediation and divorce lawyers are incompatible. They find that lawyers play an active role in ensuring the success of mediation and that mediation, in turn, helps to promote efficient case management by the lawyer. Thus, they say, we are mistaken to continue to regard the situation in 'either/or' terms; the law and mediation can be mutually complementary; such binary thinking may have utility for framing rhetorical questions about divorce reform, but it is at odds with the realities of divorce practice. The particular model of mediation utilised in Maine, which is discussed in McEwen's research, seems to incorporate the best of both worlds and, as a result, is valued by clients and embraced by lawyers:

> Divorce mediation is a process that contrasts markedly with the model assumed by much of the commentary. Rather than being an alternative to litigation, mediation draws in divorce cases which are among the most heavily litigated. Rather than demanding that legal rights fade into the shadow of informality, mediation makes legal rules and rights a key reference point through the participation of lawyers. Rather than being an informal substitute for trial, mediation serves as a relatively formal adjunct to negotiation. Rather than placing decision-making exclusively in the hands of the parties, mediation permits, even strengthens, the ability of lawyers to influence decisions. And rather than leaving parties unassisted in the face of pressures of mediators and stronger parties, mediation interposes lawyers as advisors (McEwen *et al.*, 1994, p. 183).

In this model of mediation, the focus is on resolution of the disputes associated with divorce, in a framework which nevertheless can take account of rights and responsibilities, and which recognises that issues of relative 'power' need to be addressed. However, there are other models[30] of mediation which are more therapeutic in orientation, and whose value is seen to lie in their ability to take account of the psychological processes of separation and divorce. Here, the difficulty in separating law from mediation is compounded by the confusion of boundaries between therapy and mediation.

Margulies and Luchow (1992) are not alone in characterising the legal system as inadequate to meet the psychological needs of the parties.[31] They argue that the legal system actually interferes with the psychological tasks that have to be accomplished,[32] and regard mediation as a more appropriate procedure for this reason. Like much of the literature in this area, this analysis is limited by the implicit conception that both the adversarial process and mediation are unitary modes of dispute resolution and, in their focus on 'the family', they fail to separate out the different needs of individual family members.[33] In addition, it presupposes that divorcing individuals are able and willing to behave in a rational manner, despite conflict and emotional turmoil. In Carbonneau's account, there is no strict dividing line between mediation and therapy. He states that:

> [M]ediation is neither an adjudicatory nor a therapeutic process...[it] endeavours to achieve the pragmatic end of adjudication - the finality of determinations - by simultaneously addressing the practical and emotional dimensions of marital conflict (Carbonneau, 1986, p. 1167).

This is very different from the models of mediation which are generally employed in Britain, where practitioners are at pains to delimit mediation as a dispute resolution procedure, quite distinct from any therapeutic process (see, for example, Roberts, 1990, 1997). The need to keep the boundaries distinct was a point made in the *Finer Report*:

> But the deliberate attempt to expand and systematise the welfare function, which is an essential part of the Family Court concept, carries risks as well as advantages, which can only be eliminated by clear thinking and firm practice regarding boundaries and priorities: (*Finer Report*, 1974, p. 174).

In Canada, Kruk (1993) advocates a therapeutic/interventionist approach to family mediation as the most effective and efficient means of promoting 'co-operative parenting' after separation.[34] In this account, 'shared parenting' refers to a post-separation arrangement that attempts to approximate (as closely as possible) the parent-child relationships in the original two-parent home; both parents not only have equal 'rights' with respect to their children's welfare and upbringing, but also have active responsibilities within the daily routines of their children's care and development. Whilst it can of course be argued that such a characterisation of shared parenting flies in the face of the realities of the continued gendered division of labour over child-care in the majority of households, this equality rhetoric constitutes an increasingly dominant discourse both in legal divorce and in rationales for the switch to mediation. Kruk regards the dominant British mediation (the structured, short-term, future-focused, neutral) model as inadequate to secure the aim of co-operative shared parenting, and advocates instead that a therapist-mediator is needed to help parents arrive at and implement a 'parenting plan'.

He envisages five overlapping phases to the process of mediation: assessment, to determine whether shared parenting is going to be possible; education, to ensure that the parties understand the process and understand about the children's needs; advocacy, to actively promote shared parenting as the arrangement best suited to meeting children's needs; facilitation of negotiations towards the development of the shared parenting plan; and continuing support during the implementation of the plan. As Kruk points out, his model is a 'radical alternative' (p. 258) to more traditional models of mediation. However, despite its rhetorical appeal, it is questionable whether such a model could find acceptance at present in Britain, as many of the premises of the therapeutic/interventionist model are in direct conflict with the valued norms of our non-therapeutic and non-interventionist approaches. In particular, mediation has been 'sold' in Britain as a dispute settlement procedure which allows the parties themselves to retain control of both process and outcome, and those who advocate mediation have been at pains to ensure that the boundaries with therapy are not blurred in any way. Kruk's notion that the goals of mediation be defined as therapeutic, and that the mediator's role be highly interventionist, is incompatible with the stated norms and values of mediation in Britain.

However, despite prevalent ideals, the extent to which mediators may already engage in therapeutic strategies, or routinely depart from strict neutrality, needs to be considered. In Britain, Dingwall and Greatbatch (1994) report that mediators in their study, however unwittingly, did influence both the process and the outcome of mediation, a finding that these authors see as incompatible with the value of 'party control' in mediation. Dingwall (1988) asks: 'Does mediation really offer a party-controlled settlement process or is it merely substituting the insidious influence of the mediator for the open decision of the judge?' (Dingwall, 1988, p. 151).[35]

Kressel *et al.* (1994) consider the impact of different mediator styles in custody mediation. They identify two main styles: the settlement-orientation and the problem-solving style, where those who adopted the former style were much less likely to depart from neutrality than those who adopted the latter style. However, the authors found that it was the problem-solving style, involving therapeutically oriented interventions, particularly in cases where destructive conflict was expressed, which produced more frequent and durable settlements. The main difference between the two styles is that those mediators who adopt the problem-solving style are concerned with seeking out and addressing the sources of the conflict, and thus do not shy away from issues concerning the past. This approach is contrary to the model prevalent in Britain, where the focus is on the future, with parties being discouraged from dwelling on the past.

Helm *et al.* (1992) argue that divorce mediation and psychotherapy can be interdependent, and that when they are practised collaboratively, specific benefits can result to divorcing people. The main rationale for the involvement of therapy with mediation, whether as part of the mediation process[36] or as a parallel procedure, is the recognition that divorce is not just a legal event, but is a powerful emotional process, in which intense feelings surface, feelings which are likely to have an impact on whichever dispute resolution procedure is used.[37] Feelings of anger and resentment, of betrayal and frustration, are not conducive to rational discussion, negotiation or decision-making, and for this reason, mediation in matrimonial disputes tends to be rather less successful than mediation in other types of dispute where the emotional issues are not so prominent.

Helm *et al.* (1992), whilst recognising that mediation and therapy are different enterprises, nevertheless point out that there are overlaps between the two processes. Both are concerned with recognition of underlying issues, facilitation of communication and enhancement of self-esteem. Both can facilitate the dissolution of a marriage. Helm *et al.* recommend that mediators and psychotherapists could effectively work as a team, with the therapist attending mediation sessions, in helping divorcing people resolve their disputes. With the aid of therapeutic input, mediators are freed to attend to the concrete issues, and their neutrality and objectivity is in less danger of being compromised, thus making it more likely that the ideal of party control can be realised. By contrast, the therapist may intervene in the mediation to facilitate the resolution of emotional issues, or to alleviate distress. It is important, however, that although such therapists will need mediation training, they should act *as* therapists, in order to avoid role-conflict.[38]

Roberts (1988), however, makes a strong case against such developments. Commenting on the British situation, he expresses a concern that 'all mediation carries with it the risk of unregulated manipulation and coercion' (p. 146). This risk, he says, is increased if mediation is associated with any form of therapeutic intervention, and for this reason he takes the view that mediation should remain distinct from both adjudication and counselling.[39]

Divorce Mediation: Research on Process and Outcome

In this section of the review, we discuss the research findings from a range of mediation studies. Most mediation research derives from the USA,[40] with British research still very much in its infancy.[41] In Britain, claims on behalf of mediation and commentaries about it far outweigh the volume of research which has actually been carried out in this country. Irving and Benjamin (1995)[42] review fifty representative studies in three sections: process studies, studies of mediation outcomes and studies of the predictors of successful mediation. As they point out, however, the results of research should be interpreted with caution, not least because comparability across studies is low, reflecting the heterogeneous character of mediation in the USA.

As regards 'process studies', Irving and Benjamin report that, 'the handful of process studies available are only weakly comparable' (p. 413). Nevertheless, they go on to draw two 'tentative conclusions' from the data. First, mediator styles vary. 'Successful' mediations, measured in terms of the production of agreements, are characterised by 'flexible' mediator responses to couple interactions. These mediators tend actively to intervene in the interaction, encouraging 'productive exchanges' and discouraging 'destructive conflict'. Secondly, the location/setting of mediation practice (public or private, mandatory or voluntary, its relation to local statutory regime) shapes what mediators do. Court-based mediators are less 'flexible', but data on this particular point is lacking, and many questions remain unanswered.

On the issue of 'outcomes', Irving and Benjamin identify six outcome indicators[43] that emerge from the research: agreement rate, client satisfaction, gender differences, co-parental relations, cost and follow up. Agreement rates[44] vary between 40% and 60% for complete agreement, and between 10% and 20% for partial agreement. These rates are consistent across court-based and private mediation, voluntary and mandatory cases, and domestic violence and high conflict cases.[45] Irving and Benjamin (1995) state that 'several studies report that mediation clients were more likely to reach voluntary agreement than their counterparts in litigation, in both the USA and in Britain, and to do so in less time' (p. 414). However, this conclusion may be stretching the findings of a number of studies rather too far, as there has never been a randomised controlled trial in which the outcomes of litigation has been compared with mediation. Of the two British studies to which the authors refer, one is an evaluative study of child-focused mediation,[46] and the other is an analysis of the question of 'party control' in the process of mediation.[47] Neither of these studies contains any data upon which the outcome of mediation could be compared with that of litigation. This small point, however, does raise questions about the thoroughness and the objectivity of Irving and Benjamin's review. Davis (1988) makes the important point in relation to 'outcomes' that 'settling' does not, as an end in itself, occur to most people. Rather, people are concerned with the quality of justice that is available to them,[48] and 'settlement' does not have any necessary relationship with 'justice'.

Irving and Benjamin (1995) also report that 'compared to their litigated counterparts, mediated agreements were both different and better' (p. 415). However, we are given no indication of the criterion for 'better' which the authors, or the researchers whose studies are cited, actually employ. One example[49] is given: 'mediated agreements were more comprehensive and more likely to favour shared parenting' (p. 415).

Irving and Benjamin's conclusions that these data 'suggest that family mediation is efficient and effective...and yields agreements that are comparatively complete and comprehensive' (p. 415) and that 'court-based and private mediation appear equally effective' (p. 415) are over-optimistic conclusions which, we would suggest, are not wholly borne out by the studies they review. Conclusions such as these may therefore be seen as part of the 'rhetoric' of mediation. One reviewer calls the book 'an excellent blend of scholarship and practice' and states that 'the authors have done a service to the profession by skilfully reviewing and integrating this literature',[50] thereby uncritically accepting the work on its own terms and failing to apply the standards of critical scrutiny which are expected in academic writing. Such reviews, in turn, contribute to what has become very powerful rhetoric.

As regards the issue of 'client satisfaction', Irving and Benjamin (1995) report that studies reveal between 60% to 80% of clients reporting 'high satisfaction' with both the process and the outcome of mediation. But no figures for client satisfaction with litigation or adversarial negotiation are offered for comparative purposes.[51] It should also be noted that the reader has no way of knowing how these levels of satisfaction might or might not be linked to the nature of the samples investigated. For example, are levels of satisfaction higher when mediation is voluntary than when it is court-mandated? Are they higher when mediation is child-focused than when it covers all issues?

On the thorny question of 'gender differences'[52] Irving and Benjamin (1995) are at pains to show that mediation research has taken account of feminist critiques of mediation. They conclude that results suggest that both women and men 'are treated fairly in mediation' and that 'the data provide a potent rejoinder to the feminist critique of mediation...The data reviewed...make clear that mediators have heard women's complaints and have responded in ways that protect the rights of both women and men' (p. 416-417).

As regards co-parental relations, Irving and Benjamin (1995) report mixed findings. Some studies found up to 76% of respondents reporting improvements in co-parental relations, including decreased conflict and improved communication, whilst others report limited or no change. Again, difficulties in interpreting the data may arise because of the mixture of mandated and voluntary mediation, and therapeutic and non-therapeutic mediation across the studies reviewed.

On the question of cost, Irving and Benjamin (1995) note that proponents of mediation often argue that mediated settlements are cheaper than litigation. In general, this point is supported by research, although there are some contradictory findings, and caution must be exercised when assessing the costs of any service. For example, comparing the cost of litigation with that of mediation is not as straightforward a task as it might at first appear, particularly where mediation is court-based, or includes a therapeutic component, and where parties who mediate also utilise, in varying ways, legal services.[53]

As regards follow-up studies, there are only a few longitudinal studies that have looked at questions such as the durability of mediated agreements. Again, the findings are mixed, and it is difficult to make comparisons across studies because of such matters as sample selection effects and variations in mediation practice. Nevertheless, Irving and Benjamin (1995) draw the following conclusion: these data, they say, 'speak in unequivocal terms to mediation efficacy in regard to agreement durability, compliance and satisfaction' (p. 420). Again, we would suggest that this conclusion is not warranted by the data the authors discuss.

Irving and Benjamin also review a range of studies that have addressed the issue of the 'predictors of agreement' in mediation. They point out that 'there is no consensus among researchers as to the best predictors of mediated agreement' (p. 420). Rather, there are many factors to be taken into account, including client attributes, financial parity, client communicative competence, and socio-economic status. Also important are the interactions between client and mediator attributes, mediation model, mediator conduct and the nature of the dispute(s) to be mediated. Efforts to identify the necessary 'attributes' of clients who are likely to be amenable to mediation remain 'at a rudimentary stage of development and are as yet of little practical utility'.[54]

In view of the uncertainties which persist, the complexities involved, and the caution which must be exercised when interpreting the results of a wide range of disparate research studies, it is not a little surprising that Irving and Benjamin (1995) are able to draw a definitive conclusion from their review. They state:

> The research shows, first, that mediation is highly effective. The majority of clients (both women and men) reach agreement (in whole or in part), report satisfaction, consider it fair and responsive, and, on follow up, tend to comply with their agreement and resolve difficulties informally. Secondly, mediation is also efficient, requiring limited time and expense to reach settlement (p. 422).

These are strong claims[55] but, in a separate paragraph, the authors do point out that the trends they have identified are subject to multiple interpretations, and at least one prominent researcher[56] has concluded that mediation is no better and no worse than litigation. The authors, however, believe that mediation certainly has the potential to be better than litigation, and they advocate therapeutic mediation, within an 'ecosystems' perspective, as the most promising way forward.

D'Errico and Elwork (1991) investigated the question of whether self-determined divorce and child custody agreements were 'really better' than adjudicated ones. They began from the premise that the main advantage of mediation is seen to be the self-determined character of the agreements reached in that process. As we have seen from the research reviewed so far, mediation is widely thought to lead to greater satisfaction and greater compliance with the agreement reached, less post-divorce conflict between the spouses and better emotional adjustment. D'Errico and Elwork, however, state that 'in reality, however, these claims have not been clearly and consistently demonstrated, and their validity is still in question' (p. 105). The results of their study show that couples who perceived themselves as having actively participated in reaching their own agreements were indeed more satisfied with them. These same couples, however, reported more post-divorce conflict and more emotional maladjustment. Custody satisfaction was positively correlated with emotional maladjustment, and the authors therefore conclude that self-determined agreements can have negative consequences. The authors explain this finding on the basis that persons who are able to be co-operative during the divorce process are likely to develop post-divorce arrangements that require continued co-operation, but this requires more frequent interactions which create opportunities for conflict: 'In summary, co-operation requires many divorcing couples to do that which they were unable to do while married' (p. 111).

In a similar vein, Walker (1993), drawing on a range of research studies in which she has participated, considers whether co-operative post-divorce parenting is a real possibility or just a 'pipedream'. She argues that the vision of 'happy-ever-after' post-divorce families ignores the complexity of transitions facing separating families, and the emotional, social and economic stresses which parents experience for many years. She concludes that we may be expecting too much of divorcing parents and failing adequately to address the sometimes conflicting needs of different family members.

Walker (1994) reminds us that the social, emotional and economic realities of divorce present a formidable barrier to the achievement of co-operative post-divorce relationships: 'We have found that as financial pressures bite, resentment increases, communication is strained, and conflict is not unusual for many years following divorce' (p. 3). In their four year follow-up study[57] of couples who mediated children issues on divorce, Walker and her colleagues found that a third of parents had serious financial problems which tended to exacerbate the psychological distress. They also found low levels of communication between ex-spouses concerning the children, with half of them having no contact at all with each other. As Walker states, this situation is clearly at odds with the philosophy of shared parental responsibility that is now so valued. She concludes that the long term happiness of some divorced parents is dependent upon them having as little contact as possible with each other; clearly, the best interests of parents and children do not always coincide.

Kelly *et al.* (1988)[58] report on a comparison between mediated and adversarial divorce. As there are so few studies that have attempted to make such a comparison, it is worth looking at it in detail. It should be noted, however, that this study was not a randomised controlled trial, in which couples were randomly assigned either to a mediation or an adversarial 'condition'. The participants were people who *chose* either to litigate or to mediate and, thus, whilst legitimate comparisons may be made between the characteristics of the two groups, it is difficult to draw definitive conclusions about the relative effectiveness of mediation and the adversarial process.[59] This study addressed three main questions: (i) are couples who choose mediation different from those who opt for the more traditional adversarial route? (ii) is mediation more effective in reducing psychological distress? and (iii) what factors distinguish those people who complete mediation from those who do not?

Two samples of divorcing people were studied at five points in time, beginning with (voluntary) entry into the mediation (212 people or 106 couples) or the adversarial process (225 people including 47 couples),[60] and ending two years post-divorce. Respondents were interviewed, completed demographic data forms and postal questionnaires. On demographic criteria, the mediation sample was different from the adversarial sample on a number of measures. Those who mediated were significantly younger, less likely already to have separated, were more likely to have completed college or graduate studies, and more likely to have children under 18.

The authors investigated possible differences between the mediation and the adversarial groups in respect of marital communication, the decision to divorce, spousal interactions, and co-parental relationships. There was no difference between the groups on the amount of open conflict reported in the last few years of the marriage; 50% of both groups reported that they 'often' or 'always' had conflict. There was also no difference in the quality of marital communication between the two groups; communication generally ranged from 'very poor' to 'adequate'. There were no significant differences between the groups on a measure of attitudes towards the divorce, although there were gender differences, with women more likely to have initiated the divorce and more likely to have positive attitudes towards it. Group differences were found on some personality measures; mediation respondents were more likely to have a view of their spouses as more powerful and more honest and fair, and less likely to report that their spouses took advantage of them. There was no difference between the groups on a measure of the partner's perceived ability to compromise, and there were no differences in self-ratings of co-operation.

Eight-two per cent of the mediation sample had children, as compared with 52% of the adversarial sample.[61] The authors suggest that couples with children are more likely to come into mediation because they are searching for a more 'amicable' way of resolving their disputes. Adversarial respondents did perceive themselves as being less able to co-operate on matters concerning the children, and were less likely to have discussed how they were going to organise co-parenting arrangements.

The authors go on to discuss psychological reactions to divorce: they conclude that divorce creates a heightened level of psychological distress and symptomatology. There were no differences between the groups on measures of hostility or anger; women, however, were significantly more angry than men, with 60% reporting anger. Anger was correlated with 'depression' about the divorce and with perceived stress. It was also associated with reported poor co-operation, and higher marital conflict.

At time 1 (on entry into mediation or on entry into the study)[62] 69% of the total sample were experiencing moderate to high levels of depression. The mediation sample reported significantly higher levels of depression, stress and guilt. The authors suggest that this may reflect the inability of these people to behave in a rejecting and hostile way and they state that:

> Guilt and depression engendered by the divorce, and a greater sensitivity to their spouse's feelings, may in fact lead such men and women to choose mediation as a more humane way of divorcing (Kelly *et al.*, 1988, p. 464).

At time 2 (mediation completed or six months after time 1), both groups' scores on the psychological measures had decreased, but respondents remained significantly more symptomatic than a normative sample on most measures. Thus, these decreases may be attributable to the passage of time, rather than to the dispute resolution procedure *per se*. The authors conclude that their findings do not support the hypothesis that mediation is significantly more effective in reducing psychological distress and dysfunction.[63] 'Co-operation' improved in both groups, but the change was significantly greater in the mediation group.

As compared to Time 1, at Time 2, the mediation respondents were less positive about their divorces. The authors suggest that:

> It may well be that, as a result of communicating directly and effectively enough with each other to be able to reach a series of agreements, the mediation respondents became more ambivalent about their pending divorces. It seems reasonable to speculate that the ability to resolve these issues together in a co-operative, problem-solving context may create more doubts, particularly if the mediator effectively contained the clients' conflict (Kelly *et al.*, 1988, p. 465).

The authors conclude that their expectation that the mediation group would be beneficially more affected by the process than the adversarial one was over simplified. They estimate that mediation may not be suitable for as many as 60% of couples who try it. Forty-three per cent of their sample terminated mediation before agreement on all issues was reached. The terminators were not distinguished by any demographic characteristics, or on measures of marital conflict, anger, psychopathology or communication. What was related to terminating mediation was the presence of current ties (such as not being separated) at entry into the study; the authors suggest that withdrawing from mediation may be a way of trying to hold on to the marriage.

The study investigated the reasons terminators themselves gave for termination, and found that cost was the most frequent reason given. Secondly, a cluster of feelings relating to being 'overwhelmed' and a 'lack of empowerment' emerged; people believed that they had neither the resources nor the strength to continue. Interestingly, women were significantly more likely than men to cite this lack of empowerment. Thirdly, a cluster of feelings relating to the respondent not being able to tolerate being with the spouse emerged, but there were no gender differences. Significantly, there were no differences between terminators and completers at time 1;[64] the authors draw no such conclusion, but it might be suggested that such differences as did emerge between those who terminated and those who completed, must have arisen during the mediation process itself. The question therefore arises, not discussed in this paper, as to whether mediation might actually be detrimental for some people. This observation also raises questions about the meaning of the finding, in this and other studies, that even people who terminate mediation sometimes express 'satisfaction' with the process.

Divorce Mediation: The British Debate

A debate has arisen in Britain primarily focused on two related issues: party control and balancing power in mediation. Some of the earliest British studies on mediation were carried out by Gwynn Davis and his colleagues at Bristol.[65] Davis' book, *Partisans and Mediators* brought together evidence from five separate research studies, which began in 1978. Davis sees the case for family mediation as having been built upon the twin pillars of 'cost reduction' and 'child welfare', but he argues that there is no simple relationship between the practice of mediation and the pursuit of these objectives. As regards child welfare, he argues that favourable outcomes in this respect cannot be guaranteed, because of the inevitable tension between 'vigorous pursuit of child welfare objectives' and the achievement of 'party control' in mediation. He observes that:

> Empowering the disputants may be one aspiration, but it is equally plausible
> to regard the practice of the new mediators as underpinned by their strongly
> pro-child and pro-family values (Davis, 1988, p. 58).

Similarly, there are problems with the assumption that more
widespread use of mediation will result in legal aid savings. He points out
that mediation only *appears* to be cheap, because it is performed by
volunteers or its costs are absorbed into the Probation Service budget. He
argues that a better case for mediation may be made in terms of (a) the
highly idiosyncratic nature of family conflict, (b) the fact that future
contact between family members may need to be sustained and (c) family
members are presumed to share certain values, although their individual
interests may be in conflict.

Davis (1988) discusses the thorny question of inequalities in
bargaining power. Early feminist critics in Britain (for example,
Bottomley, 1984, 1985) regarded this as one of the most problematic
aspects of the move towards informality in family law. Mediators
themselves have not ignored the problem, but they tend to regard the issue
of 'inequality' in a broader (and less political) way. Parkinson (1986), for
example, identifies a number of 'inequalities' in bargaining power
(including intellectual, verbal, access to resources, emotional and
physical); because 'power' is conceived in this way, it follows that no one
person necessarily holds all the power at any one time. Part of the task of
the mediator, according to Parkinson, is to mitigate these power
imbalances, if truly voluntary and lasting agreements are to be reached.
But, she does not consider in any depth the techniques that can be used to
address this question. Notably, also, Haynes' work (1993), which has been
influential in Britain, did not explicitly address the question of mitigating
power imbalances in the process of mediation.[66] Similarly, discussion
devoted to the question of power imbalances is absent from the collection
of papers in Fisher's book (1990), although individual authors do mention
such things as 'balancing power' as among the 'goals' of mediation.[67] The
task for mediators becomes, in Roberts' words, 'to offset inequalities of
bargaining power without loss of impartiality' (Roberts, 1990, p. 93). But
we are given no indication as to *how* this may be done, and the essential
tensions between mediator neutrality and the possible need for
interventions to ensure fairness in the negotiation process are not
discussed.

Roberts (1997) mentions some of the ways in which mediators can
'offset' inequalities of bargaining power between the parties. Three main
ways are described: first, the mediator should ensure that the parties

themselves recognise any inequalities that exist. Secondly, the mediator must ensure that both parties have all the relevant information. Thirdly, it is the responsibility of the mediator to ensure that both parties participate freely and fairly in the negotiations. Mediators, she says, also have a duty to intervene if an outcome is being consented to that is patently unfair. In her discussion of these guidelines for good practice, Roberts adopts a broad and pragmatic view of the meaning of 'inequality' which includes a range of factors (such as emotional and social vulnerability, *de facto* care and control of the children) beyond simple financial and material circumstances. For example, she argues that a non-resident father is in a weaker bargaining position than a resident mother. Roberts' assumptions about 'power' in marriage and divorce lead her to focus on 'bargaining power' within the mediation process, to the neglect of broader inequalities, such as those which are gendered and of structural and discursive origin, which have been of concern to feminist commentators (see, for example, Fineman, 1991, 1995; Grillo, 1991).

Haynes (1988) points to the difficulties in defining 'power'; power is the property not of a person, but of a social relation and, in divorce, it has many manifestations. Haynes defines power as 'control of or access to emotional, economic or physical resources desired by the other' (p. 278). For him, 'power' is interchangeable with 'influence' (p. 278) or 'social influence' (p. 281). One partner may exercise power in one aspect of a relationship, whilst not in others, and power is often linked to the different 'roles' played by different people in the family. Thus Haynes suggests that unitary power is not possessed by one partner all of the time. He sees the tasks of the mediator as including to enable 'transfers of power' between areas and between spouses, and to maintain an overall 'balance of power' between the parties. Haynes reasons that where one partner wields visible power, it is necessary for the mediator to identify the 'compensations' which the apparently powerless party receives in the transaction:

> The loss of power experienced by one spouse in the marriage is usually compensated by some real benefits to that spouse in another area. In a typical "macho" marriage, the loss of identity by the wife in becoming subordinate to the husband paradoxically gives her power in the relationship. The subordinate condition is a desirable resource to the husband because he needs her in that subordinate position in order to maintain his macho sense of himself. If the wife can threaten the stability of that resource by threatening to decrease her subordination and therefore the value of the relationship to him, she, in turn, exercises power in an apparently powerless situation (Haynes, 1988, pp. 279-280).

Most men have more power in their marriages in the area of finances and decision making, and most women have more power in their marriages over relationships and the children. Thus in a typical adversarial divorce, the husband wields his power through the support and asset distribution while the wife wields hers through the children (Haynes, 1988, p. 280).

Thus, he argues, the mediator needs to determine the various 'power attributes' that each partner has, and discover where that power lies, and whether it is 'sufficiently imbalanced to adversely effect (*sic*) the negotiations'. Haynes sees the mediator as having a responsibility to correct such imbalances as are likely to interfere with the couple's ability to negotiate a fair agreement. How is this to be done?

Haynes begins his discussion of this issue by setting out five areas of power (or 'social influence') which the mediator should assess and, where necessary, make the appropriate intervention to effect balancing:

1. *Informational Power:* Power imbalances which are the result of one party having more information than the other are relatively easily corrected in mediation: the mediator can ensure that all the relevant data are provided and can be shared.
2. *Referent Power:* This refers to the desire of the parties to maintain a joint referent. Examples include the family's standards of fairness, or the 'interests of the children', or the approval of the mediator, any or all of which may be invoked, either overtly or covertly, to effect a change in position of one or both spouses.
3. *Legitimate Influences:* What Haynes refers to as 'legitimate influences' relate to traditional concepts of rights as arising from particular roles. For him, a paradoxical aspect of this form of power lies in 'the power of the powerless'; for example, a powerless spouse can legitimately expect help (financial or otherwise) from the powerful one. It becomes necessary for the mediator to intervene to 'break' legitimate power relationships where their maintenance would result in an unfair outcome, but Haynes admits that such interventions are problematic, insofar as they involve challenging established patterns of behaviour.
4. *Expert Influence:* One or other party may use expertise to gain an advantage over the other. In mediation, however, the mediator retains the crucial expert power, which can then be shared, and used for mutual benefit.
5. *Coercive Influence:* Coercion and rewards are seen by Haynes as opposite sides of the same coin. But mediation can diminish the

power of one spouse to reward or punish the other, for example, by 'reframing' threats into constructive statements or even promises, or by directly challenging threats.

Thus, the mediator needs to make an assessment of the couple along all of these dimensions, as an ongoing process with reference to the concrete issues under discussion. However, as Haynes points out, the question of the various manifestations of interpersonal power (as distinct from social power) also needs to be addressed. Here, the mediator has to obtain a sense of the pattern and dynamics of the power relations in each individual couple. The mediator may then employ one of three basic strategies. First, identifying with the person under attack; here the mediator directly intervenes to stop destructive behaviour. Secondly, forbidding an issue; here the mediator obtains the agreement of the couple that certain issues (for example, the views of third parties) be excluded from the mediation. Finally, control of communications; here, the mediator prevents one person from dominating by taking control of and structuring communications, and restating the position of each party in a more neutral way. Concluding his chapter, Haynes states that the mediator, although not a therapist, can accomplish therapeutic interventions, whilst being clear to the parties that s/he is not conducting therapy.

What is clear from this brief examination of Haynes' account is that he appears to see no problem with the type of interventions he utilises for managing power relations. However, academic commentators have taken a different view.[68]

There have been some heated exchanges between mediators and academics in the UK over these issues. In the late 1980s and early 1990s, Dingwall and his co-workers began publishing the results of their research into mediator-client interactions in Britain. For example, Dingwall and Greatbatch (1991) report the findings from a study of 79 mediation sessions which they tape-recorded and analysed using a form of conversation analysis. Their central finding went right to the heart of the issue of 'party control' in mediation; they found mediators to have extensive power to influence both the process and the outcome of mediation, power which was used both positively (to encourage some outcomes) and negatively (to discourage others).[69] [70] Roberts (1992), writing as a professional and someone involved in mediation practice, took issue, not just with these findings, but with the research more generally, criticising both the methodology the researchers had adopted and their understanding of the basis of mediation.

In their response, Dingwall and Greatbatch (1993) drew attention to the distinction between the advocacy of mediation as a preferred form of dispute resolution by a leading practitioner, and the social scientific analysis of this new form of dispute resolution. They reiterated their concerns about the 'overselling' of mediation by practitioners, and the production of 'facile answers' in response to important questions of social policy. They saw these processes, from a sociological point of view, as understandable aspects of the expansion of a new occupational jurisdiction. Roberts (1994), in reply, drew attention to the problematic relations between theory and practice, and the respective contributions of academics and practitioners,[71] and she pointed out that academics, too, have their own professional interests to protect. Academics, she argued, are also guilty of oversimplifying claims about mediation. In the final article in this exchange, Dingwall and Greatbatch (1995) reiterated their belief that it is the proper role of the social scientist to provide critical comment on new occupational orthodoxies. This debate, it seems, reflects the differing values and commitments of practitioners and academics.

Under the scrutiny of the social scientist the premises, practices and values of mediators have been problematised and politicised. These debates signify not an 'attack' on practitioners by academics, but an attempt to make explicit the power of the mediator, and to cut through the rhetoric of mediation. Social scientific analysis helps us to attain some understanding of mediation as a new practice and as a new occupational group. Like the legal system which it, in part, replaces, mediation contributes to the regulation of the behaviour of citizens through the deployment of particular discourses that address particular social concerns. The impact of such critiques is that mediation is not a politically neutral activity[72] and it is the legitimate concern of the social scientist critically to scrutinise social policy developments.

Divorce Mediation: British Evaluation Work

In recent years, there have been two major projects that have evaluated mediation in Britain. The first (Ogus *et al.*, 1989) was carried out at the Conciliation Project Unit (CPU) (now the Relate Centre for Family Studies) at the University of Newcastle on behalf of the Lord Chancellor's Department (LCD). The brief of the CPU was to provide the LCD with information to enable a decision to be made whether a publicly funded conciliation service should be established. To this end, the project entailed the collection of data from existing schemes, to compare the costs of different types of schemes, and to assess their effectiveness.[73] At the time this research was carried out, the out-of-court schemes were concerned with child-focused conciliation, and were not 'comprehensive' as many schemes are today.

The second major piece of evaluative research (Walker *et al.*, 1994) was also carried out at the University of Newcastle. In 1990, funding was provided by the Joseph Rowntree Foundation for the development of five pilot projects in comprehensive family mediation,[74] and the research team was invited to evaluate the five projects. The aims of the research included to evaluate and compare the effectiveness of the range of approaches to comprehensive mediation, having particular regard to the views of 'consumers', and to assess costs. We will briefly discuss the main findings of these two studies in turn.

First, on the question of cost, Ogus *et al.* (1989) report that their research did not provide support for the idea that the 'effects of conciliation on cost more than outweigh, or even substantially mitigate, the resource costs of providing it' (p. 349). However, the authors did find some slight evidence of a tendency for conciliation to lead to cost reductions (reduced litigation costs, etc.), but these were relatively minor. In summary, the authors state that 'the results of our statistical analysis of costs indicate that conciliation, whether court-based or independent, involves significant net additions to the overall resource cost of settling disputes'(p. 349).

On the question of the effectiveness of conciliation, the authors report difficulties in reaching firm conclusions, not least because the conciliation intervention itself was variable, in both nature and the length of the process. In addition, problems of 'causality' remain difficult to resolve. Without a randomised controlled trial, or even an adequate control group, difficulties in attributing causality are likely to render firm conclusions difficult to draw in evaluative research such as this.

However, the authors did find that, in general, users reported that agreement was reached on some issues in 71% of cases, in which 74% of people described themselves as 'satisfied' with the agreements reached. The court-based services, in particular where judicial control was 'high', were less successful than other forms of conciliation in this respect, with independent schemes the most successful. As regards any improvement in the quality of relations between former spouses, there was no evidence in this study that conciliation had either a positive or a negative impact on relationships. Users of independent schemes did seem to experience improvements in psychological well-being, but, again, problems of attribution and causality remain. The authors point out that this could well have been a function of the greater length of time parties spent in the independent schemes. On the question of user satisfaction, 15% reported feeling dissatisfied whilst some 75% said they would recommend conciliation to others.

Thus the findings of this initial study were not such that the authors were able unequivocally to make recommendations on the desirability of setting up a national service. The authors identify five factors which they regard as contributing to the effectiveness of conciliation: first, the 'difficulty' of the case; more complex cases are more difficult to resolve, whether by mediation or otherwise. It should also be noted that 'difficulties' in a case have many origins and take many forms, and many difficulties (such as those associated with poverty or gender inequalities) cannot be addressed, let alone resolved, within divorce dispute resolution alone. Secondly, the issues involved; it is unusual for couples to be in dispute over a single issue and, once one is resolved, the dispute may become focused on another. The third factor is type of conciliation; the independent services seemed to have an advantage over court-based programmes in that more time was allowed for settling disputes, and consequently more detailed explorations of the issues could be made. People felt under less pressure to agree in the private schemes than they did in the court environment. The fourth factor is users' understanding of conciliation; the authors note that information needs to be provided, so that people come to conciliation knowing what to expect and what will be expected of them. Finally, the overlapping of legal, judicial, welfare and conciliation processes may be a further source of confusion that limits effectiveness. Thus the authors conclude that mediation should not be mandatory, should not be focused only on child related issues and should be clearly differentiated from other processes.

Turning now to the report of Walker *et al.* (1994),[75] 102 couples[76] underwent comprehensive mediation during the research period in the 5 centres. Of these, 58% referred themselves. Fifty-six per cent of couples reached the end of the process and drew up a *Memorandum of Understanding* which set out details of the agreements they had reached. They attended an average of 6 mediation appointments over 21 weeks, taking up 16 hours of mediator time.

The authors found that during comprehensive mediation, 80% of couples reached some agreement (41% on some issues and 39% on all issues). Twenty per cent failed to reach any agreement at all. Just over half were satisfied with the outcome of mediation, whilst 18% expressed dissatisfaction. The authors also report, contrary to the findings of the earlier study, that mediation had beneficial effects on communication between the spouses and on the reduction of bitterness and tension. As regards the question of costs, many of those using the service regarded it as a cost-effective alternative to the legal process. But the authors found that the costs of providing mediation varied between services and, in general, was heavily subsidised by practitioners working for low rates of pay.

The main problem with this study, as with any 'evaluative' research, is the lack of a control group; it is not possible to say, on the basis of this study, whether mediation is any better or any worse than litigation or solicitor-led negotiation on a range of measures. In addition, the generalisability of these findings is further limited if it is borne in mind that the people who mediated had, in general, chosen to do so. Nevertheless, this research undoubtedly played a significant part in the development of government proposals to reform the divorce law, now set out in the Family Law Act 1996.

McCarthy and Walker (1996) have further developed the work of the Newcastle group of researchers. They conducted a three-year follow up study of 113 people (by postal questionnaire), in which they assessed the longer-term impact of mediation, and compared the experiences of those who used comprehensive mediation (29%) with those using child-focused mediation (71%). They found that almost two thirds of people said that they were glad they had used mediation, whilst 25% wished that they had not done so. People who used the all-issues mediation were more likely to say that they were glad they went; 70% said that it had helped them to reach agreement about money and property, and 60% agreements about children. Sixty-six per cent felt that they had been helped to reduce conflict. Those using all-issues mediation were more likely to reach agreements than those whose mediation was focused on children's issues, and their agreements about children were more likely to last. The authors point out that reaching agreement should not be seen as the 'be all and end all' of mediation, because mediation might produce other benefits, such as improving communication, reducing bitterness and enhancing negotiating skills. Only three respondents in this study did not employ solicitors during divorce. The authors conclude that reaching agreements during mediation can have a significant impact on the quality of life after divorce and also on the cost of getting divorced, and that mediation has a vital role to play in the remaking of co-operative relationships after divorce.

One of the problems which besets mediation research and which certainly applies to the evaluation studies we have discussed, is the lack of baseline data from which comparisons may be made. Thus, for instance, levels of conflict, co-operation and communication, prior to the mediation intervention, are not known, and thus, nothing definitive may be said about 'improvements' in these areas.

Gender Issues in Mediation

The matter of gender issues in mediation continues to be debated, both in Britain and abroad. In the USA, Grillo's analysis of the 'process dangers for women' in mediation (Grillo, 1991) attracted trenchant rejoinders that occupied an entire issue of the *Family and Conciliation Courts Review* in 1992.[77] In Britain, Bottomley (1984, 1985) began the debate.[78] It may be that the issues involved will never be resolved; feminist analyses begin from very different premises from those adopted by many practitioners and proponents of mediation. Feminist critiques begin with an implicit acceptance that, despite the formal equality which women now have before the law, they continue to be disadvantaged, in relation to men, by substantive inequalities which are perpetuated by social discourses in which women, as a group, are discursively positioned as the 'other' of men, and in which gendered polarities are produced and reproduced.[79] It follows that women have particular interests in the divorce process which are different from, and may be in opposition to, those of men. By contrast, those who embrace mediation do so from a very different perspective; for them, gendered parity of bargaining power may be assumed to be present, and the possibility of women's and men's separate and competing interests in divorce tends to be overridden by a focus on the interests of children or on those of 'the family' as a whole.

Thus, there is a sense in which the concerns of these different interest groups both bypass and deny each other's premises,[80] and true resolution of the issues has proved impossible to achieve. Both interest groups work with a clear set of values. In the case of feminism, those values relate to the feminist project as a whole; in the case of mediation, those values relate to beliefs about what is presumed to be in the 'best interests' of children. For obvious reasons, the latter set of values more easily feeds into and feeds off the dominant discourses that make their appeal to 'objectivity' through their links with child welfare science.[81] The feminist argument sees mediation as assisting in the preservation of the gendered *status quo*, and to that extent, mediation appears as inherently conservative. That the gender debate no longer rages as fiercely as it might, perhaps is testimony to the power of the dominant social discourses which render feminist accounts marginal,[82] and which tend to elevate mediation to the superior status of an obvious 'common sense'. That feminists seem reluctant to tackle the issues head on may also reflect the inherent dilemmas in feminist attempts to engage with law, dilemmas which have become particularly acute with the post-modern deconstruction of 'women' as a category and a unified interest group. [83]

Let us consider the feminist critiques, and the responses to them, in more detail. Bottomley (1985) argued that, in the present social structure, feminists should be extremely wary of the appealing image of mediation, which she saw as inseparable from broader changes in family law which themselves were likely to be detrimental to women. For her, mediation was both an alternative to the legal process and a development within it which, in accordance with Donzelot's thesis (Donzelot, 1980) 'cloaks continuing intervention and supervision of families by courts and related agencies which is rendered benevolent by images of caring and the welfare of children' (Bottomley, 1985, p. 163). She argued that, whilst the relations of feminists to the formal law is necessarily ambivalent.

> [I]n the present situation the use of lawyers, arguments around rules and the procedural safeguards of formal justice may well serve women's interests better than regulation through a more informal, welfarist approach which seems to emphasise party control and choice (p. 164).[84]

For Bottomley, the shift from public to private ordering in family law is a deeply worrying development; she sees an exchange of one form of regulation for another and states that:

> [P]rivate ordering can only be detrimental to women; economic, social and psychological vulnerability all militate against the image of the equal bargaining situation which is presumed to be present in mediation for it to be a truly mutual agreement (p. 179).

Existing power relations are therefore affirmed.[85] Thus, Bottomley argues, women are likely to suffer in three ways from mediation: they face their former partner with a lack of equality; they face a seemingly neutral mediator who is likely to be purveying dominant social values that are oppressive to women; and mediation prevents women bringing their specific problems and needs in relation to the family into the public arena of formal justice where fairness and equity are at least possibilities. Formal justice, she argues, offers three crucial things: substantive rights, procedural safeguards and the possibility of mitigating power imbalances between the parties.

Roberts (1996, 1997), in defence of mediation, states that criticisms of mediation such as those raised by Bottomley, rest on two assumptions which she sees as mistaken; first, that women do not know what they want and cannot speak for themselves and, secondly, that where women do seek co-operation with former partners, they are seen as acting against their own best interests. Roberts' main objection to these assumptions, and to feminist criticisms, is that they, in her view, lack empirical support. By contrast, she adduces research evidence that addresses issues of relative bargaining power and gender fairness in mediation. On the question of bargaining power, Roberts (1996) argues that personal power relationships are complex and multi-faceted; both parties may feel vulnerable in different ways on divorce, and situations are never static: 'Rarely are the disadvantages stacked all one way' (p. 8).

Further, she states that mediation cannot be expected to remedy the social and economic inequalities that undoubtedly exist.[86] On the question of gender fairness in mediation, Roberts (1996) says that problems of power differentials exist as much in the traditional legal process as they do in mediation, and the adversarial system may even introduce new inequalities.[87] Roberts (1996) then goes on to consider the empirical evidence, and argues that there is none to support the notion that women are disadvantaged by mediation; on the contrary, she says, 'there is a growing body of research showing high levels of satisfaction among women in relation both to the process and outcomes of mediation' (p. 9).

However, in citing American and Australian studies to this effect, Roberts perpetuates a notion of mediation as a unitary practice, and fails to take account of such limitations in the applicability of research findings as have previously been discussed in this review. Thus, there is considerable slippage between mediation as practised in particular ways, in particular countries, in particular historical circumstances, with particular client groups, addressing particular issues, and having particular relations with the judicial system, and a mythical 'mediation' which does not and can not exist.[88] In addition, contradictory findings are ignored.[89] More significantly, perhaps, Roberts' analysis is largely confined to the question of women's and men's 'satisfaction' with mediation, and she argues that mediation is neither inherently good nor inherently bad for women's interests. Roberts actually ignores many of the substantive points made by feminist critics, which is not surprising, as her starting premises are those of a practitioner and are very different from feminist concerns.

In a lengthy article, Grillo (1991), an American law professor and herself a mediator, presents a sustained and detailed critique of mediation[90] that has provoked a range of responses.[91] The crux of her argument is that mediation fails women because it does not adequately respect their struggles and their lives.[92] Grillo begins from feminist premises, and draws in material, such as women's and men's relative income levels, and their respective earning capacities (which are affected by their relative investments in domestic labour, including childcare), which substantiate the idea that gendered inequalities[93] continue to exist at both structural and personal levels. She also considers how different gendered identities are manifested and expressed at a psychological level. She argues that it is only when these aspects are fully taken into account that mediation can be considered in context, and can be seen to be a process that ultimately supports the *status quo* of gender relations.

Grillo presents a powerful critique of the claimed neutrality of mediators, which rests on an analysis of the 'unacknowledged perspectives' (p. 1585) which underpin their approach. Mediators, she argues, exert a great deal of power. This power is exercised under the guise of a neutral mediation process; it manifests itself in such basic procedural matters as the setting of the ground-rules for mediation regarding who talks and what is talked about, procedures which are themselves informed by ideological assumptions about appropriate male and female behaviours and, more particularly, about 'the family'. In contrast to the power exercised by lawyers and judges under the formal law, the crucial issue here is that mediator power is hidden and unacknowledged, it is masked by the rhetoric that the parties are reaching their own decisions.[94]

Grillo is not accusing mediators of acting in bad faith. On the contrary, she states:

> A mediator will always be influenced in mediation by her own values. These values may be personal, or they may be derived from the mediator's professional training, or the community in which she lives. The mediator may not disclose, or perhaps even recognise, her reliance on such values. It may appear to the mediator, as to any of us, that her perception of the world is objectively true (Grillo, 1991, p. 1592-93).

Thus, Grillo makes the point that 'party control' does not extend as far as the 'normative issues' which are at stake in mediation.

Grillo's paper appeared to cause some consternation in the world of mediation commentary. This chapter will now look briefly at the range of responses to it which were made in a series of articles published in a single issue of *Family and Conciliation Courts Review* in 1992. First, Grillo's paper is 'summarised' by the editor, Hugh McIsaac. But, his summary presents only a limited view and, notably, the feminist premises upon which Grillo's analysis is based, together with the detailed reasoning and empirical support she provides for those premises, are not addressed. Rosenberg (1992) then presents a lengthy defence of mediation. Significantly, he begins by simply restating many of mediation's claims. His paper begins:

> Mediation has won praise from the bar, from numerous participants and practitioners and from scholars as a tremendous breakthrough in dispute resolution. It empowers the parties by enabling them to be the ultimate decision-makers, and it allows the parties to reach agreements that take into account important facts that are often ignored in judicial decision-making. Mediated agreements are much more likely to satisfy the parties to a dispute than are court orders, and are more likely to be followed than are court orders (Rosenberg, 1992, p. 422).

Rosenberg goes on to explicate three main points at which he takes issue with Grillo. First, he states that Grillo misrepresents what actually happens in mediation, and that the examples she uses are examples of the 'worst possible abuses of the process'. Secondly, he points out that many states have already enacted legislation that addresses Grillo's concerns. Finally, in contrast to Grillo's assertion that mediation holds 'process dangers' for women, he states that 'it is generally helpful to women and men, and an overwhelming number of women and men who have been through mandatory mediation approve of it strongly' (Rosenberg, 1992, p. 423).

He concedes that poorly conducted mediation is unlikely to be either helpful or effective, and that some people will find mediation distasteful. Rosenberg is clearly working with a 'use-abuse' model of mediation. He is able largely to dismiss Grillo's critique by adopting the view that she has focused too much on the 'abuses' of mediation; in adopting this model, he is able effectively to side-step Grillo's main criticisms, indeed, the fundamental point of her paper. For Grillo adopts no such 'use-abuse' model. The force of her criticism lies precisely in her identification of the *fundamental premises* of mediation as detrimental to women's interests. Rosenberg does not address this important point.

Similarly, Duryee (1992), in the same issue of the journal, takes issue with Grillo primarily on the grounds that her argument 'resists resting on available research'[95] (p. 507). But Duryee herself 'resists' recognition that Grillo's paper is primarily a discussion of the hidden *premises* of mediation, supported by examples from actual cases of which Grillo has knowledge. She goes on to discuss the 'evidence' to counter Grillo's arguments but, like Roberts (1996, 1997), she fails to problematise the status of such evidence and, more importantly, she fails to acknowledge that the arguments Grillo makes cannot be decided on the basis of 'evidence' alone. Grillo's point that the issues are fundamentally *political* ones is simply ignored. Saposnek (1992) continues the same line of argument by alleging that Grillo's central argument 'rests on poor scholarship' (p. 490). For this reason, he says, her thesis is simply not credible.

The response to Grillo's work, insofar as it ultimately seeks to undermine her academic credibility, effectively silences her critique of mediation. Such tactics, of course, come as no surprise to feminist scholars; they have learned to expect such rejoinders. But, the nature of this response to her work perhaps is what best illustrates Grillo's points; the 'process dangers for women' in mediation rest on the hidden assumptions which are embedded in the dominant discourses which seek to preserve the gendered *status quo*, such that any challenge will be likely to be met with fierce resistance.

The Question of Domestic Violence

In Britain, until the domestic violence provisions of the Family Law Act 1996 came into effect, the legal provisions regarding domestic violence remained complex and confusing.[96] These complexities arose from the fact that there were several jurisdictions under which some form of protection from violence could be sought, involving family, civil and criminal law. The 1996 Act provides for a more unified procedure. Looking at domestic violence in the context of 'no fault' divorce and the new emphasis on mediation as the preferred dispute resolution procedure, however, raises new problems.

The Booth Committee (1985) on Matrimonial Causes Procedure expressed concern about injunction[97] proceedings on three grounds: first, such proceedings were seen as having the inherent propensity to exacerbate bitterness and conflict between couples; secondly, the report expressed concern that the inevitable urgency with which such cases are treated left little room for the alleged abuser to seek advice and to prepare his case; thirdly, they pointed to the lack of effective sanctions against applicants who seek this relief 'without just cause'. In addition, the ever-rising costs of injunction proceedings, like those of matrimonial causes more generally, has been an important factor in discussions about the future of Legal Aid.

An issue that is closely related both to the feminist critique, and to the question of whether mediators can or should attempt to 'mitigate' power imbalances, is that of domestic violence. Abuse in the home, whether of women or of children, is one manifestation of gross gender and age-related imbalances of power.[98] There are differing views on whether mediators should attempt to mediate such cases and, if they choose to do so, what is the best way to go about it, and how more equitable balances of power are to be achieved without compromising the neutrality of the mediator.

Haynes' manual (1993) includes a section on 'the problem of abused spouses'. He recognises that spouse abuse is a frequent occurrence, and that its presence interferes with the ability to negotiate a fair agreement. He states that 'the problem for the mediator is to recognise what are the indicators of spouse abuse and decide what special provisions are required when spouse abuse is evident' (p. 35). He goes on to list six indicators of spouse abuse that the mediator should look out for at the intake interview. If abuse is suspected, the mediator may wish to talk separately with each spouse, and can use this opportunity to 'assess the safety issues and help empower the victimised partner' (p. 36). Such individual interviews are confidential. Haynes has developed a procedure for abuse cases, which he sees as enhancing the woman's rights and opportunities to negotiate a 'reasonable settlement'. It is crucial, in Haynes' scheme, that the abuser admits that abuse is present; if not, the mediation should be terminated. If the couple do agree that abuse is present, there are a number of rules that must be followed, as conditions for staying in the mediation. These are that the abused spouse must obtain an injunction, the abusing spouse must leave the family home immediately, and agree not to go there while the mediation is in progress, and contact with the children must take place away from the family home at some neutral spot.

However, what is missing in Haynes' account is any discussion about precisely how mediation in abuse cases should proceed, once the safeguards he mentions have been put in place. The reader is left to wonder about how the power imbalances, of which abuse is but one manifestation, are to be dealt with during the mediated negotiations. It is as though domestic violence is seen as an isolated, or easily containable problem, which has nothing to do with broader power relations, and is amenable to a straightforward technical solution.

Parkinson (1986) included a section on 'managing open and violent conflict' in her discussion of the role of the conciliator in separation and divorce. She took the view that, whilst mediation is in no sense a panacea for domestic violence, it may enable some couples to gain control of their violent feelings, and enable couples to talk to each other in a way they could not have managed on their own, thus diffusing tension.[99] For her, conciliation should not be used as an alternative to an application for an injunction; where there is the real possibility of violence, it can be appropriate in conjunction with court proceedings and legal advice. Practical steps can be taken to maximise the possibility that further abuse of the victimised spouse will not occur at least around the time of the mediation sessions. However, Parkinson gave no details about the precise techniques which mediators might employ to manage violent conflict.

In Britain, National Family Mediation recognises that mediation is unlikely to succeed where there is domestic violence and has produced a policy statement in relation to domestic violence and mediation, which requires each participant to make a fully informed and voluntary decision to enter mediation, after all safety issues, including screening for domestic violence, have been fully considered. Thus it is recommended that all services must routinely screen for domestic violence before mediation starts (Roberts, 1997).[100]

In the early 1990s, in the wake of the proposals for reform of the divorce law, several commentators raised the issue of domestic violence. The journal of National Family Mediation, *Family Mediation*, devoted a whole issue to this subject in 1993. Articles appeared in the legal and socio-legal press in 1994, specifically addressing the question of family violence in the context of divorce reform and, in the USA, the influential *Family and Conciliation Courts Review* devoted nearly a whole issue to papers on the subject in 1995.

Kaganas and Piper (1993) begin with a recognition that, in Britain, little is known about the extent to which mediators are aware of the impact of domestic violence on the process and outcome of mediation. For them, the separation period represents a time of intensified danger for women, whose partners may resort to violence as a way of reasserting their control in the relationship; thus, mediation takes place at a time when many women are at their most vulnerable. They raise the question as to whether it is reasonable for people in these circumstances to be expected to negotiate with an abuser. There are those who believe that the mediation process can be suitably modified to take account of abuse and to mitigate its effects,[101] and there are those who take a contrary view, that a background of intimidation is not conducive to fair and equal bargaining. Lack of a clear consensus on what constitutes 'abuse' militates against resolution of the debate, and these authors suggest that any working definition must focus of the effects of abuse; it is not enough, simply, to ask women whether abuse has occurred.

Marianne Hester and her colleagues have carried out extensive research into the negotiation of contact arrangements in families where there has been a history of wife abuse.[102] Hester and Pearson (1993) see the issue of the safety of women as intimately linked to the question of the welfare of children; violence does not always (or even usually) stop on separation, and often contact times are used by violent partners to continue with the abuse and to attempt to continue to exercise control. They highlight the problem of achieving true agreement between spouses in such situations; mediation might provide the opportunity for a violent partner to continue the battle. Thus, there are problems with mediation's tendency to focus on the future and not the past. Hester and Pearson argue that, only by understanding the past, can proper provision be made to ensure the safety of abused spouses and their children.

Hester *et al.* (1994) argue that the premium placed on conciliation by the Children Act 1989 has made it more difficult for women leaving violent men, and that children are being put at risk as a consequence of the neglect of issues of violence by a range of professionals who deal with contact arrangements on separation. They argue that one of the major shifts brought about by the Children Act has been a commitment to the idea that contact with the non-resident parent will always be commensurate with children's welfare. From their interviews with court welfare officers and mediators, these researchers found that most equate the best interests of the child with contact with the non-resident parent at all costs; in this context, the safety of both women and children can be compromised. It seemed that, such was the dominance of this assumption, that the idea that children's welfare might be compromised by contact was unthinkable. They give examples of extreme cases in which contact with violent fathers was arranged, to the detriment of the children concerned. In one case, contact was arranged with a father recently released from prison for the manslaughter of the mother. The last time the children saw their father was when he killed their mother with an axe. In another case, contact was arranged with a father recently released from prison for the attempted murder of the mother. The father repeatedly stabbed the mother in the court welfare offices, witnessed by the children. Importantly, many mothers in this study also went to great lengths to facilitate contact between children and their fathers, believing that it was in the interests of their children for them to do so.

Hester and Radford (1996) report on the outcomes of the completed research project and suggest that the interim reports from their work are beginning to have some positive impact on professional practice.[103] One of their main findings is that:

> Contact tends not to work in circumstances of domestic violence. In only seven out of fifty-three cases in England and two out of twenty-four cases in Denmark was contact eventually set up so that there was no further abuse and harassment of the mother or the children (p. 3).

The main reason for the failure of contact to 'work' in the vast majority of cases was attributable to men's continuing violence and abuse. The majority of women were assaulted by their partners after separation, and all of the post-separation violence was linked in some way to child contact. Contact was only stopped when there was very strong evidence that the child was suffering as a result of seeing the father. The professionals tended not to make any effort to find out about violence and abuse; where it did come to light, many minimised it or dismissed it as irrelevant to contact. The research report recommends that contact should not be presumed to be in the best interests of the child where there is or has been domestic violence; instead, the authors argue that, in these cases, there should be a presumption of 'no contact', with the possibility of contact only if this can safely be arranged.

Hester *et al.* (1997) report on the results of their national survey, carried out in 1995-96, of court welfare and voluntary sector mediation practice in relation to domestic violence.[104] As a result of their research on domestic violence and child contact, there has been an increased focus on domestic violence by both court welfare officers and voluntary sector mediators, and the probation service has issued national standards for family court work which includes specific reference to domestic violence. Court welfare and mediation services have developed practice guidelines. The survey research was intended to assess the impact of recent changes in practice. The researchers found that although some professionals had adopted specific procedures for identifying cases where violence was an issue, most had not and continued to rely on other professionals or on women themselves to bring these issues out into the open. As Piper and Kaganas (1997) and Kaganas and Piper (1999) argue, there remains a general lack of any systematic means of identifying domestic violence.

Hester *et al.* (1997) found that three main approaches characterised the practice of court welfare officers; these ranged from a 'safety-oriented' approach,[105] through 'impartial report writing' to an 'agreement-focussed' approach. Half tended to use a mixture of approaches, but only 16% used primarily the 'safety-oriented' approach. Mediators' practice was characterised by two main approaches: 'safety-oriented'[106] and 'emphasis always on mediating'. Only 10% of mediators used the 'safety' approach. The researchers also found that the professionals tended to employ broader definitions of domestic violence than had been the case in the previous research, but about 25% of mediators were reluctant to incorporate psychological or emotional abuse into their definition. Mediators were also concerned about potential 'gender bias',[107] preferring (in contrast to court welfare officers) to regard violence or the potential for violence as 'mutual'. The authors recommend that a 'zero-tolerance' policy towards domestic violence, supported by appropriate advertisements, be implemented and publicised.

Johnston (1993) called for greater understanding by mediators of violence and is concerned with how best to ensure safety. She reports on two studies of mediation with high conflict families carried out in the USA, more than three-quarters of which had a history of physical aggression. She identifies five different types of violence: (1) ongoing, episodic male battering, (2) female-initiated violence, (3) male-controlling violence, (4) separation/divorce trauma, and (5) psychotic reactions. The findings include that parent-child relations are significantly impaired in violent families, and that children are likely to be subjected to violent attacks too. The implications of these data for mediation are that a greater understanding of the complexities of violence in families is needed if domestic violence, in the context of divorce, is adequately to be addressed by mediation as *both* a mental health question and a social-moral issue. Johnston is clear in her view that mediation can proceed where there has been domestic violence, but providing that an adequate assessment of the 'type' of violence has been made.[108] Sun and Woods (1990) consider how best to identify violence at intake and how to make decisions about the appropriateness of mediation in the light of the outcome of the 'screening' process. Where mediation proceeds, they emphasise the importance of planning carefully to ensure safety, including picking up on subtle cues of abuse during mediation and closing sessions safely.

Corlyon (1993) expresses concern that many serious allegations, made in divorce petitions, pass unaddressed in the divorce process. She points to the problems inherent in the priority accorded to securing the child's contact with the non-resident parent in the absence of full investigation of all the issues, including allegations of violence. An alarming 64% of unreasonable behaviour petitions filed by women contain allegations of violence, some very serious, with death threats in 19% of cases. Children are not always protected from such violent encounters, yet contact with the abuser is only very rarely denied. The evidence presented by Corlyon challenges the assumption made in the White Paper (Lord Chancellor's Department, 1995) that people tend to rely on allegations of unreasonable behaviour to secure a quick divorce. These cases in fact proceed much more slowly, and often involve, for example, injunctions and orders for welfare reports. Court-based conciliation in such cases often terminates with issues remaining unresolved, but independent mediation can be more successful in taking the heat out of arguments. Thus, like other papers in the issue of *Family Mediation* devoted to domestic violence, this research points to the pressing need for the issue of violence to be taken seriously; allegations of 'fault' may reflect the nature of a relationship in which the behaviour of one partner *was* a real cause for concern, which has implications for the future arrangements for children. Thus, Corlyon questions the wisdom of mediation's focus on the future, to the exclusion of the past:

> The assumption that divorced parents are about to enter a new era of civility, mutual respect and shared parenting responsibilities in which the past can be simply erased is one which rests very uneasily with parents who have experienced each other's worst behaviour (Corlyon, 1993, p. 15).

Fisher (1993) reports on the incidence of violence in one family mediation service: 23% of cases involved abuse.[109] Craig (1993) discusses the effects of violence in terms of the theory of 'learned helplessness' (Seligman, 1975). She suggests, however, that mediation can be empowering in such cases insofar as it may help family members to learn more constructive and egalitarian ways of decision-making.[110] Morkham (1993) writes as a co-ordinator of a mediation service and considers the risk of violence to both clients and staff, and the measures that can be taken to minimise that risk, which obviously have resource implications.

Questions about mediation and domestic violence were raised in the debates which led up to the passing of the Family Law Act 1996.[111] Kaganas and Piper (1994a) express concern that the divorce reforms might result in reduced disclosure of abuse that would endanger women and children during the period of 'reflection and consideration' prior to divorce. They feel that the separation of issues of abuse from the divorce itself may be ill-advised, and could lead to agreements being reached in mediation which are contrary to the interests and safety of the abused spouse. Kaganas and Piper (1994b) advocate comprehensive screening for abuse, which concentrates on the effects on the victim, prior to mediation.[112] These authors are sceptical about the apparent optimism with which some mediators regard the possibilities of redressing power imbalances in mediation, an optimism that they see as being undermined by research that shows existing interaction patterns are resistant to change in mediation.[113] Like others in this debate, Kaganas and Piper also question the wisdom of suppressing discussions about the past.

Raitt (1996) takes up some of the points raised by Kaganas and Piper (1994b) and she takes as 'axiomatic that the effects of abuse are incompatible with mediation as a consensual process' (Raitt, 1996, p. 12). Like Kaganas and Piper (1993), she believes that the definition of abuse[114] employed will have an impact on the effectiveness of screening measures; women may have difficulties both in recognising that they have been abused and in admitting it. The divorce reforms do not encourage women who may have been abused to opt out of mediation. On the contrary, abused women may well be reluctant to incur the possibility of financial penalties (in the form of being denied access to Legal Aid) or to be responsible for frustrating the mediation process. Additional pressure to mediate comes from the ideology that 'conflict' is what 'damages' children, and that children do best when they can maintain relationships with both parents.[115] It is not uncommon for mediators to express these apparent 'truisms' in mediation and 'the best interests of the child' can be actively invoked to promote agreements between former spouses.[116] Such powerful discourses are becoming increasingly difficult to resist, but the point is that the deployment of such discourses is likely to place an abused women in an impossible situation; she is likely to believe that the welfare of her children will be forfeited if she is unable to behave amicably and co-operatively.

Raitt (1996) argues that a criterion of 'the best interests of the child' should be used to supplement the criterion of the 'impact of abuse' in screening for mediation. This principle has long been operative in the legal process, but, as Raitt points out, there is little evidence that mediation too upholds that principle. Research is now beginning to establish links between wife and child abuse (see, for example, Hester and Pearson, 1993;

Mullender and Morley, 1994); the policy implications are profound, but have not yet been fully explored. As Raitt observes, there may be circumstances in which the interests of children are best served by their parents having no contact with each other.[117] This observation is supported by other research on children and divorce (for example, the study by Maccoby and Mnookin, 1992).

However, what Raitt overlooks in her analysis is the way in which conceptions of 'children's best interests' have increasingly become synonymous with an extension of father's 'rights' (Brophy, 1985, 1989; Harne and Radford, 1994; Hooper, 1994). Mediation already claims to address itself to children's interests,[118] and the divorce reforms are founded on a belief that mediation is better equipped than the adversarial system to promote children's interests, insofar as the new procedures are designed to minimise 'conflict'. Raitt's solution is naive, given current dominant discourses about children's welfare; if her suggestion was taken up, ironically, there is a danger that it might result in the real needs of women and children becoming more marginalised. If, however, there were to be a reformulation of what actually constitutes the interests of children, which took into account over-simplified notions of 'conflict', and took into account the links between wife and child abuse, and moved away from the simplistic notion that contact is beneficial in all cases (regardless of the circumstances), the situation might be quite different, and Raitt's suggestion could be a very constructive one.

The debate about the appropriateness of mediation in the context of past violence, or where the possibility or threat of further abuse remains, seems unlikely to be settled on the basis of evidence alone. These are profoundly political issues which resonate, not only with those in the 'gender' debate, but also with issues raised by the emergence of mediation as a new profession.[119]

Dispute Resolution and Ethnic Diversity

Irving and Benjamin (1995) present a overview of research on the question of family mediation and ethnicity which they regard as 'a critical but neglected dimension of practice' (p. 306). They point out that, in most of the mediation literature, ethnic diversity is assumed to vary in circumscribed ways, around a common mean, centred on white, middle class couples. Something similar can be said about research in Britain;

here, in fact, there is very little which has been published on the subject, a circumstance that is telling in itself.

An article by Schuz (1996), 'Divorce and Ethnic Minorities', published in the UK, is written by someone who lives and works in Israel. She points to the problems inherent in a situation where members of minority ethnic communities may obtain civil divorces, yet find barriers to religious divorces in their communities, or find that religious divorces are not recognised. She states that 'in a pluralist society, the state cannot abdicate all responsibility for the problems caused by differences between the civil law and the religious law of its ethnic minorities' (Schuz, 1996, p. 150). She suggests that recognition of the legal institutions of ethnic minorities is what is required, rather than to impose British civil institutions upon them. But, there are other aspects of cultural diversity that Schuz does not discuss. The fundamental questions which arise must be 'how appropriate is the model of "the family", which underlies divorce law, for all cultural groups in Britain?' and 'how appropriate are Euro-centric dispute resolution practices?'

In the pluralist and multicultural society, which is Britain today, 'the family' no longer takes a unified, traditional, easily recognisable form; instead, family structures and relationships are characterised by multiplicity, diversity and change (Elliott, 1996) and, in this context, divorce becomes a process replete with a multitude of meanings. As Irving and Benjamin (1995) point out, the family therapy and social work literatures have only recently begun to give prominence to questions of ethnicity in discussions of clinical practice; such changes have yet to filter through to the divorce literature.

The recent divorce reforms have been largely silent on this issue (Day Sclater, 1995). Gale (1994), in a short article, calls for mediators to be trained in the 'impact of culture' such that they might manage their clients' negotiations more effectively; without taking culture into account, no 'valid generalisations' about clients' behaviour can be made.[120] The question of ethnicity in relation to family mediation (as in relation to divorce more generally), sadly, remains largely unexplored territory.[121]

In conclusion, it can be said that, in the current state of our knowledge about divorce dispute resolution, it is not possible unequivocally to say that mediation is 'better' than adversarial negotiation, or *vice versa*. Our decisions about this issue depend very heavily on the premises we employ, the priorities we have, and the goals that we aim for. Mediation currently has found favour with our legislators, but this rests less on a sound research base than it does on the cultural dominance of a child welfare discourse and on a new form of political correctness that assumes gender equality and shuns the expression of strong feelings. Importantly, however, this idealisation of mediation will be subject to some harsh 'reality-testing' when the divorce provisions of the Family Law Act 1996 are implemented.[122] At this stage, the assumptions that have been made about the capacity of divorcing people to behave rationally and co-operatively, and to be able to put their emotions to one side 'for the sake of the children' will be tested. As we discuss in chapters 5 and 6, there is every possibility that, despite the persuasive powers of the dominant discourses of welfare and harmony in divorce, the psychological coping strategies of divorcing people will severely test the aims of the legislation.

Notes

[1] The term 'mediation' has generally replaced 'conciliation' in the UK, as the latter perhaps has connotations of 'reconciliation'.

[2] See, however, recent work by the Bristol researchers (Bailey-Harris *et al.*, 1998), in which they argue that the increased frequency of litigation and longer delays in Children Act cases may be attributable to the primarily 'settlement orientation' of contemporary courts and professionals.

[3] This assertion, however, has been the subject of some debate in Britain, discussed later in this chapter. As Ingleby's work also shows, it is difficult to draw a clear dividing line, in adversarial proceedings, between the respective inputs of the solicitor and the client in terms of either process or outcome. He sees solicitor-client input as existing on a continuum (Ingleby, 1992, p. 136). Thus, he questions the notion that divorcing parties necessarily lose control over their dispute when they seek legal representation (Ingleby, 1992, p. 139).

[4] It should be said, however, that, in Britain, the traditional legal process is not always or necessarily adversarial in nature. In recent years, there has been an increasing trend for the courts in family matters to encourage conciliatory approaches, particularly in children cases, through the use of court welfare officers in a conciliatory role. By the early 1990s some courts were already applying a conciliatory framework to the settlement of financial and property matters, and this area of family law is currently under review, involving ancillary relief pilot schemes (see Diduck, 1999). The existence of the Solicitors' Family Law Association, formed in 1982, whose code of practice demands a conciliatory approach by its members, is testimony to the fact that even bipartisan negotiations are not necessarily conducted in an adversarial fashion. Similarly, as Davis (1988) pointed out, certain aspects of our family law no longer conform to an adversarial model of justice.

[5] The question of where and why, precisely, 'conflict' in divorce arises is difficult to answer. In the White Paper (Lord Chancellor's Department, 1995) it is seen as attributable to the fault-based and adversarial nature of divorce proceedings. By contrast, a psychological perspective would see conflict as necessarily present in the separation process (see, for example, Vaughan, 1987/1993; Johnston and Campbell,

1988). One prominent mediator took the view that 'conflict often results from failed communication rather than from incompatible needs and goals' (Parkinson, 1986, p. 53). In addition, it should be pointed out that 'conflict' would better be seen as a complex and multidimensional, rather than a unitary phenomenon. Little is known about the dynamics and processes of conflict in divorce, or how these map onto the formation and resolution of disputes.

6   See Cockett and Tripp (1994).

7   As Davis *et al.* (1994) state: 'For most divorcing couples, a decision of the court is as remote a prospect as the summit of Mount Everest viewed from base camp' (p. 253).

8   Randomised controlled trials (RCTs), in which participants are randomly assigned to one or other condition in the experimental design, are useful in research where the aim is to determine the relative efficacy of one treatment over another. They are widely used in medical research.

9   But a similar percentage in the British study (Davis, 1988) reported that their solicitor had been 'very helpful' (p. 87).

10   See also Davis (1988) who states that 'only a small proportion of initially contested applications are finally adjudicated. For the most part, the law and the court provide a framework for negotiation' (pp. 2-3).

11   See Davis (1988), Ingleby (1992) and Davis, Cretney and Collins (1994).

12   See Sarat and Felstiner (1995).

13   For a collection of papers bringing together British and American contributions, see Dingwall and Eekelaar (1988).

14   In Britain, the Solicitors Family Law Association has a code of practice which explicitly provides for a conciliatory approach to be adopted by its members.

15   Davis (1988) p. 114. In this study, the researchers found several instances where *both* parties felt that their respective solicitors had been too ready to make concessions to the other side.

16   Simon Roberts (1988) characterised the situation in Britain as one of 'bewildering diversity' (p. 144).

17   See also Ingleby (1988).

18   See Davis, Cretney and Collins (1994) Chapter 3.

19   *Wachtel v. Wachtel* [1973] Fam. 72, CA.

20   On narratives of divorce, see Riessman (1990), Day Sclater (1997a). Divorce narratives are discussed further in chapter 6.

21   See Sarat and Felstiner (1995), chapter 2.

22   This is so whilst children themselves continue to be denied any real or substantive 'rights'. See Roche (1995, 1999).

23   In a brief, though trenchant, critique of recent shifts away from the formal legal process towards non-adversarial forms of dispute resolution, Nader (1992) argues that the rise to prominence of a discourse of 'harmony' turns plaintiffs into patients needing treatment, with adverse consequences for the basic freedoms of human citizens.

24   These authors are commenting on the situation in France.

25   It should be noted that the French tend to draw very much on psychoanalytic approaches, in marked contrast to the prevailing climate in British mediation. Mediation groups in France often work as part of a centre, where divorce counselling, mediation and contact services for children are offered. Further, in the French context of a codified legal system, it is likely that the distinction between litigation and

negotiation will have a different meaning than it does in the British context. I am grateful to Lorraine Radford for these points.

26   The same can of course be said about mediation.

27   As Morrison (1987) points out, this raises a number of ethical issues. If mediation constitutes the practice of law, the question arises as to whether and under what conditions divorce mediation can be provided by lawyers without violating the code of legal ethics.

28   In the USA, not all states mandate mediation in divorce. In those which do not, the majority of referrals to mediation come from lawyers. See Bruch (1993). British research (Walker *et al.*, 1994) shows that many people first hear of mediation through their solicitors or are referred to mediation by their solicitors.

29   The authors are reporting on American research, and on divorce dispute resolution in the state of Maine, where divorce mediation is mandatory when there are issues concerning children, and where mediation an *all* disputed issues is encouraged. In addition, lawyers regularly attend mediation sessions, a situation which is very different from that envisaged in Britain under the provisions of the Family Law Act, 1996.

30   For a discussion of the different models of mediation in the USA, see Silberman (1982). For a discussion more relevant to Britain, see Roberts (1988).

31   In fact, they discuss the psychological needs of 'families', as though families contained no conflicts of interest in terms of psychological needs.

32   In arriving at this conclusion, these authors employ a stereotyped picture of the adversarial process which is greatly at odds with the evidence which has previously been discussed in this review. For example, they refer to the 'toxicity of the adversary system' (Margulies and Luchow, 1992, p. 502).

33   These authors express an increasingly prevalent view that divorce 'rather than being the death of the family...is now regarded as a reorganising event for the family' (Margulies and Luchow, 1992, p. 491). This issue is discussed further in chapter 1.

34   Research by Dillon and Emery (1996), in which separated parents who had been randomly assigned to either mediation or traditional adversarial methods for resolving child custody disputes were surveyed nine years post-settlement, found that non-custodial parents in the mediation group reported more frequent current contact with their children and greater involvement in decisions about them.

35   In their recent work, Greatbatch and Dingwall (1997) have investigated how mediators and disputants manage their interactions. They have found that disputants do not always rely on mediators to initiate exits from their arguments; rather they often close their argumentative exchanges without assistance, using practices that are common in ordinary conversation, though oriented towards the conventions of mediation.

36   As advocated, for example, by Kruk (1993) and Johnston and Campbell (1988).

37   Day Sclater and Richards (1995).

38   The same point can of course be made in respect of lawyers in mediation.

39   Davis makes a similar point when he says 'we find...that a form of 'conciliation' is undertaken by practitioners whose principal concern is with the repair of family relationships on a 'family therapy' model. Apparently, mediation is regarded as an appropriate extension of these activities, if not actually synonymous with them. This of course sits uneasily with any desire to promote 'party control'; the greater the

emphasis on professional expertise, the more the parties will tend to be confirmed in their inferior 'client' role' (Davis, 1988, p. 58).

[40] For reviews, see Pearson and Thoennes (1985, 1988); Irving and Benjamin (1987, 1995); Vermont Law School Dispute Resolution Project (1987). See also Roberts (1997).

[41] See, for example, Piper (1993), Davis (1988), Dingwall and Eekelaar (1988), Freeman (1996), Parkinson (1986), Ogus *et al.* (1989), Davis and Roberts (1988).

[42] These authors are advocates of 'therapeutic family mediation' which they locate within an 'ecosystemic' orientation to family processes. For a favourable review of the book, see Bahr (1996).

[43] It should be noted that outcome studies have not attempted to address the issue of the relative equity of mediated agreements. As long ago as 1987, at an international conference, there was a call for 'some information about whether mediation produces more or less equitable agreements' (see Singer, 1987). See also Pearson (1991).

[44] It is not clear from the discussion whether the agreement rates relate only to child-related issues, or to all issues in the divorce.

[45] As the authors make no distinction between therapeutic and non-therapeutic forms of mediation in arriving at these figures, it is not possible to say anything about the influence of different forms of mediation on agreement rates, which would seem to be particularly relevant in cases of high conflict and gross power imbalances.

[46] Ogus, Walker and Jones-Lee (1989).

[47] Dingwall (1988).

[48] This point is supported by the findings of Davis, Cretney and Collins (1994).

[49] Deriving from the work of Koopman, Hunt and Stafford (1984) whose study focuses on child-related agreements.

[50] Bahr (1996), p. 805.

[51] Irving and Benjamin (1995, p. 416) state that these figure compare favourably with that of 65% for legal services in divorce, but they give no indication of the study from which this figure is drawn. In any event, it should be noted that this comparison does not warrant the conclusion that clients are, in general, any more satisfied with mediation than they seem to be with litigation, a point which is contrary to the spirit, if not the letter, of Irving and Benjamin's review.

[52] Discussed in more detail in a separate section of this chapter.

[53] One criticism which was made of the British evaluation studies was that, in assessing cost, the researchers did not take sufficient account of the fact that some of the mediators in the sample were charging lower than market rates for their work, and that incidental legal costs were not included in the calculation. Davis (1988) points out that there has been encouraged 'a form of false accounting under which mediation *appears* to be cheap because it is performed by volunteers, or by divorce court welfare officers whose costs are absorbed within the Probation Service's overall budget' (Davis, 1988, p. 55).

[54] Irving and Benjamin (1995), p. 421. It is noteworthy that there were calls as long ago as 1987 for focused research in this area. See Vermont Law School Dispute Resolution Project, 1987. As Irving and Benjamin (1995, p. 425) point out, the most effective use of mediation involves matching clients amenable to it with the particular service model best suited to their needs. That 'mediation' is seen as a unitary mode of dispute resolution, and that screening for amenability is not routinely carried out, and that clients are not matched to the mediation model which best addresses their needs,

are factors which are likely to militate against the success of any wholesale introduction of mediation in the present state of our knowledge. As Irving and Benjamin point out, our knowledge base in this respect remains incomplete.

55 It may be, as Irving and Benjamin point out, that research agenda in mediation have been too driven by policy-based funding. This relationship is problematic, because policy makers have traditionally had very restricted interest in outcomes, and there is a great need for a distinction to be drawn between pragmatic and fundamental research in this area. See, for example, Dingwall and Greatbatch, 1993, 1995.

56 Pearson (1991).

57 This is a follow up to the evaluation of child-focused conciliation services reported in Ogus *et al.* (1989).

58 See also Kelly (1991).

59 The authors do not make this proviso.

60 The authors do not comment on the possible significance of the fact that the mediation sample consisted of couples, whilst the adversarial sample consisted, in the main, of people whose partners were not included in the study.

61 The point made above may have a bearing on this difference, but the authors do not say so. The impact of mandatory mediation in child-related disputes in California is also not made clear in the discussion. It is not clear whether and, if so, how many of the adversarial sample became obliged to participate in mandatory mediation over the study period.

62 On average, eight months after the decision to divorce has been made.

63 As Fisher (1994) points out, the work of Kelly and her co-workers does not show that psychological adjustment is enhanced as a result of mediation. Mediation is a process for *dispute* resolution, not *conflict* resolution.

64 Mediators also reported no differences between the groups at the first session. By the third session, however, mediators rated people who did not terminate as more willing to mediate, more involved in the sessions, less angry and having higher self esteem. Thus the authors argue that ambivalence may not crystallise until the third session.

65 See Davis (1988), Davis and Roberts (1988).

66 See, however, Haynes (1988).

67 See, for example, Roberts (1990, p. 91).

68 See also Grillo's work (1991) discussed in the section on 'gender' in this chapter. The basis of Grillo's critique is a problematising of the apolitical model of 'power' assumed in accounts such as that of Haynes, and an interrogation of the ways in which common mediator strategies reproduce gendered power relationships in a broader sense.

69 The significance of work such as that of Dingwall and Greatbatch is that it problematises these issues, issues which practitioners like Haynes (1988) appear unquestioningly to regard as legitimate practice.

70 Similar issues are also under discussion in the USA in relation to community mediation. Garcia (1995) reports on a study that explored how disputants' positions and interests were represented in mediation practice using videotaped community mediation sessions. The author concludes that self-representation in mediation is never unconstrained. Rather, the interactional organisation of mediation and the actions of mediators work to limit and define how disputants formulate their utterances. In some cases, mediators limited themselves to rephrasing, restating or

elaborating the disputant's position, but in others the mediator took the place of a disputant in the negotiations.

[71]   Similarly, in the USA, Kressel (1997) argues that a systematic understanding of professional practice can be built upon the reflective insights of skilled practitioners.

[72]   On this point, see also Nader (1992).

[73]   'Effectiveness' was seen in terms of the nature and durability of agreements reached, reduction of conflict, satisfaction and well-being of parties, and the skills of successful conciliators (see, Ogus *et al.* (1989), p. 2).

[74]   Experienced mediators were trained in comprehensive mediation according to the Haynes' model. In some services, mediators worked in pairs. Lawyers did not attend mediation appointments, but were available for consultation by mediators, and clients were free to consult their own solicitor alone, or another jointly with their spouse. In some cases, welfare rights advisors were available to be consulted.

[75]   See also *Social Policy Research Findings*, No. 48, February 1994, Joseph Rowntree Foundation.

[76]   Of these 102 couples, it would seem that client views about comprehensive mediation were gleaned from only 54 users of comprehensive mediation who returned their questionnaires.

[77]   For a supportive assessment of Grillo's work, see Nader (1992).

[78]   In the context of a feminist critique of legal practice more generally. See Brophy and Smart (1985).

[79]   See, for example, Okin (1989), Smart (1989), Naffine (1990), Fineman (1991). See also Collier (1995, 1999) on the ways in which family law produces (heterosexual) masculinities.

[80]   See, for example, Roberts (1996) where feminist concerns are only narrowly conceived, and are addressed at the level of women's and men's reported 'satisfaction' with mediation. See also the chapter in Irving and Benjamin (1995) which deals with feminist concerns.

[81]   On the problematics of such linkages see, for example, Dingwall and Eekelaar (1986), King (1991).

[82]   The dominant discourses render interventions benevolent by a reliance on 'the twin rhetorics of science and concern' (Bottomley. 1985, p. 170); thus welfarism is rendered unproblematic, even though it overrides the procedural safeguards of formal justice. The Finer Report also recognised that 'to promote welfare is an unusual function for a court of law' (*Finer Report*, 1974, p. 174).

[83]   See, for example, Jackson (1993); Duncan (1994) and Lacey (1998). See also Day Sclater (1996c).

[84]   See also Dingwall and Greatbatch (1994) on the question of 'the virtues of formality'.

[85]   Fineman (1991) makes a similar point in discussing what she calls 'the illusion of equality'. For her, equality in family law seems to be assured by the equal application of the same rules to women and to men. She argues, however, that this merely reproduces existing inequalities, and states that true equality could only be achieved by the application of 'equality of results' principles. This would, however, necessitate some form of positive discrimination or affirmative action, which in themselves are precluded by the 'equality of rules' principles with which the law functions.

[86]   Roberts does not address Bottomley's point that the formal law can go some way to mitigating such power imbalances, but instead seems to regard them as immutable, or as irrelevant to divorce dispute resolution.

87   Roberts is adopting a broad use of the word 'inequality' here, and referring to such things as personal differences in choice of lawyer and lawyer style, rather than structural inequalities which attach to gender categories.

88   Other methodological problems with mediation research include sample size and selection, the lack of proper control groups, and the problems caused by placebo effects. Other problems relate to the unclear boundaries between mediation and the judicial system, and mediation and therapy.

89   For instance, some authors have noted that men tend to be more satisfied than women with mediation, and mothers are more likely to feel that they fared better in litigation. For a discussion of this evidence see Grillo (1991).

90   Grillo (1991) is writing about mandatory custody mediation in the state of California. Many of her criticisms, however, are equally applicable to non-mandatory mediation. Even in California, where mediation has been mandated by the court since 1981, there is great variation in practice across counties, and practice is continually evolving, and therefore it is impossible to make a distinction between its therapeutic and non-therapeutic forms.

91   See the articles in the *Family and Conciliation Courts Review*, vol. 30, number 4 (1992).

92   Grillo (1991) also make the point that the traditional judicial process is patriarchal in character, and so cannot be relied on to protect or further women's interests in any event.

93   Mediators use a range of techniques to 'balance power' between the parties, but their claim that this adequately addresses potential problems rests on the premise that the mediator can recognise power imbalances when they occur. But the perception of inequalities depend on the perspective adopted and, in any event, interventions to 'correct' power imbalances arguably fly in the face of the mediator's claim to be a neutral facilitator. As Grillo argues, 'The existence of partiality, countertransference, and projection on the part of mediators explains why mediators' attempts to redress imbalances cannot necessarily be relied upon to meet the problem of unequal bargaining power' (p. 1592).

94   Grillo (1991) also discusses the ways in which racial prejudices intersect with sexism in the dominant discourses and in the implicit assumptions made by mediators. She also raises the important point that mediators, being human, are not immune from the processes of identification and projection, transference and countertransference, which again remain unacknowledged and which must undoubtedly affect both the process and the outcome of mediation: 'Partiality comes in many forms...impartiality is a myth' (p. 1587). Thus, allowances need to be made for failures of neutrality. The judicial system is, of course, not exempt from similar criticisms, but the crucial difference is that formal law is a public process and a matter of record, and problems may be exacerbated in the context of the more private informalities of mediation.

95   This 'defence' of mediation is echoed in Britain in the work of Roberts (1996, 1997).

96   For a detailed discussion of the new law, see Horton (1996).

97   Injunctions to protect abused spouses were commonly sought in domestic violence cases.

98   The recent linkages which have been reported between spouse and child abuse seem to be having the effect of making policy makers more concerned about the issue of spouse abuse than they have been hitherto. (See Burton *et al.*, 1988, Mullender and Morley, 1994; Hester and Radford, 1996; Hester *et al.*, 1997).

99   Citing a 'case example', Parkinson argues that 'the irrational fears and anger which had culminated in outbursts of violence became more manageable in the presence of a neutral third person who provided a safe and sufficiently controlled environment where irreconcilable needs could be looked at more calmly and rationally' (Parkinson, 1986, p. 122). It is thus noteworthy that Parkinson adopts a psychological explanation of the violence, to the neglect of any discussion of power and coercion in intimate relationships. In the case example which she gives, however, both parties were encouraged to take legal advice and that advice, moreover, was communicated by the solicitors concerned to the mediator; this combination eventually led to an agreed separation.

100   The question of what happens to those people who are 'screened out' of mediation remains an open one. See Kaganas and Piper (1999).

101   See, for example, Haynes' work discussed above.

102   See also Hester *et al.* (1997) for a report on a national study of court welfare and mediation practice and domestic violence (discussed below).

103   See, for example, *Re D (Contact: Reasons for Refusal)* [1997] 2FLR 48 and *Re H (Contact: Domestic Violence)* [1988] 2FLR 42.

104   The survey also aimed to inform further developments by finding and examining examples of 'best practice'. Questionnaires were sent out in 1995 to all court welfare officers and National Family Mediation mediators in England and Wales and to voluntary sector mediators in Northern Ireland. The response rates for court welfare officers was 94% (teams) and 41% (individuals). For mediators the response rate was 94.9% (services) and 43.8% (individuals).

105   This was concerned with identifying domestic violence, and ensuring safety both within the family proceedings process and in relation to outcomes. Some were using a 'screening' approach across all aspects of their work, but there was a lack of *systematic* screening.

106   This involved the identification of domestic violence via separate meetings, and with ensuring safety in the mediation process and in any outcomes decided on by the clients. Mediators were also in the process of developing 'screening' procedures, although many believed that clients for whom abuse was an issue would 'screen themselves out' by not coming to mediation. The researchers detected a 'large gap' between the actual practice of individual mediators and the suggested practice in NFM guidelines regarding screening. Some mediators were found to be acting in a way 'entirely contrary' to the guidelines, arguing that knowledge of clients prior to the first session would compromise their impartiality.

107   Yet gender issues are the key to understanding and effectively tackling domestic violence. See Burton *et al.*, 1998.

108   Johnston, however, gives mediators (rather then women themselves) the power to define the appropriateness of mediation in these circumstances, with obvious consequences for women's perceived empowerment.

109   As Fisher points out, this is likely to be an underestimate, as the figures were collected before implementing a policy of interviewing new clients separately.

110   Craig raises, but does not discuss, the feminist point about how far balancing power and empowerment in mediation are realisable ideals, and how far they are merely rhetoric.

111   For a discussion of these debates, see Kaganas and Piper, 1999.

112 This suggestion has also been made by others, and has now begun to be acted upon. See, for example, Roberts, 1997. See also Hester *et al.*, 1997 for a recent survey of practices in this respect.

113 e.g. Bryan (1992).

114 In their recent survey of professional practice, Hester *et al.* (1997) report that there is wide variation in definitions of abuse employed in the practices of court welfare officers and mediators, with the latter less willing to include psychological or emotional abuse, and less willing to acknowledge the gendered basis of domestic violence.

115 The extensive research of Hester and her co-workers indicates that most abused mothers continue to believe that it is in the best interests of their children for contact with abusive fathers to continue. See Hester and Radford, 1996.

116 See Walker and Robinson (1990) for an example of this in the context of 'reframing' in mediation. Roberts (1997) states that 'Children provide the common interest and the mutual inducement for collaborative effort' (p. 139).

117 Hester and her co-workers suggest that there may be circumstances in which the best interests of the child are served by having no contact with the father. See also Hooper, 1994.

118 Roberts (1997), for example, states that 'There has long been a consensus that mediation can enhance children's interests' and 'Family mediation has long been identified with a greater concentration on the needs of children...There is also a common view that mediation offers the 'best setting' for the voice of the child to be heard' (p. 139).

119 Where there is or has been violence and abuse, it has been suggested that mediation may be less applicable to and more problematic in negotiating contact and child care then in relation to purely financial matters (see Hester *et al.*, 1997). However, issues of gender and power (discussed earlier) would still feature.

120 See also Shah-Kazemi (1996).

121 For further discussion of the paucity of research in this area see Piper and Day Sclater, 1999.

122 Implementation of the divorce provisions of the Act is unlikely to take place before 2000.

3 The Psychology of Divorce: A Review of the Literature

JULIE JESSOP

Introduction

There has been a tendency over the last few decades for research into divorce to view the process as traumatic, and to focus primarily on the negative effects for children. However, there is a growing body of research that focuses on the effects of divorce on adults, and widens the debate to include the positive as well as the negative aspects of the divorce experience. As Veevers (1991) points out:

> It must be remembered that *at least* half of [these] people...actively sought a divorce with the implicit assumption that reclaiming a single status would enhance the quality of their life experience (p. 102) (italics in original).

This chapter aims to review the more recent research that has been conducted into adults' divorce experiences with regard to psychological adjustment and well-being, and to look at the factors which have been identified as salient to outcome. First we will look at the methodological and theoretical limitations which continue to confound research into divorce, and which need to be held in mind when analysing and evaluating research findings. We then consider levels of psychiatric symptoms and suicide that have been associated with divorce, followed by a review of research that focuses on identity, attachment and psychological adjustment. Issues of gender difference and the specific issues of parenthood are then covered and differential outcomes based on age and ethnicity are examined. The conclusion draws together the main themes that have been identified in the literature and looks at whether the research shows evidence of a shift towards a more 'normative' view of divorce.

Methodological and Theoretical Limitations of Divorce Research

As Kitson and Morgan (1990) point out, research on the consequences of divorce has shown 'laudable improvement' in methodology during the past decade. Unfortunately, the complexities of isolating divorce variables from economic, social and psychological factors remain problematic. Furthermore, owing to the emotional nature of the subject being studied, problems connected with data collection, selection bias and statistical significance still abound.

Because of the limitations of cross-sectional studies, and those that rely on retrospective data to capture the essence of divorce as a process, there has been a growing move to conduct longitudinal studies. Nelson's (1994) study, however, highlights the problems associated with this: when attempting to follow a group of 35 recently divorced women over a six year period, only 11 were contactable at the last follow-up date. One of the main reasons for the high attrition rate is the transitional nature of divorce and changing financial circumstances which, for many people, necessitates a change of residence whether involuntarily, through choice, or on remarriage.

The geographical mobility associated with divorce also makes it difficult to meet sample quota, and, as the study by Gray and Silver (1990) illustrates, this can often lead to a marked gender difference in response rates. One way of overcoming this difficulty was pursued by Simons *et al.* (1993); they managed to achieve a 99% response rate by paying respondents $175 to participate in their study. This method of obtaining samples is, unfortunately, not an option for most researchers, especially in a political climate which is more concerned with research which would lead to the stabilisation of the 'traditional family' than in helping to overcome the consequences and stigma attached to divorce; even if payment were a possibility, the problems of selective uptake would still be present.

Amato and Booth (1991) found that whilst their data showed clear trends leading in one particular direction they were unable to show significant differences owing to small sample sizes. This meant that, as far as they were concerned, their 'analysis almost certainly underestimated the strength of the associations between divorce and attitudes' (p. 320). It is because of the fact that specific criteria are difficult to meet that studies are often too small to allow quantitative analysis, and therefore the majority of conclusions drawn by researchers can at best be tentative.

The issue of selection bias was addressed by Arditti and Keith (1993), whose study of father-child relations found a higher rate of involvement and child support payment than would generally be expected. They believe that the main reason for this was that fathers who agreed to take part in the study were atypical and more involved with their children than men in general. Whilst studying fathers directly, rather than gauging their involvement through mothers' reports, is obviously a step in the right direction, the effects of selection bias show that caution has to be exercised in interpreting results and making generalisations.

Difficulties of classification and comparison can also result in misleading conclusions being drawn. Kurdek (1991), for example, points out that seemingly straightforward classification into married and non-married may lead to those who have remarried being included with those who have never been divorced, and the non-married group containing those who are cohabiting. As Wallerstein (1991) stresses, direct comparison between the married and divorced obscures the multiplicity of sub-groups within each category; these groups are not homogeneous, and treating them as such can lead to seriously misleading conclusions.

Although the problems associated with the 'measurement' of divorce 'effects' have been highlighted by various researchers, Arditti and Madden-Dedrich (1995) point out that what research should really be looking at is 'how people define the situation in which they find themselves' (p. 231). It is this emphasis which informs the majority of feminist studies of the divorce experience, and which is moving away from the constraints of 'objective' methodologies which supply us with statistics but do little to increase knowledge of how divorce feels to individuals and how they make sense of it.

Alongside these methodological issues, divorce research has also been characterised as exhibiting what Irving and Benjamin (1995) see as 'a dearth of theory'; when theory is invoked it is often based, either explicitly or implicitly, on a conception of the 'normal' family containing two (married) parents. Thus divorce, by default, is seen as psychopathological. As Wallerstein (1991) states:

> [I]t is the lack of theoretical clarity as well as the challenge of method that has contributed so substantially to the equivocal, sometimes conflicting conclusions that have been reached by different investigators (p. 349).

Another factor which has to be taken into consideration when looking at research into divorce is its country of origin. Whilst this chapter assesses research from a variety of different countries, it must be remembered that cultural, legal and religious (Nathanson, 1995) differences often make the direct comparison of divorce experiences and outcomes tenuous.

In an attempt to increase our understanding of the divorce process, it is necessary to devise methodologies which encapsulate the complexities of divorce and uncover both the social and personal features which make up individual experience. It is also necessary to be guided by theoretical concepts which take into account the multiplicity of family forms and which acknowledge the validity of such diversity, rather than relying on traditionalist views of the 'nuclear family'.

Psychiatric Symptoms and Suicide

In *Marital Breakdown and the Health of the Nation* (McAllister, 1995), it is stated that depression has been studied extensively, and the relationship with marital conflict and divorce has been shown repeatedly. This, together with the fact that 'there is clear evidence that the divorced have a much higher admission rate [to psychiatric units/mental hospitals] which at times approaches ten times that for married individuals' (p. 17), emphasises the strong association between marital status and mental health. (See also Richards *et al.* (1997), and Gottman (1998) for similar US findings).

Elliott *et al.* (1992), in a study which involved the analysis of the nationwide *Health and Lifestyle Survey*, reported that when respondents were asked whether they had ever suffered from 'severe depression or other nervous illness', marital status was found to be the most important predictor of depression, with the divorced/separated most likely to answer in the affirmative and the single least likely. They also found significant sex differences, with women almost twice as likely to report depression than men (22.6% v. 11.7%). Other factors which were significant in this study included age and social class, with those in semi-skilled/unskilled occupations and those older, being more at risk.

Although women are generally more likely to suffer from depression than men, Livingston Bruce and Kim (1992), in a longitudinal study of American health survey data, found that men undergoing divorce or separation during the course of the study were 9.3 times more likely to experience major depression than married men. This figure is significantly higher than the corresponding figure for women, with the prevalence of major depression in women who experienced marital disruption being 3.1 times higher than those who were happily married. Thus it would appear that whilst marital disruption leads to higher levels of major depression in both men and women, it is men who are substantially more likely to suffer first onset due to separation or divorce.

As well as separation and divorce being linked with depressive episodes, many studies have highlighted the increased risk of suicide for those undergoing marital dissolution. McAllister (1995) points out that 'relationship breakdown is one of the major causes of suicide worldwide, and the differential in mortality rates by marital status is huge' (p. 21). Studies of suicide rates in America and Canada (Wasserman, 1990; Trovato, 1991; Leenaars *et al.*, 1993; Lester, 1997a), Denmark (Stack, 1990), Finland and Norway (Stack, 1989) all point to a higher risk of suicide for those who are not married, with the divorced group having a suicide rate that is 3 to 4 times higher than for those who are married (Stack and Wasserman, 1993).

In assessing the risk of suicide for those who are separated or divorced, it is important to take account both of those who contemplate or attempt suicide and of those who succeed. The study conducted by Elliott *et al.* (1992) included 20 qualitative interviews which revealed that two respondents, one man and one woman, had attempted suicide as a direct result of marital disruption. Arendell (1986), when studying the effects of divorce on mothers, found that 26 of the 60 women she interviewed had contemplated suicide during the divorce process.

Hu and Goldman (1990), in an international comparison of differential mortality rates in 16 developed countries, found that married people experienced greater longevity over those who were unmarried in the vast majority of countries, even when factors such as socio-economic status had been controlled for. They also found that in most countries mortality rates were higher for men than women[1] and, worryingly, that the differential between the married and the unmarried had increased over the last few decades, with divorced and widowed men in their 20s and 30s being at particular risk (in some countries up to ten times higher than their married counterparts). Reasons put forward for such differential mortality/suicide statistics have been based on ideas of marriage as protective, or on the selection hypothesis, with those being depressed/physically unhealthy/suicidal as less likely to marry in the first place or more likely to encounter marital dissolution. The belief that marriage is protective is, in part, associated with the Durkheimian perspective, which sees marriage as one of the most important forms of social integration, a proposition that seems to hold true across many developed countries (Fernquist and Cutright, 1998).

Stack (1990) argues that because social support is a major factor influencing the risk of suicide, the differences between suicide rates for men and women could reflect the fact that women are more likely to maintain family and social relationships after divorce. This hypothesis finds support in the findings of two recent studies (Solomou *et al.*, 1998; Lester, 1997b), in which suicide rates were positively associated with divorce for men but negatively associated for women.

Although the exact causal mechanisms between mortality and marriage are unclear, there is no doubt that separation and divorce, as McAllister *et al.* (1995) point out, continues to be detrimental for both mental and physical health. Divorce adversely affects a large percentage of people, and there is a need for research to be undertaken which can isolate the variables that lead to increased depression and morbidity, and decreased mortality for those experiencing divorce. It is also necessary to ask why these trends are continuing, given that divorce has been a persistent feature of society for over twenty years.

Identity

Most social commentators and researchers now acknowledge that divorce constitutes a process rather than a discreet event. Kitson and Morgan (1990), in their decade review, define part of the 'adjustment' process as the development of 'an independent identity that is not tied to the status of being married or to the ex-spouse'; however, the formation of a separate identity can be problematic for a number of reasons. Clulow (1990), for example, (unusually) adopts a psychodynamic perspective and emphasises that marriage is critical to a sense of self (see also Berger and Kellner, 1964); in outlining the similarities and differences between divorce and bereavement, he stresses that whilst both involve coming to terms with loss and the search for new meanings, 'when marriage breaks down there is a loss not only of a partner, but also of self'.

Although the process of coming to terms with the breakdown of a marriage involves the creation of a separate identity for both men and women, Kahn (1990) argues that because women are more likely to see marriage and the home as a source of identity, and to feel responsible for making it happy, when it fails a woman not only loses that identity but also sees herself as a failure. Based on clinical studies, Kahn believes that 'the ex-wife syndrome' is a relatively common psychological 'disorder' which stops women from forming a separate identity away from the ex-spouse and ultimately from 'completing' the psychological tasks of divorce. Chandler (1991), similarly, considers the formation of a new identity from a woman-only perspective, and highlights that because, historically, a woman's goal has been equated with marriage, divorced women are faced with 'the difficulties of forging a new identity and of making sense of a world which disparages women who are alone' (p. 68).

Colburn *et al.* (1992), in a cross-sectional study of 268 respondents who divorced during 1983/84, found that whilst, in general, the divorce experiences of men and women were converging, there was a marked gender difference in how separate identities were formulated. They found that 29.9% of men 'appear to create new identities through participation in new intimate relationships' (p. 103), compared to only 11.6% of women. They conclude that:

> [M]ales and females do differ in their ways of constructing a new identity. Males are more likely to externalise the problem of adjustment through a romantic solution. Females are more likely to cite changes in themselves and the experience of independence as the basis for a new identity (p. 105).

Similarly, the research of Cohen and Savaya (1997) considers how Moslem women recreate identity through 'inner resources' rather than external influences. Whilst emphasising that the divorce experience is not always negative, Chiriboga *et al.* (1991), in a longitudinal study of divorcing men and women, point out that:

> [D]ivorce is a transition that robs people of social involvements that form the basis not only of validation of one's position in society but also of one's sense of identity: who one is (p. 291).

Emery and Dillon (1994), looking at the divorce process from a clinical standpoint, believe that one of the main tasks associated with divorce is the renegotiation of relationships and the redefinition of boundaries. This task, they say, is hampered by the lack of 'normative expectations' surrounding divorce, and the fact that there is no ritual which signals the ending of one relationship and the beginning of another (see also Clulow, 1990; Chandler, 1991; Veevers, 1991).[2]

The creation of an identity separate from the ex-spouse when children are involved makes the process even more complex. As Emery and Dillon (1994) point out, not only do those divorcing have to 'disentangle ongoing parental roles from spousal roles that have ended' but, in order to move forward, must be able to 'grieve the end of the relationship and grapple with the challenges to their identity'.[3] The work of Maccoby and Mnookin (1992), following over 1,000 divorcing families over a three year period, also highlights the fact that 'separating spousal roles from parental roles is not an easy matter' (p. 24).

Simon (1992), considering the salience of parental identity in role strains and psychological distress, found that parental identity is more salient in women's self-conceptions than in men's. This, he believes, is due to the continuing 'sociocultural conceptions of adulthood which emphasize the primacy of motherhood for women's social self' (p. 26). His research also shows that those men who scored highly on levels of 'parental commitment' were actually slightly more affected by 'role strain' than women. This finding, he believes, may reflect a wider societal shift which is questioning the basic concepts of masculine identity and highlights the ambiguity presently surrounding this issue (see also Collier (1995) for further discussion on the debates surrounding changing masculine identities). Maccoby and Mnookin (1992), however, stress that fathers in pre-divorce families, on average, 'are considerably less involved' (p. 26) with their children than are mothers, and this obviously has implications for gender differences in all parental identities.

The fact that the majority of mothers continue their role as primary care-givers to children after divorce may preclude the necessity for any major shift in role identity, and therefore could act as a buffer to other changes in identity which have to be negotiated during the divorce process. These factors highlight some of the complexities associated with the concept of identity and illustrate the need for caution in assessing research into the relevance of identity on divorce adjustment.

Attachment

The creation of a new identity is also confounded by continuing 'attachment' to the ex-spouse, and concern over this issue has prompted an increase of research into the relationship between ex-spouses. Berman (1985) believes that the formation of a new life and commitments is based on the ability to detach from the ex-spouse, and that this is one of the major tasks involved in the divorce process (see also Kahn, 1990). Masheter (1991), however, argues that continuing attachment is not always 'maladaptive', and found that 'divorce did not necessarily terminate the relationship, even when the couple had no children or one or both partners were remarried' (p. 105). In her study of 265 respondents who had been divorced between two and two and a half years, 82% had contact with each other at least occasionally, 50% monthly and 25% weekly, and 43% of the sample reported friendly feelings towards the ex-spouse, with only 21% stating that the relationship was hostile. She also found that, rather than contact being due to continuing joint parenting responsibilities, 'contact was friendlier and quarrelling less frequent for those without children than with children' (p. 103). However, whilst Masheter's work supports the notion of an amicable or harmonious divorce based on a continuing attachment, she acknowledges its limitations due, in part, to selection bias and the fact that the study was unable to establish whether frequent contact was the cause of friendly feelings, or *vice versa*.

The multiple problems associated with maintaining attachment was highlighted by Kitson and Morgan (1991),[4] who stressed that:

> [C]omplex marital bonds must be severed - a difficult task since the partner was viewed as a 'good choice' initially and not all of the marriage was bad. Following divorce there is a growing social and legal expectation that couples will maintain a civil (meaning both 'civilised' and 'legal') relationship until the children reach a minimum age of 18. This socially and legally mandated continuity asks a lot of people who could not tolerate living together.

Kahn (1990), claims that, as far as women are concerned, all connections between ex-spouses have to be terminated in order to 'complete' the divorce process. She believes that the 'we can still be friends' fantasy is frequently reinforced by society, which holds up the 'amicable divorce' as the ideal, if only 'for the sake of the children', but is not possible if women are to gain autonomy and a new sense of self. Goodman (1993), however, in a study of men and women who had been divorced at least 15 years, found that whilst interaction with former spouses was generally minimal, greater interaction was related to better mental health and well-being.

The differing conclusions drawn by researchers regarding the relationship between continuing attachment and adjustment to divorce, reflects the difficulties caused by the lack of norms and expectations available to those divorcing (Kahn, 1990; Clulow, 1990; Veevers, 1991; Emery & Dillon, 1994). Metts and Cupach (1995) emphasise that because there is no culturally shared framework for post-divorce relationships, the first months after divorce is a period when the ex-partners have to actively negotiate new boundaries. The problems associated with defining these boundaries are, however, highlighted by Colburn *et al.* (1992) who found that 22% of men and 21% of women in their study reported having had sexual relations with their ex-spouse since the divorce was finalised. (See also Arendell (1986) who found that 20 out of the 60 women she interviewed had had sex with their ex-husband in the year following divorce, and four had continued a sexual relationship for considerably longer than that.)

The creation of a separate identity and attachment to the ex-spouse are both linked to the divorce process, and how these matters are resolved has obvious implications for 'adjustment'. What is less certain is how these factors interact and the extent to which such interaction poses a threat to a positive resolution. As with other aspects of divorce adjustment, individual experience varies, and whilst for some people creation of a new identity is dependent on a complete cessation of attachment, for others this would either be impracticable or undesirable.

Psychological 'Adjustment'

There is growing support for a transitional or crisis model of divorce which stresses the varying 'stages' of psychological adjustment throughout the divorce process (Wallerstein and Blakeslee, 1989; Chiriboga *et al.*, 1991; Gray and Shields, 1992; Steefel, 1992). Booth and Amato (1991) explored different models of divorce adjustment and found support for the crisis model in that stress was high during divorce but reduced following divorce in the vast majority of cases. They point out that even those whose pre-divorce resources and outlooks (such as low income, low education, unemployed women and those who had been left) made them more likely to suffer psychosomatic symptoms in the initial post-divorce period, had regained equilibrium after two years. (It should be noted, however, that unlike the majority of studies, Booth and Amato specifically considered people who did not have children.)

A longitudinal study by Nelson (1994) which charted a group of 35 women, from seven months to six years post-separation, and compared them with a control group of married women, found that although the separated women reported lower income and more life strains, there was no significant difference in emotional well-being. In fact they found that women in the first few years after separation reported a more growth-orientated coping style which led to greater autonomy, increased confidence and more positive life changes than married women. These differences, however, diminished over time, such that at the six year interval no significant differences were evident.

Bursik (1991a) studied 104 women, 36 without children, 35 with young children and 33 with children over 18, who were in the early stages of the separation/divorce process and again one year later. She found that although there was no significant change to overall well-being and physical health, scores for emotional health were higher at the follow-up, and most expressed general feelings that things were better. Unchangeable factors such as age and children were not strongly associated with adjustment for any of these women. However, non-traditional attitudes towards sex roles, and relationships with the ex-spouse characterised by low levels of acrimony, were found to be highly correlated to several measures of positive adjustment at both times.

Using the same sample, Bursik (1991b) also considered the effects of divorce on ego development. Whilst she acknowledges that divorce is disruptive and can lead to disorganisation and regression,[5] she believes that the overall outcome can be positive. Regarding the issue of how women adapt to and integrate disequilibriating life-events such as divorce over a one year period, she found that on measures of self-esteem, life satisfaction, mood disturbance, stress symptoms and physical health there was 'support for the hypothesis that marital separation and divorce...may foster ego development' (p. 305). Thus, although divorce may be stressful, the ability to 'master' the events, and the creation of coping mechanisms, can lead to opportunities for increased growth and development.

The impact of divorce on social support networks (Chandler, 1991; Diedrick, 1991; Colburn *et al.*, 1992; Simons *et al.*, 1993; Garvin *et al.*, 1993) has been found to play a large part in psychological adjustment. Hughes *et al.* (1993), for example, found that whilst most women reported an initial loss of friends and in-laws directly after divorce, within six months the mean number of friends had increased, although not significantly, from 14.8 to 16.7. There was also a change in the structural and interactional characteristics of the participants' social networks over this time, with an increase in social activity opportunities, rather than practical support, being linked positively with psychological adjustment based on measures of emotional health, mastery and self-esteem.

Miller *et al.* (1998) studied the distress of widowed and divorced women and found that it was the 'type' of support received which was pertinent to lowering distress, with the widowed gaining more benefit from practical help, and the divorced benefiting more from having someone to listen to their personal problems. Waggener and Galassi (1993) highlight the fact that it is not the number of people involved in the social support network but, rather, the perceived satisfaction which is the important determinant of outcome. They found that, in most cases, social support satisfaction was a better predictor of self-esteem, depression, anxiety, interpersonal sensitivity, somatic symptoms and total symptoms than social support frequency. Dissatisfaction with social support was positively correlated with total symptoms and negatively correlated with self-esteem.

As mentioned previously, attitudes towards sex roles have also been found to influence psychological outcome (Amato and Booth, 1991; Pledge, 1992). Bursik (1991a), in fact, found these to be 'among the strongest predictors of women's emotional health, well-being and physical health' (p. 159), with those showing higher masculinity scores on the Personal Attributes Questionnaire adjusting much better. Pledge (1992), in a review of the literature on the impact of marital separation or divorce, also found that women with a less traditional sex-role orientation showed better adjustment to the divorce process.

Thiriot and Buckner (1991), however, looking at the post-divorce adjustment of 204 custodial parents (90% of which were women), found that sex-role expectations did not substantially affect divorce adjustment. Whilst acknowledging that the research is inconclusive, Veevers (1991) states that:

> Whether or not nontraditional persons are actually better able to cope with the divorce transition, they may be better able to define their experiences in positive terms, a process which itself lowers their stress (p. 114).

The adoption of non-traditional sex-role attitudes may also be indicative of a stronger sense of identity that can be utilised as a means of counteracting the changes that the divorce process engenders.

However, the difficulties associated with correlating attitudes and outcome was highlighted by Amato and Booth (1991) in a longitudinal study of people's attitude changes as a consequence of divorce. They stress the point that the direction of causality is not clear because liberal gender role attitudes may have either preceded or followed divorce. These contradictory research findings highlight both the methodological and theoretical problems connected with studies of divorce and illustrate the complexities associated with isolating individual 'variables' in psychological studies. Indeed these factors are something that cannot be separated from the impact of 'divorce' on psychological 'adjustment'.

Gender Differences in Divorce

Studies of the different experiences of men and women with regard to divorce provide conflicting results with respect to both effects and outcome (Volgy, 1991; Synge, 1994). There is general area agreement, however, that women are more likely to suffer psychological stress prior to divorce (Diedrick, 1991; Colburn *et al.*, 1992; Pledge, 1992; Kincaid and Caldwell, 1995), but men suffer more post-divorce (Wadsby and Svedin, 1992; Livingston Bruce and Kim, 1992). One of the explanations advanced for this gender difference involves the idea that those who initiate divorce will adjust better (Veevers, 1991; Margulies and Luchow, 1992), and women are more often the initiators of formal proceedings. However, it must be remembered that the person who files the petition for divorce is not necessarily the 'initiator' either of the proceedings or of the marriage breakdown, and that issues of control and measurement are fundamental to any definition which is to be useful in understanding the consequences (Rossiter, 1991).

Gray and Silver (1990), conducted a study of 45 couples who were asked to 'tell their story'. They linked cognition[6] and adjustment and found that 'perceiving oneself as having had control over the separation was clearly associated with successful adjustment to the breakup' (p. 1189). They also reported that men and women both assessed the women as having had slightly more control over the divorce process, and that there was no gender difference in the capacity of respondents to see themselves as 'victims' of the situation. Thus it would appear that being able to perceive the other person as the villain of the piece, regardless of initiator status, leads to better psychosocial adjustment and resolution of the break-up.

A Swedish study by Wadsby and Svedin (1992), which included the assessment of 47 ex-couples, concluded that the changes as a consequence of divorce were significantly different for men and women in several areas, and that in most cases women faired better than men. They believe that initiator status is significant in differential outcome (60% of women in their study had initiated the divorce), and that it ratifies other studies that show women suffer more psychological distress prior to divorce. Their study found that whereas 40% of women thought that the marriage had been bad for 2-5 years, this belief was shared by only 25% of the men, and although 42% of men believed that the marriage had been in trouble for less than a year, only 17% of women held this view. With regard to psychological well-being and self-confidence, assessed by visual analogue scales, Wadsby and Svedin also found marked discrepancies between the outcome of divorce for men and women; 72% of women reported that their mental well-being had improved since the divorce, and only 18% felt it had been impaired, this contrasted respectively with figures of 28% and 45% for men.[7] They also reported that 84% of women had more self-confidence (6% less), against 37% of men (23% less). One of the reasons which could account for this discrepancy is the fact that 50% of the men experienced a loss of social relationships after divorce, and 35% of men stated that they had no one to talk to about their experiences (10% of men felt that they had no need to talk to anyone).

It should be pointed out, however, that Wadsby and Svedin's sample contained a disproportionate amount of women who were in full-time, highly paid employment, which would not only have alleviated any financial pressures, but would also have increased their self-confidence. Bisagni and Eckenrode (1995), explored the role of employment on divorce adjustment and the psychological well-being of women, and found that work identity was positively associated with higher self-esteem and low levels of distress. They postulate that employment not only involves greater social interaction and support, but also that it leads to a sense of meaningfulness and productivity, and can be a positive distraction from emotional problems caused by the divorce (see also Pett *et al.*, 1994).

Gender differences in reaction to the psychological stress of divorce were also found by Horwitz *et al.*, (1996), who reported that whilst women were more likely to show significantly greater increases in depression than men, men reported far more alcohol problems than women. Studies which look at the different divorce experiences and outcomes of men and women, therefore, need to be placed within a wider social context which takes into account both societal norms and expectations, and also the economic redistribution which occurs as a result of divorce (Arendell, 1986; Maclean, 1991; Furstenberg and Cherlin, 1991; Morgan, 1991; Maccoby and Mnookin, 1992). Most families with children are still based on a 'traditional' division of labour (Maccoby and Mnookin, 1992), with the man taking on the role of economic provider and the woman being responsible for the emotional and nurturing aspects of family life, and therefore divorce will obviously have differential outcomes based on gender. These issues are particularly relevant to the following sections on mothers and fathers, and need to be addressed with regard to whether it is the divorce process itself which is problematic or continuing gender inequalities.

Mothers

A large proportion of research into the effects of divorce on adults has tended to focus primarily on women as mothers, this representing the most common subgroup of divorced women, (for an exception see Booth and Amato, 1991, who, as mentioned above, studied the effects of divorce on those without children). Arditti and Madden-Dedrich (1995) use a feminist framework as a basis for collecting data and understanding how mothers make sense of the divorce experience. They believe this method provides 'a means for understanding how individuals go through or make sense of difficult events in their lives' (p. 230). Their research also emphasises the problems for divorced mothers by family-centred discourses in which 'motherhood, within the context of a heterosexual marriage, is seen as the standard by which all other mothers are judged'; they believe that 'those mothers who do not share this social context...are invisible and marginalised' (p. 231). When conducting a qualitative content analysis of written accounts provided by 80 divorced women, they found that loss and guilt were predominant emotions, and that many women felt 'overburdened by the responsibilities of [single] parenthood' (p. 238).

However, they also found that, balancing the negative aspects of the divorce experience, many women gained confidence and had better relationships with their children: they wrote of positive outcomes and 'of unexpected happiness and serenity' (p. 241) for both them and their children. It appears that, for these women, the most cogent factor in coping with the many problems inherent in single-parenthood was the ability to focus on the benefits of the divorce rather than the negative aspects. The generalisability of this study, however, is limited owing to the fact that the respondents had had particularly difficult divorces and relatively low levels of father involvement.

Garvin *et al.* (1993) studied 56 divorced mothers, and compared the differences between those who remained single and those who had remarried. They found those who remained single had significantly higher levels of stress and psychiatric symptomatology, and scored significantly lower on measures of self-esteem and satisfaction with social support. One of the biggest external differences between the two groups, however, was income; the average income for the divorced-single group being $14,000, whilst the average for those who had remarried was significantly higher at $42,000. This leads them to argue that rather than divorce *per se* being responsible for higher levels of depression and poorer social adjustment, it is the effects of 'economic hardship, social isolation, and increased work and parenting responsibilities that single parents are both more exposed to and more vulnerable to'(p. 239). (See also Buehler and Legg, 1993.)

Irving and Benjamin (1995) state that 'divorced women in the United States and Canada can expect a 30% decline in their pre-divorce annual income, with about one third likely to drop below the poverty line in consequence' (p. 56).[8] This situation is also reflected in the U.K.: Maclean (1991) points out that in 1984 over 55% of one-parent families (the majority of which are female-headed) relied on state benefits as their main source of income. Secondary problems associated with economic hardship have also been highlighted by Simons *et al.* (1993) whose study found, among other things, that those single mothers who were under severe economic pressure reported both high exposure to negative events and low social support, which, in turn, were associated with psychological distress and ineffectual parenting practices.

The type of custody arrangement after divorce is also a salient factor for single mothers. Arditti and Madden-Dedrich (1997) found that mothers with sole custody gained more parenting satisfaction than those who had joint custody arrangements (see also Baker and Townsend, 1996). However, both Kahn (1990) and Chandler (1991) emphasise the difficulties of parenting for single mothers, and argue that because lone parenting is measured against the ideal model of the 'normal' two-parent family, there is always something missing, and that women are often left to feel they are a poor substitute for 'proper' parenting. However, whilst stress and depression for mothers is usually high immediately following divorce, this does tend to diminish over time as routines are established (Lorenz *et al.*, 1997).

Chandler (1991) believes that one of the problems stems from ambiguity 'as mothers feel they should be more available, that the children should, in the absence of the father, have more of them, while also feeling resentful that they have to give so much and that the children tie them to the home' (p. 141). This ambiguity can also lead to problems of discipline as single mothers lose the parental echelon of power and aim for a less hierarchical and more democratic/permissive relationship with their children. Kahn (1990) believes that, indeed, these mothers represent a new form of matriarchal household. Unfortunately, in a society which continues to see single mothers as deviant and undesirable (Rice, 1994), and with persisting wage disparity, lack of social support and child care (Arditti and Madden-Dedrich, 1995), the benefits which could accrue from this new family form are often over-shadowed by the material and psychological pressures which it brings.

Morgan (1991) posits the view that economic inequalities in society disadvantage all women, and that marriage merely provides temporary insulation from these inequities, as such women who leave marriage, for whatever reason, will automatically experience a decline in economic well-being. However, divorce can have adverse economic effects for both men and women; Cohen (1996), in a study of both maternal and paternal single households, found that the economic situation was a strong predictor of family well-being. In fact it was found that single-parent families with a good economic situation actually had a higher sense of family well-being than two-parent families.

Nevertheless, the economic consequences of divorce do have profound repercussions for a large majority of women, especially mothers. This aspect of divorce cannot be separated from the psychological effects, and many of the problems associated with single motherhood can be seen to be linked as much to the lack of economic provision as they are to the lack of the physical presence of a husband and father.

Fathers

Although, as noted above, divorce research has focused more on mothers, by definition, there must be an equal number of divorced fathers. Within research, however, emphasis has usually been placed on their role as economic providers and the provision (or not) of child-maintenance.[9] This emphasis can be seen as a reflection of the father role in general, and the fact that even in 'intact' families, men's involvement with childcare activities and the responsibility they carry for children is marginal compared to that of women (Hochschild, 1989; Marsiglio, 1991; Seltzer, 1991; Arendell, 1995; Sanchez and Thomson, 1997). Indeed, as Maccoby and Mnookin (1992) point out, in pre-divorce families mothers 'are overwhelmingly more likely to be the person *responsible* for the children', are likely to have three times more face-to-face interaction with children, and 'in terms of the time spent as the responsible parent, mothers outweigh fathers nine to one' (p. 26).

Over the last decade, however, there has been a growing body of research on the structural constraints and psychological adjustments which affect fathers on divorce (O'Brien, 1992; Ambrose *et al.*, 1993; Cohen, 1995). This shift is also reflected in the fact that in 1993 the *Journal of Family Issues* devoted a volume to fatherhood (as did the *Journal of Divorce and Remarriage* in 1995). Umberson and Williams (1993) conducted in-depth interviews with 45 divorced fathers and found that not only did these men report substantially higher levels of parental role strain than did married fathers, but that they exhibit higher rates of psychological distress, alcohol consumption and mortality.

Seltzer (1994), writing from a child-centred perspective, claims that 'at divorce, men typically disengage from their biological children', and that 'because marriage is a short-term institution, men's relationships with children are also short-term' (p. 235). In part, this proposition is based on her earlier work conducted into the relationships between fathers and children who live apart, which found that 30% of children had no contact with their father on divorce, and that only 25% had weekly contact.

Although Furstenberg and Cherlin (1991) also argued that levels of post-divorce paternal disengagement were due to the fact that 'men see parenting and marriage as part of the same bargain - a package deal' (p. 38), others have argued that this view is overly simplistic. For example, Kruk (1992) believes that not only is fathers' disengagement due to the threatened or actual loss of children, but that it is connected inversely with the strength of the father-child relationship pre-divorce. From a sample of 80 divorced fathers in both Scotland and Canada, half with regular contact and half 'disengaged', he found 'disengaged' fathers actually reported higher levels of involvement/attachment pre-divorce.[10] He explains this discrepancy as a reaction against a 'visiting' relationship which in no way resembled, for these men, 'real' fatherhood, and which resulted in the loss of attachment, role and identity. The two main influences on this outcome are seen as the ex-wife's support of the father-child relationship, and a legal system which Kruk sees as not only biased against men, but which he sees as fostering antagonism between the ex-partners. As evidence of bias he states that 'in 55% of all cases in the study, lawyers actively discouraged fathers from pursuing custody; only 12% agreed with or encouraged it' (p. 90).

Fathers' dissatisfaction with the adversarial system was also found by Arditti and Allen (1993); in their study of 87 men they state that 'fathers expressed strong negative feelings about discrimination from the legal system' (p. 461). They also point out that whilst there is a wealth of research into the economic hardship of women following divorce, that many men, especially those on low incomes, also suffer a severe reduction in finances.[11]

Bruch (1992), however, emphasises the legal bias against women rather than men,[12] and stresses that whereas courts often impose movement restrictions on custodial mothers, the same rarely applies to fathers. The problems with the adversarial nature of divorce litigation have been highlighted by various commentators (Margulies and Luchow, 1992), and are among the main reasons put forward for a move towards compulsory mediation in divorce. However, Bruch points out that because mediation rests on the need for 'neutral solutions' based on compromise, women are more likely to be disadvantaged due to on-going power imbalances in the relationship.[13] Emery *et al.* (1994) found that men who mediated their divorce settlement were substantially more satisfied than those who litigated, and women who mediated were significantly less satisfied at follow-up than those who litigated.

Another salient factor relating to paternal involvement which has received growing attention is that of the continuing ex-spousal relationship[14] (Masheter, 1990, 1991; Maccoby and Mnookin, 1992; Neale and Smart, 1997). Researchers which have identified different patterns of parental communication have argued that a continuing relationship based on high levels of conflict is not only 'bad' for the children (Rodgers and Pryor, 1998), but is also connected with loss of paternal contact over time.[15] However, even the in-depth studies of fathers' adjustment to divorce (see, for example, Simpson *et al.*, 1995), are unable to identify exactly what mechanisms and processes, psychological and/or practical, work to produce different outcomes.

The issue of paternal rights and responsibilities is a recurring theme in both the divorce literature and legal debates. Smart and Sevenhuijsen (1989), for example, bring together a collection of papers which show how current ideas about the 'welfare of the child' and 'fathers' rights' can work against women.[16] Smart (1989) argues that 'the more men's interests and children's interests are seen to coincide, the more mothers are disempowered' (p. 10). In these dominant discourses, single mothers (and fatherless families)[17] have been linked with delinquent and maladjusted children; this has become part of a public perception supported by political rhetoric.[18]

Additionally, as Furstenberg and Cherlin (1991) point out, in placing too much emphasis on the role of divorced fathers, we may be attempting to 'engineer' a direct role for fathers in divorced families that does not often exist in 'intact' families. Whilst there is no doubt that some men obviously suffer great emotional turmoil on divorce and in relation to the subsequent redefinition of the relationship with their children, it would appear that a large proportion still see disengagement as an expedient option; the economic effects of this decision on women, together with the psychological effects on those children who are effectively abandoned, should be held in mind when assessing research into fathers and divorce.

Age and Divorce

It has been hypothesised that older divorcing people would suffer more psychological problems and be less able to recover equilibrium than younger people, and that this would be especially so for older women (Uhlenberg *et al.*, 1990; Morgan, 1991). Longitudinal studies such as that by Wallerstein and her co-workers (see, for example, Wallerstein and Blakeslee (1989)) have, however, produced some contradictory findings. They found that whilst women who were over 40 on divorce, and who had actively sought the divorce, continued to have no regrets 10 years later, 50% of those over 40 who had not wanted the divorce found it very difficult to establish a new identity and still felt intensely lonely even if the marriage had been bad. They also found, however, that men over 40 followed a similar pattern and that even though they had a higher rate of remarriage than women, 50% had not remarried 10 years later and felt isolated, lonely and socially deprived.

Chiriboga *et al.* (1991), found that whilst women over 40 were initially more stressed by the divorce, they were actually coping better than younger women (and men) later. This, they believe, could be due to the conflicting demands made on younger adults of being a parent and being single again. Although the number of people aged over 65 who are granted a divorce each year is minimal (1.1% of divorces in 1980 occurred in the 65+ age group), this, nevertheless, comprises a sizeable minority. Hammond and Muller's (1992) study showed that divorced men in this age group had poorer adjustment than women, and that women, when asked to compare life now with a year prior to separation (including parenting, social life and overall happiness), reported higher scores of satisfaction. Nevertheless, whilst women were more likely than men to turn to others for support during the separation period, they did not do so as much as either younger women or younger men. An atypical finding of this study, however, was that no differences were found in the financial scores for men and women; this contradicts the vast majority of studies which show that older women are more likely to suffer economic disadvantage, thus raising questions about methodological reliability.

Gander (1991) compared post-divorce adjustment factors among people over 50 and younger people and found that although younger people anticipated the divorce more than those 50+ (40% v. 28.5%), that nevertheless the older people 'experienced significantly less conflict after the divorce than the younger group did' (p. 183). However, no significant differences between the groups were found on measures of conflict experienced during the divorce itself, or in general post-divorce well-being.

The accumulation of disrupted relationships for the elderly has been seen as deleterious to relationships between parents and their adult children and to other social ties (Goldscheider, 1994). This study found that men, in particular, were prone to isolation as they lost their 'kin-keepers', and that even if they remarried, they were more likely to lose touch with their biological children and to have weaker ties with step-children. This finding is also supported by the work of Solomou and her colleagues (Solomou *et al.*, 1996, 1999). Their study of the elderly found that lone men had the lowest scores for social engagement. They also found, however, that whilst there was a clear association between earlier divorce and reduced likelihood of home ownership, there was no indication that the experience of divorce was associated with any long-term effects on health. (It should be noted that this study excluded all those who were mentally or physically frail.) Overall it would appear that when factors such as economic circumstances are taken into account, age at divorce is not a strong predictor of psychological adjustment.

Ethnicity

There is relatively little research which looks at ethnic differences with respect to divorce adjustment, and often studies which try to isolate differences find that sample sizes make it impossible to make statistical analyses (Neff and Schulter, 1993). Sudarkasa (1993) maintains that, in respect to African American households, marital stability is not the same as family stability, and that 'blood' kin continues to be a salient factor. Thus, although divorce research often refers to the fact that 'blacks have a higher risk of divorce than whites' (Irving and Benjamin, 1995), this has to be looked at in a wider socio-historic and cultural context. Indeed, Sudarkasa argues that single parenthood and divorce are 'adopted in the face of the demographic, economic, political and social realities of Black life in America' (p. 86) and, as such, can be seen as a mature decision in light of circumstances.

Bowman's (1993) work on the economic marginality of Black men focuses on the problems for husband-fathers who take on roles and then are denied the opportunity to fulfil them through traditional channels. This work emphasises the importance of socio-economic circumstances in isolating ethnicity as a salient factor in divorce.

Whilst research into ethnic differences is sparse, there is a growing body of literature which looks at divorce from a cross-cultural perspective in an attempt to separate cultural from universal aspects of divorce outcome. Amato (1994), for example, compared recent literature on the impact of divorce in India and America, and also interviewed divorcees, officials and researchers connected with the divorce process in India. Whilst he highlights the fact that divorce creates stress in both countries and that factors which facilitate divorce adjustment are also similar in both cultures, religious and cultural differences make comparison difficult (most of the research he looked at in India was based on Hindu marriages). Women came out as more disadvantaged than men in both countries although, as could be expected, American women faired better than their Indian counterparts; this he links with 'inequality' between men and women which he says is greater in India than in the USA. The continuing financial dependence of many Indian women on men, and the social stigma attached to divorce, causes increased emotional distress for these women and the difficulties of social adjustment are greater because, as Amato points out: 'Community disapproval...is stronger for women than men' and 'when a marriage breaks up, people are inclined to feel that it is the wife's fault' (p. 212). There is also a much lower rate of re-marriage for Indian women and this, together with the fact that the only 14% of adult women are in paid employment, means that many women have to turn back to the family for financial support. (See also Siganporia, 1993.)

One aspect which is clear from the majority of cross-cultural comparisons, especially within the Western world, is that divorce is still highly correlated with increased risk of depression, morbidity and decreased mortality rates in all countries; what is less clear are the causal mechanisms and processes which operate to produce this state of affairs.

Discussion

The difficulties of studying 'divorce' are reflected in the conflicting research findings and the various different emphases which researchers place on aspects of the divorce experience. However, whilst there is a growing recognition that viewing divorce in purely negative terms tends to result in an emphasis on negative outcomes, researchers appear to have done little to bring about a more positive attitude towards divorce or to foster a perception which may help people negotiate the experience with better understanding. It would appear that social stigma and feelings of individual 'failure' still abound.

Research which focuses on issues of identity and attachment often give rise to opposing conclusions, as individual circumstances and personality traits mean that there is no single factor which is responsible for better or worse 'adjustment'. There can also be confusion as different studies use different measures of adjustment and control for divergent variables. Although there has been a move away from cross-sectional studies towards more longitudinal research, which assists in identifying the relative salience of individual and biographical factors, this research needs to encompass a wider selection of people, and to follow people for much longer, both pre- and post-divorce. There is also a need for research that relies on data from the whole family rather than on individual perceptions, and a need to conduct more prospective studies to address the limitations inherent in retrospective studies.

Studies which have focused on parenthood still tend to use a two-parent paradigm and therefore see single-parenthood as a truncated system which gives rise to socio- and psycho-pathology. Implicit normative models of 'family' are assumed in many studies, as well as in legal decision-making and divorce dispute resolution practice (see, for example, Neale and Smart, 1999); these assumptions exist in profound tension with the realities of the diversity of family forms in contemporary society. Recent research which emphasises co-operative models of parenting after divorce are inclined to equate better child-parent relations and better outcomes for children with more frequent contact or joint custody arrangements, although the research findings on this issue are contradictory and controversial (see, for example, the recent review by Rodgers and Pryor, 1998). The current dominance of the welfare discourse can be seen to be reflected in both research and legal practice and, as we discuss in chapters 5 and 6, plays an important part in the ways in which divorcing people themselves make sense of their experiences.

Studies which identify gender differences in divorce adjustment often overlook structural and substantive inequalities and continuing wage disparities. These factors, and their economic consequences, mean that comparisons of psychological adjustment based on gender are often spurious. Whilst there is a growing amount of research which looks specifically at the divorce experience of men, and which obviously adds to the body of knowledge concerning divorce, the emphasis on 'men's rights' (Collier, 1995) should be set within a wider context which acknowledges that recent divorce reforms, whilst attempting to be gender-neutral, have actually served to lessen the financial burden faced by men on divorce at the same time as they have increased the practical and emotional burdens on women. As discussed in chapter 2, considerable tensions exist, in both law and research, between dominant ideologies of gender-neutral 'parents' and the continuing discursive construction of women and men, mothers and fathers, as gendered beings.

Studies which focus on factors such as age and ethnicity highlight the multi-dimensional aspects of divorce adjustment, but are often too small in number to afford generalisable results. In addition, most studies suffer from problems of identifying the direction of causation, and most do not even attempt to specify the processes that produce different outcomes. Sampling biases have led to the majority of subjects being white, middle-class and female.

There is no doubt that the traditional research indicates that there are a range of psychological adjustments which have to be made during the divorce process; the divorce process occupies a period of dislocation and anxiety which lasts for differing lengths of time and has differing consequences depending on an individual's specific personality, biography and material and social circumstances. However, it seems that the need for divorcing individuals to battle against a dominant ideological stance which holds up 'the family' as the cornerstone of society, and which increasingly decries single-parents as burdens on the state, is unlikely to facilitate those adjustments. This, for many, surely compounds the negative aspects of divorce and hampers changes which could help alleviate guilt and distress.

Conclusion: The Need for a Psychosocial Approach to Divorce

As shown in this chapter, the psychology of divorce has not been a neglected area of study. But it was also seen that research into the psychological reactions of adults to divorce has been beset by a range of methodological and conceptual difficulties (Kitson & Morgan, 1990) and it has been said there has been a lamentable dearth of theory in this field (Irving & Benjamin, 1995). Mainstream psychological and psychiatric research on divorce has tended to concentrate on the quantitative assessment of psychological states, to the neglect of any understanding of the processes and personal meanings involved. A focus on personal meanings and experiences has, however, been difficult to achieve within the traditional psychological paradigm. As Henriques *et al.* (1984/1998) have noted, orthodox psychological research rests upon particular methodological criteria as well as an implicit view of the nature of 'the individual' as separate from the social world. Thus the investigation of experiences and meanings has inevitably been constrained by the empiricist and rationalist assumptions of the traditional paradigm.

By contrast, recent 'social constructionist' approaches in the social sciences, especially those that focus on the structuring significance of language and discourse, may have more to offer in the way of understanding subjects' own worlds. This study was located in an emerging paradigm of 'narrative' research, a newer approach which has usefully been applied to understanding how people make sense of divorce (Riessman, 1990a, 1991,1992; Day Sclater, 1995b, 1997a, 1998b, 1999; Day Sclater and Yates, 1999).

The vast literature on the psychology of divorce reviewed in this chapter seems to suffer from two main limitations: first, studies on the alleged 'effects' of divorce on children predominate. Secondly, where adults have been the focus of study, the research has tended to focus on the quantitative measurements of psychological states, to the neglect of people's experiences. Within the traditional paradigm, psychological research has documented people's 'adjustment' to divorce, sometimes conceived as a series of 'stages' (comparable to those in bereavement). The result has been the further entrenchment of a pathologised image; divorce represents an emotional trauma from which people 'recover' in a predictable way over time, they are seen as getting back to 'normal' as time goes by.

Our study has departed from this traditional paradigm in a number of ways, and for a number of reasons.[19] The starting point for developing this 'psychosocial' approach to divorce was an acknowledgement that traditional psychology adopts a limited view of the human subject, as unitary, coherent, and rational, leaving little room to understand human inconsistencies, contradictions, irrational impulses and emotions, and unconscious processes. This traditional picture of 'the individual' is deep rooted in both psychology and law but has been challenged on a number of fronts; in particular, post-structuralist theories have emphasised the complexities, contradictions, fluidity and situatedness of human subjectivity which cannot be captured by a traditional approach.[20]

The development of a 'psychosocial' approach has several important consequences. First, it means that different research questions are generated; we are no longer just looking for evidence of how 'individuals' adjust to divorce, and return through a series of predictable stages back to 'normality'. Instead, we are looking at how people make sense of their experiences, and how the social world in which they live and act contributes to the personal meanings they create about the worlds they leave behind as well as those they aspire to. Secondly, adopting a psychosocial approach means developing a new methodology appropriate to the kinds of issues we want to study; we did not just want to measure internal psychological states, using quantitative scales, but wanted to use a qualitative approach which permitted subjects to articulate accounts of their experiences in their own words. Understanding how people make sense of their experiences means paying particular attention to the language that they use to tell about their experiences; focusing on the stories that people tell to make their experiences meaningful and understandable to others is the essence of our approach. The next chapter sets out full details of our approach, methodology and the assumptions and theoretical arguments which underlie it.

Notes

[1]   Hemstrom (1996), however, in a study of 44,000 Swedish deaths, argues that when other factors are controlled, gender differences are smaller than is usually believed.

[2]   Chandler (1991) highlights the fact that Judaism is the only religion that provides a ritual which would aid the psychological transition from a shared identity to a separate one.

[3]   This view was also put forward by Robinson (1991) in *Family Transformation Through Divorce and Remarriage*. She argues that 'One of the major tasks of the divorce process is that in which the divorcing partners who are also parents redefine their parental roles, while relinquishing those of husband and wife' (p. 67).

[4]   Quoted in McAllister (1995) *Marital Breakdown and the Health of the Nation* (2nd edn), p. 28.

[5]   See Kelly (1982).

[6]   See also Christensen and Shenk (1991) and Granvold (1994) who apply a cognitive approach to marital dysfunction and the effects of divorce.

[7]   Colburn *et al.*'s (1992) study of gender and the divorce experience also showed discrepancies in well-being with more than twice as many men than women agreeing with the statement that nothing good had happened since the divorce.

[8]   See also Arendell's (1986) work on divorced women. She stresses that economic hardship is more pertinent to divorce outcome than psychological aspects of divorce adjustment.

[9]   Studies have shown that in many cases the number of men paying child maintenance payments is less than 50%, and that even when full maintenance is paid it does not

exceed 15% of the husband's gross income for two children (Maclean, 1991; Maccoby and Mnookin, 1992).

[10] It should be noted that Kruk relied on fathers' own retrospective accounts. It is not possible assess fathers' actual attachments to their children from such accounts.

[11] See also Collier (1999) for a discussion of the ways in which men are beginning to position themselves as the new 'victims' of divorce in the context of what some have caled a 'crisis in masculinity'.

[12] See the section on 'gender' in chapter 2 for a fuller discussion of these points.

[13] Saxton (1993) states that divorce attorneys point out that divorcing parties typically have no advocates, which gives the husband an advantage.

[14] Such support is not always forthcoming owing to the fact that some families feel that their responsibility has been fulfilled by the provision of a dowry (which is not returnable on divorce). Because of the stigma attached to divorce there is also a very low number of women in a similar situation who can be called upon for help or support.

[15] See Kaganas (1999) for a fuller discussion on the relations between contact, conflict and risk of harm for children.

[16] See also Collier (1995, 1999); Day Sclater and Piper (1999); Day Sclater and Yates (1999); Kaganas (1999); Neale and Smart (1999) for some recent contributions to the gender debate.

[17] See Dennis and Erdos (1992).

[18] See also Smart (1997); Neale and Smart (1997); Smart and Neale (1997). For a critical discussion of the work of Smart and her colleagues, see James and Richards (1999).

[19] Full details of conceptual and methodological framework are given in chapter 4.

[20] See, for example, Hollway (1989). Recent theorising also emphasises the crucial links between embodiment and subjectivity: see, for example, Grosz (1994); Shildrick (1997); Gatens (1996).

4 Theory and Method for a Psychosocial Approach to Divorce

In this study we have been interested in the ways in which the psychological processes in divorce interact with the practices of dispute resolution. Despite calls for further research integrating the two (for example, Vermont Law School, 1987), little is known about these interactions.[1] This is, perhaps, partly a consequence of the fact that the psychological aspects of divorce have been conceived of and 'measured' in so many different ways, and partly a consequence of the great diversity in dispute resolution procedures. But we would also argue that this is partly a consequence of the limitations of the traditional paradigm.

Several commentators (for example, Arditti and Madden-Dedrich, 1990, Riessman, 1990a) have pointed out that, despite the broad literature on the psychological aspects of divorce, very little is actually known about the range of divorce experiences and the personal meanings which they hold. The search for general 'truths' about divorce, which has characterised orthodox approaches, has tended to eclipse any quest for understanding diversity or individual experiences, and there has been little attempt in mainstream research to explain or theorise the psychological processes involved in 'adjustment'[2] or the psychodynamics of dispute resolution. There is a sense in which traditional work has 'naturalised' the psychology of divorce, and has failed to see experiences of divorce, and their expression, as socially constructed or historically contingent.[3]

The main objective of this project was to investigate the relationships between the psychological processes of separation and divorce, and dispute resolution discourses[4] and procedures (as linked and mutually dependent social and psychological phenomena), using a qualitative, multiple case study approach (Rosenwald, 1988). In our theoretical framework,[5] the relationships between psychology and dispute resolution were conceived in dynamic, mutually constitutive terms (Day Sclater, 1995b). The project therefore set out, not only in pursuit of 'findings', but also to develop an appropriate theoretical and methodological framework for an interdisciplinary, psychosocial approach to divorce. Because our approach departs from orthodox ones in a number of ways, this chapter describes our orientation and the possibilities it offers, and explains the rationale for studying the psychology of divorce in this particular way.

Whilst traditional psychological research may illuminate certain aspects of the divorce process, it is of limited value in understanding individual experiences holistically; these experiences are decontextualised in the research process and personal meanings tend to be left out of account. The measurement of internal psychological states, and the cataloguing of individual 'adjustments' to divorce, which characterise the psychological literature, rest upon a 'black box' (cognitivist and rationalist) view of the subject which, in turn, depends upon a limited view of 'the individual' and renders 'the social' peripheral. By contrast, the psychosocial approach, which this study develops, seeks to overcome the individual-society dualism and to regard, instead, the human subject as social at its core. This chapter demonstrates how a psychosocial approach resists the traditional sociological/psychological disciplinary boundary, and uses concepts and methods that deliberately and routinely transgress such boundaries.[6]

Applying this approach to divorce implies a need to theorise the individual-society interrelationship. It also implies moving beyond the idea that psychological processes in divorce are likely to 'affect' dispute resolution in some causal manner. In our framework, dispute resolution processes and discourses are just as likely to 'affect' individual psychological processes as *vice versa*, and the 'causal' paradigm is abandoned in favour of an interactive model which emphasises the mutual constitution of individual feelings, cultural discourses and social structures. A psychosocial approach thus involves recognising the ways in which discourses of divorce provide frameworks within which divorcing people think, feel and act, and make sense of their experiences; it implies a recognition of the interrelationship of human agency and social structure, and a commitment to understanding the ways in which human subjects act to negotiate, resist or reproduce broader social structures. Crucially, dispute resolution procedures depend upon human subjects engaging with them and, from a psychosocial viewpoint, human activities are seen ultimately to depend upon how the subject constructs meaning in the context of her or his immediate circumstances and life history.

The Critical Psychology of the Subject

In developing this psychosocial approach to divorce we owe an enormous debt to what has been called the 'critical psychology' movement (see, for example, Henriques *et al.*, 1984/1998; Ingleby, 1986; Squire, 1989; Bakhurst and Sypnowich, 1995; Parker and Spears, 1996; Fox and Prilleltensky, 1997; Ibanez and Iniguez, 1997). Henriques *et al.* (1984/1998) opened the way to a critical and psychodynamically informed approach to psychology when they identified the weakness of orthodox psychology's construction of 'the individual' within an individual-society dualism. They saw that 'the individual' had been constructed as an object of study and as a site for social regulation and administration (see also Rose, 1990; Burman, 1994; Morss, 1995). They argued that the unitary, rational individual of orthodox psychology was an historical product; it had no necessary relation to the way people actually were, but was a particular construction, a product of psychological theorising, which was intimately linked to a larger project of social regulation in which psychology, as a discipline, was engaged.

Influenced by post-structuralist theories, Henriques *et al.* advocated a new way of thinking about people, one which saw rationality as only one part of humanity and which took account of unconscious as well as conscious processes (see also Ingleby, 1986). They adopted the term 'subjectivity' in place of 'the individual' to reflect a broader conception of the person, incorporating both psychological and social dimensions. For Henriques *et al.*, human subjectivity is diverse, multiple, fragmentary, contingent, not wholly rational and potentially contradictory. They challenged the orthodox idea that subjectivity is internal, private and personal and argued instead that it was relational and discursive, produced and reproduced in social relationships throughout life. Importantly, subjectivity is seen as having no essential coherence; rather it is contingent upon the discourses, relationships and practices with which individual subjects engage.

The Importance of Language and Discourse

In critical psychology, a significance is accorded to language, at both an individual and a social level, which is absent in traditional psychology and sociology. In orthodox research, language is merely a means of communication; people say what they mean and mean what they say, and language is a transparent medium by which 'reality' is reflected and conveyed in a meaningful way. On this view, meanings are given in language and hence are more or less self evident. By contrast, a critical approach problematises meaning and challenges this mimetic view of language; it sees language, not as reflecting experience, but as constitutive of it. Parker (1992), for example, talks about the 'turn to language' in psychology as having its origin in the work which drew attention to the importance of meaning and the accounts people gave of their actions, in ethnomethodology and in analytic philosophy. He sees an attention to language as a response to the 1970s 'crisis' in social psychology (Parker, 1989). Crucially, language is seen as not only constitutive of experience, but also of subjectivity itself. We shall have more to say about this in a moment.

Importantly, however, language is not a politically neutral system, but is organised in discourses, some of which are more dominant than others at any given time (Laclau and Mouffe, 1985; Fairclough, 1989, 1992; Plummer, 1995). According to Derrida (1978a, 1978b), signifiers only achieve their meaning in specific discursive contexts; thus, the fixing of meaning can, at best, be only temporary. But an emphasis on the crucial importance of language need not lead us to conclude that the construction of meaning is something that is externally, rather than internally, achieved; that would be a mere reversal of the orthodox position in psychology. The task becomes one of recognising the constitutive contributions of both the inner and the outer worlds in meaning-making.

It is important not to lose sight of the fact that it is people who engage with discourse and who use language; as Giddens (1991) argues, human agency must not be subsumed under the imperatives of all-powerful external structures, but neither must those structures be ignored. Further, it is crucial not to lose sight of what is subjective about subjectivity, for 'selves' are not just language and discourse, or the effects of those things. Parker (1992), for example, wonders about what is going on in people's heads when they use discourse. Vice (1996) goes further, and asserts that 'all discourse is inhabited by the unconscious' (p. 6).[7] The implication here is twofold and reciprocal: without particular psychological structures (conscious and unconscious), people would not and could not engage with particular discourses and, conversely, particular discourses presuppose, construct and perpetuate particular psychological constellations. Lacan (1957/1966) argued that unconscious processes depend upon the workings of language, and it follows that the workings of language, therefore, reflect something about unconscious processes (see Hollway, 1989).

Work in literary, media and film studies (see, for example, Williamson, 1978; Belsey, 1980; Lapsley and Westlake, 1988) has usefully addressed these complications of meaning production. Out of this work arises the idea that meaning is never finally achieved, but is an ongoing process, in which inner and outer continually interact in such a way that they are, ultimately, inseparable from each other. This work has addressed the crucial problem of how it is that things come to 'mean' anything at all. The idea has emerged that meaning is as much to do with 'form' as it is with 'content', is as much to do with the external world as it is with the internal one, and that the individual producer of meaning can never be the ultimate guarantor of that meaning, because of the dynamic processual nature of meaning, and because the audience interprets from its own vantage point. Thus, meanings have come to be regarded as far from fixed, given or self evident; instead they can be seen as multiple, partial, contingent, and as having elements of both the manifest and the latent (as in dreams in Freudian theory).

As Williamson argues, the real person stands in the gap between signifier and signified, between what *means* and what *it means* (Williamson, 1978, p. 41). On this view, the subject is not simply either a receiver or a creator of meaning; he or she makes meaning because language 'calls upon' her or him to do so. These insights depend heavily upon Althusser's concept of 'interpellation' (Althusser, 1971). According to Althusser, 'all ideology hails or interpellates concrete individuals as subjects'. Thus, discourses invite us to create ourselves in accordance with the way they have already created us, but this need not mean that the human subject is simply constituted by pre-given structures. Rather, we need to think about the ways in which these invitations, interpellations, these 'hailings' are received by the subject, conceived of as a subject-in-process.

One way of thinking about the constitution of the subject in discourse is provided by the concept of identification; we can see a discourse as presenting us with the invitation to identify with an image of ourselves, implied by the discourse (for example, the image of 'patient' in medical discourse). Lacan's revisioning of Freud's theory is useful here as a means of understanding the psychological processes involved, and the psychological investments people make in such identifications. According to Lacan, it is through relating to a mirror image of ourselves that we first become aware of ourselves as individual beings, separate from others (Lacan, 1966/1977). (The 'mirror' here may be thought of either literally or metaphorically.) In identifying with the image, however, the subject becomes split and, in an important sense, alienated from itself, for the image offers an imaginary unity of the self which is nevertheless 'Other', at a distance from the embodied self. It is in this 'primitive' psychological process that the roots of subsequent identifications lie and, we might say, the processes of discursive interpellation are anchored.

On this argument, interpellation in discourse involves both the creation of an identity and an alienation from it. The recurrent desire to recreate the presymbolic imaginary self, which is a condition of humanity, is channelled in interpellation, as the subject seeks to merge with the image. Discourses offer us an image which is Other, but they invite us to become the Same, and the perpetual motive for the processes of identification which ensue, is insatiable desire, the need to make good the 'lack' which is inherent in subjectivity. Thus, Lacan's work indicates to us the very profound psychological investments which people make in being 'hailed' by discourse; there is an affective dimension in operation, involving both conscious and unconscious processes.

It is important, however, to return to the issue of human agency. Discourses may provide the scaffolding for the structuring and restructuring of subjectivities, but they should not be regarded as ultimately determining. As Kaplan (1983) has put it:

> Discourses cannot simply control/contain all within their compass, so that gaps open up through which change can take place. The gaps, that is, permit points of resistance which enable new articulations, which, in turn, begin to work on and to alter the dominant discourse (p. 18).

This is an important point because not only are there a wide variety of, often competing or contradictory, discourses available, but the subject is always *more* than that which identifies, for the moment, with the discursive image (for example, I may identify myself as 'patient' within medical discourse, but my 'identity' is not singular, and I may simultaneously claim to be a woman, a white woman, a mother, a worker, and so on). Thus there is always an excess of identity that a single discourse cannot hold. Further, because a single individual must necessarily always exceed the identities assigned, there is a sense in which any identity involves misrecognition.

In psychology, Davies and Harre (1990) have similarly begun to theorise the relationship between discourse and psychology through their concept of 'positioning'; the implication of their argument is that the human subject is constituted through language.[8] Davies and Harre argue that discourses provide a range of 'subject positions' (such as 'wife' or 'father' in familial discourses, or 'doctor' and 'patient' in medical discourses) which individuals may take up (often unwittingly), negotiate or actively resist. In this way, discourses provide social frameworks within which aspects of subjectivities are produced. Discursive positions therefore signify cultural positions and relations; they are terms which transcend the actual persons who might be defined by means of them, and the terms (which are often binary, such as 'mother' and 'father') each sustain their value, not through any reference to the 'real', but through its relation to the others in the discourse (Silverman, 1983, p. 182). Therefore, when a subject positions him or herself in discourse (for example, 'I am a mother'), in psychological terms they are identifying with a particular signifier within a closed system of signification.[9] The concept of discursive positioning therefore opens up the way for a psychological understanding of the operation of discourse, and a basis for a psychodynamic explanation of how, in speaking, the subject is simultaneously being spoken. Let us now consider the implications of foregrounding language and discourse for the research design and methodology.

Methodological Implications

The Research Interview

One immediate consequence of according priority to language is a need to be clear about the nature of the research interview. Traditionally, the interview in social scientific research has been a means of collecting data; the researcher asks the questions and the respondent provides the answers. At the start of this study, we felt the need to re-think the whole nature of the interview process, because we wanted subjects to talk to us about their experiences, using their own words, and articulating their own concerns, rather than providing their responses within the parameters we, as researchers, had set. The main focus of interest was in how subjects themselves told about their experiences of divorce and dispute resolution, and in what discourses they invoked in what ways in giving their accounts.

Traditional interviewing styles can lead research subjects into supplying particular kinds of responses, which may have more to do with interviewees' perceptions of the research and the needs of the researcher than with the way they otherwise would articulate their experiences. Collins (1997), for example, argues that interviewees seem quite ready to collude with the stated objectives of the researcher; indeed, they may feel themselves to be under a duty to comply with what they perceive the researcher wants from them. They are likely to struggle to make sense of the interviewer's questions in the light of what they perceive the researcher to be looking for and, as Chase (1995) argues, their responses will be structured accordingly. When a researcher asks what is perceived to be a sociological or a psychological question, it may do no more than to elicit what Wiersma (1988) calls a 'press release' or what Bordieu refers to as an 'official account'.[10]

Such crystallised responses tell us very little about the subject's own world of meanings. In a similar vein, but from a psychodynamic perspective, Hollway and Jefferson (1997) recognise that research subjects often employ defensive strategies in interviews, particularly when they are being encouraged to talk about anxiety-provoking or emotionally painful material. They argue that particular types of research questions can mobilise defensive barriers, whilst others are more effective in eliciting accounts which are richer in personal meanings. Chase (1995) also alerts us to the possibilities of distortions in research interviews if the interviewer is unaware of what might be culturally problematic about a particular topic or story.

Feminist researchers have long argued that in order to elicit richer material, material which does justice to the complexities, ambivalences and contradictions of our subjects' lives, it is necessary to approach the interview in a different way.[11] Based on a political imperative of letting women speak for themselves, feminist researchers have developed approaches to interviewing which prioritise, not the concerns of the researcher, but the lives and meanings of subjects themselves (see, for example, the work of the Personal Narratives Group, 1989).

Personal Narratives

In a lengthy and detailed discussion of research interviewing, Mishler (1986) argues that, if given the chance, subjects will use the research interview as an opportunity to tell their 'story'. The result is often a lengthy and rich personal narrative account of experience. The recent emphasis on the importance of narrative methodologies in the social sciences is an attempt to address some of the limitations in more traditional approaches for studying the complexities of lives and selves. In social science, 'narrative knowing' - the storying of events into order and meaning (Sandelowski, 1991) - is increasingly being acknowledged as a viable alternative to objective knowledge. The 'impulse to narrate' is seen as part and parcel of being human, manifesting itself both in lived experience (Bruner, 1987, 1990; Sarbin, 1986) and in the accounts people give of their lives (Rosenwald and Ochberg, 1992). According to White (1980), so pervasive is narrative in human culture that to raise the question of the nature of narrative is to invite reflection on the very nature of human culture:

> So natural is the impulse to narrate, so inevitable is the form of narrative for any report of the way things really happened, that narrativity could appear problematical only in a culture in which it was absent - absent or, as in some domains of contemporary Western intellectual and artistic culture, programmatically refused (p. 1).

White quotes from Barthes (1977, p. 79): narrative 'is simply there, like life itself...international, transhistorical, transcultural' (White, 1980, p. 1). Thus, at a general level, narrative is the means provided by a culture which people use to translate 'knowing' into 'telling', to articulate their experiences and fashion their identities. At a less general level, a variety of narrative forms feature as the socio-historical products of different cultures, and are informed by a range of discourses which are more or less dominant at any given time; as Plummer (1995) puts it, all stories have their time and place.

In social science, there is now a developing literature which regards personal narrative accounts not simply as static cultural entities but as 'texts in action' (Widdicombe, 1993) in which subjects actively construct their subjectivities and subjective authenticities. Narration is seen as central to the construction of identity (Personal Narratives Group, 1989; Iles, 1992). Kerby (1991) discusses the ways in which narratives and narration give meaning to what we usually call 'the self'; the self is given content, is delineated and embodied in narrative constructions, and this development of the self in narrative is one of the most characteristically human acts. Thus, on this view, the self arises out of signifying practices, rather than existing prior to them as an autonomous agent. For Kerby, the self is the 'implied subject of a narrated history' (p. 109). Steedman (1986) sees self narration as involving acts of remembering and interpretation which, in drawing on both individual biography and wider social discourses, underlies the psychosocial production of self. Freeman (1993) argues that history, memory and narrative are inseparable in the production of self in autobiographical narratives. These developments may not quite yet amount to a 'new paradigm' in social scientific research,[12] but they do enable us to challenge traditional notions of selfhood as internal and static and to address the articulation of self as a psychosocial phenomenon, in which personal activities and meanings occupy centre stage.[13]

Narrative work, however, does have some limitations. For the purposes of our discussion, the limitations in relation to human psychology are perhaps the most significant. In narrative work, the idea that subjectivities are inherent in texts is often interpreted to mean that they may be 'read off' from the texts without much ado. From a psychological point of view, such an assumption is obviously problematic. A psychologist would want to know, for example, *why* telling one's story matters, what it is about the process of narration that enables subjectivities to be constructed and transformed (Day Sclater, 1998b; 1998c). Parker (1992) drew attention to the psychological gaps in discourse analytic work when he pointed out that the question of what was going on in people's heads when they used discourse had yet to be answered. The opposite question, namely that of what language is doing in any person's use of it, however, is equally important. We have already mentioned the significance of Davies and Harre's (1990) concept of 'positioning' and that of Althusser's (1971) 'interpellation' which go at least part of the way to addressing the question of how subjectivities may be linked to culture, and we have mentioned that it is possible to read discursive positionings in psychological terms. However, the broader question of whether there is subjectivity beyond discourse[14] and, if so, what form it takes and how we might have access to it, remains largely an open one.[15]

As Plummer (1995) points out, personal narratives are not *merely* texts; rather, they are texts spoken by 'breathing, passionate people in the full stream of social life' (p. 16). Or as Rosenwald (1992) puts it: 'If people are identical with their beliefs and narratives, then only beliefs and narratives can ever be bruised' (p. 269). That is to say, the stories people tell about their lives are rooted both in the material conditions of their existence, and in the things that they do, and they also have psychological roots, relating to biography, and to passion and desire. In taking up discursive positions, living, breathing, desiring, embodied subjects align themselves with cultural signifiers which both facilitate and constrain actions, thoughts and feelings. Narratives thus mediate between embodied subjects and situations, and are reducible to neither.

The psychological investment which people make in telling stories and in discursive positioning has roots that go beyond rational activity and conscious awareness. Lacan (1966/1977), for example, sees the subject as being 'bound' to the signifier in language because, through language, the subject seeks (in vain) to satisfy desire, to make good the lack which has characterised the subject's relationship to the signifier since earliest infancy. For Lacan, it is the subject's insatiable desire which provides the motor that drives the subject's talk. This may well be so at an abstract level, and Hollway (1989) has usefully applied Lacanian ideas to the interpretation of conversational exchanges. However, the leap from Lacan's abstract concept of desire as contentless (a generalised 'lack'), from its mere existence underlying the use of any and all language, to its manifestation in narratives which have both content and form, is a problematic one which is not easily achieved without resorting to what Rustin (1997) calls 'wild analysis'.

A more pressing problem, for our purposes, derives from the recognition that the narratives produced in research interviews can no longer be viewed unproblematically as the product of the subject alone. We have already touched on the idea that the research interview is an intersubjective exchange, involving the researcher as well as the subject. The question of the complexities of the psychological processes involved in narrating arises.

Interview Narratives

Interview narratives are joint products in a very important way (Riessman, 1990b, 1992; Leudar and Antaki, 1996; Day Sclater, 1997b). Hollway and Jefferson (1997) mention, in this connection, the psychoanalytic concepts of transference and countertransference, as the invisible unconscious dynamics which operate in conversational exchanges, and may be particularly potent where there are power differences between participants in a conversation. In a similar vein, Josselson (1995) talks about interview exchanges in terms of 'empathy'; she shows how an empathetic stance on the part of the interviewer constrains the respondent's response in particular ways, such that these unseen emotional dynamics of the interview are implicated in the outcome of the research. There are other ways of theorising the emotional subtexts in research: we have discussed these phenomena elsewhere in terms of Winnicott's idea (Winnicott, 19953/1977) of the 'potential' or 'transitional' space and in terms of Bion's notion of 'containment' (Day Sclater; 1997b, 1998c).

The common ground among these perspectives is a recognition of the operation of unconscious dynamics, the existence of 'emotional subtexts' in research interviews, in the absence of which a particular story would not have been told in the way that it was. For the purposes of our discussion, the crucial point is that signification is not just a linguistic process; it is also a social, intersubjective and psychological one too.

However, as signification is located in discursive practices, it becomes also a process with a political dimension. Language is not a neutral system but is, as Fairclough (1989, 1992) amongst others has pointed out, organised in historically specific discourses in which knowledge-power relations are manifested.[16] As Hollway (1989) argues, repressions are not just psychological phenomena, but can arise as much from politically and culturally problematic significations as they can from internally motivated ones.

In this study, we have therefore attempted to employ a methodology which is well-grounded in theory. The interviews were unstructured and conducted along the lines of life-history interviewing (Plummer, 1983). Following Mishler (1986), our aim in interviewing was to permit subjects to articulate their own feelings and concerns in personal narrative accounts of their divorce experiences. As far as possible, we have avoided imposing our own concerns and categories on subjects' responses whilst, at the same time, recognising the crucial role of the researcher in the production of subjects' narratives, and the psychodynamic nature of the interview.

The theoretical background upon which our methodology depends led us to understand the expressed feelings and meanings, not as enduring properties of each individual subject but, in a dialogical way, as personalised manifestations of broader social processes. That is to say, upon analysis of the narratives, we expected to find that subjects' invocations of particular social discourses would both facilitate and constrain subjects' constructions of their experiences, emotions and identities. Some of these discourses (such as those about 'the family', 'children' and 'gender') are generally available in our culture; others, such as those that structure divorce dispute resolution, are more specific to the divorce process itself. The theoretical approach led us to regard discourses, experiences and feelings as mutually constitutive, and we were interested in the ways in which these mutual constitutions were negotiated, from a psychological point of view.

Methodology and Data Analysis

Our study was a longitudinal, prospective one; the field work was carried out over an eight month period in 1996-97. We recruited 30 participants with the help of local mediators and solicitors over a wide area in the south of England. Some subjects asked to join the study having read reports on the research in local newspapers. For eleven of our participants, who fulfilled our criteria of being separated but not divorced at the start of the study, and whose divorces were finalised at the end of the study, we collected a full range of case-study material over the period of the study; for the remainder, our data sets are incomplete owing to the difficulties, common in divorce research, of maintaining contact with participants and sustaining their commitment to research which is dealing with sensitive and emotionally painful material. The main part of our analysis has been based upon these case studies.

We collected both quantitative and qualitative data. For the quantitative data, each participant completed three General Health Questionnaires (GHQ-28) at two monthly intervals. The GHQ has been extensively validated in general practice where it is used to identify probable 'cases' of psychiatric morbidity, which can then be either confirmed or disconfirmed by means of a clinical interview (Goldberg and Williams, 1988).[17] In social scientific research, it is not used to assist in diagnosis in this way, but simply as a means of providing a quantitative assessment of psychological well-being. The GHQ-28 consists of four sub-scales (somatic symptoms, anxiety and insomnia, social dysfunction, severe depression), each with seven items. Its purpose is to detect recent changes in effect, and subjects are asked to indicate which symptoms they have experienced in the last few weeks and their severity. Most studies suggest that a threshold score of 4/5 is an appropriate indicator of possible 'caseness' in the general population.

For the qualitative data on subjective experiences of divorce, each subject was interviewed by means of in-depth, unstructured, life history interviews in which subjects were invited to tell us about their experiences of divorce and how disputes had arisen and been dealt with. Subjects were interviewed three times at two-monthly intervals. Interviews lasted, on average, one and a half hours, and were tape recorded and transcribed in full.

We also collected some semi-structured interview data in the final stage of the project. At this stage, participants were asked specific questions concerning the symptoms and feelings they had experienced, and the progress and outcome of divorce disputes.

Of our eleven case studies, two participants were men and nine were women. They were aged between 40 and 59 years (average 45 years), married for between 4 and 26 years (average 17.8 years) and separated for between one month and four years (average 16.9 months) at the start of the study. Educational qualifications of participants ranged between 'none' (4 people) and 'A Level or above' (4 people). Two participants were in full-time paid employment (both men), two women were unpaid homemakers, and the remainder worked part-time. Two women were also studying. All participants were parents; all but two had dependent children living with them (one man and one woman). Five had petitioned for divorce, and five were respondents to divorce proceedings. One participant was involved in judicial separation proceedings for religious reasons. Four participants had begun dispute resolution by mediation, but all went on to instruct solicitors to negotiate about property, finances and children on their behalf. None of the participants for whom we have a full set of data was involved in contentious litigation about any aspect of the divorce, although some of the others whom we interviewed were involved in contentious litigation about finances, property and/or children.

It needs stating that our sample is not a 'random' one and we do not make any claims about its representativeness of the sort which are appropriate in quantitative statistical studies where validity depends upon random sampling techniques. In qualitative, ethnographic work such as ours, 'theoretical' sampling is more appropriate. Our case studies illustrate a range of divorce experiences, where individual narrators provide what can be thought of as windows of understanding into the worlds they occupy. This does not mean that we have abandoned a commitment to generalisability as an important research aim, but the generalisability which derives from case studies is of a different order to that appropriate to large scale quantitative research. Rosenwald (1988), for example, points out that psychologists have tended to neglect the detailed case study of individual lives because it does not seem to contribute to the formulation of general 'truths'. However, he argues that individual cases, if brought into 'conversation' with one another, permit shared realities to be reconstructed out of individual perspectival images. It is obvious, but perhaps still needs stating, that individuals can only reveal what they are placed to reveal, and for this reason it is important to pay particular attention to the context, particularities and partialities of individuals' perspectives. It is precisely upon this range of unique experiences, and the common threads that join them, that the focus of our research has been. Our approach illuminates the nuances and complexities in the personal experience of divorce which are hidden from view in more traditional studies, at the same time as it allows us to say something about the social structuring of those experiences (Day Sclater, 1999a, 1999b).

Our analysis of the data was based upon a narrative approach (Riessman, 1993; Cortazzi, 1993; Manning and Cullum-Swann, 1994)[18] in which we focused on both the form and the content of participants' accounts. Because of our interest in the psychosocial nature of experience and emotion, we were interested to identify the social discourses which traversed the narratives; our analysis therefore utilised also a form of discourse analysis (Potter and Wetherell, 1987, 1994; Parker, 1992; Wetherell and Potter, 1992; Burman and Parker, 1993). In this aspect of the analysis we drew on Davies and Harre's (1990) work on discursive positioning; we paid particular attention to the ways in which participants invoked different discourses in telling their stories, and how they dealt with the tensions between them. We were particularly interested in how participants drew on, and positioned themselves in relation to, the dominant divorce discourses of welfare and harmony.[19] But we also wanted to go beyond what narrative analysis could tell us and to be able to say more about divorce and dispute resolution as psychosocial processes.

Despite Sarbin's (1988) brave attempt to formulate a 'narrative psychology',[20] the conceptual framework for linking 'narrative' and 'psychology' outside of a therapeutic context[21] remains undeveloped and the literature is sparse. We took the view that, as in discourse analytic work, the particularly *psychological* aspects of subjective experience and meaning had a tendency to disappear from view in narrative work. We concluded that narrative analysis, on its own, was ill-equipped to address issues of a particularly psychological character. We addressed this point by considering the common themes among the case studies and by identifying the common psychological constellations that seemed to underpin different discursive positionings. Here, the analytic process was informed by concepts from Kleinian psychoanalytic theory;[22] we used these to link narrative forms, story genres and discursive positions to psychological processes. It needs to be stated explicitly that we did not venture to 'psychoanalyse' our participants; such a project would be insupportable and unethical. Rather, we used psychoanalytic ideas to understand the narrative forms which were common when our individual case studies were brought into 'conversation' with one another (Rosenwald, 1988).

Facts and Fictions

In concluding our discussion of the theory and methodology of our work, perhaps a few words about the 'validity' of narrative work ought to be said. Our discussion so far has made it clear that personal narratives do not simply 'reflect' experience in any unproblematic way. However, it does not follow that they are *merely* fictions (Hildago, 1992). It is integral to the realist and rationalist underpinnings of western thought that we habitually draw a distinction between 'truth' and 'fiction'. Not only do we draw this distinction (it is part of 'common sense') but we also conceive of truth and fiction as two mutually exclusive and hierarchically organised categories. The dichotomy may work well for 'bare' experience, but experience which is devoid of meaning is inconceivable. Meaning is an interpretive process, an integral aspect of experience, which is not readily categorisable as either truth or fiction. Truth, itself, is arguably a rhetorical achievement, and it is for this reason that personal narratives should not be judged according to common sense or traditional scientific criteria of truth.

Discussing psychoanalysis, Spence (1982) draws a useful distinction between 'narrative truth' and 'historical truth'; there is no necessary relation between the two, and narrative truth is of an altogether different order. According to Spence, historical truth is elusive; narratives do not generate historical verisimilitude, but once a given construction has acquired the status of narrative truth, it becomes just as real as any other kind of truth. For Spence, more important than 'truth' is the adequacy of a narrative, attested by its consequences in living.

As White (1980) argues, drawing on the work of Roland Barthes, narrative 'ceaselessly substitutes meaning for the straightforward copy of the events recounted' (p. 2). He goes on to ask:

> What is involved, then, in that finding of the 'true story', that discovery of the 'real story' within or behind the events that come to us in the chaotic form of 'historical records'? What wish is enacted, what desire is gratified, by the fantasy that real events are properly represented when they can be shown to display the formal coherency of a story? In the enigma of this wish, this desire, we catch a glimpse of the cultural function of narrativizing discourse in general, an intimation of the psychological impulse behind the apparently universal need not only to narrate but to give events an aspect of narrativity (White, 1980, p. 4).

In narrative, events possess a structure, an order of meaning, which they do not possess as a mere sequence (White, 1980). Thus, in our study we have taken the view that it is more useful to think about personal narratives, not as reflections *of* experiences, but as reflections *on* them. The 'truths' they reveal are both personal and social; in Chase's words 'a major contribution of narrative analysis is the study of general social phenomena through a focus on their particular embodiment in life stories' (Chase, 1995, p. 2). As Josselson states:

> Narrative is the representation of a process, of a self in conversation with itself and with its world over time. Narratives are not records of facts, of how things actually were, but of a meaning-making system that makes sense out of chaotic mass of perceptions and experiences of a life (Josselson, 1995, p. 33).

Narrative approaches therefore challenge realist notions of truth and permit a critical engagement with the subject-in-culture as an intersubjective and psychosocial phenomenon. This is the point made by the Personal Narratives Group:

> When talking about their lives, people lie sometimes, forget a lot, exaggerate, become confused, and get things wrong. Yet they *are* revealing truths. These truths don't reveal the past 'as it actually was', aspiring to a standard of objectivity. They give us instead the truths of our experiences. They aren't the result of empirical research or the logic of mathematical deductions. Unlike the reassuring Truth of the scientific ideal, the truths of personal narratives are neither open to proof nor self evident. We come to understand them only through interpretation, paying careful attention to the contexts that shape their creation and to the world views that inform them. Sometimes the truths we see in personal narratives jar us from our complacent security as interpreters 'outside' the story and make us aware that our own place in the world plays a part in interpretation and shapes the meanings we derive from them (Personal Narratives Group, 1989, p. 261).

Rosenwald (1992, p. 271) states that:

> One need not assume that narrators represent their lives accurately or that this is even possible. It is enough to note that they believe they are doing so...No narrator is indifferent to his or her account; narratives play a role in the life they recount – if only by the dissatisfactions they cause the speaker and the stimulus they provide for the redirection of life and life story. In this sense, *they are both about the life and part of it*. This double relevance gives them their motivational and cognitive power to transform lives.

Telling and living, he says, are in a dialectic relation with each other. Rosenwald goes on to argue that life narratives are best regarded as provisional, as poised ready to 'antiquate' themselves, and as providing potential impulses to future development. For this reason, narrative 'truths' must always be partial, situated and provisional and can be assessed according to their 'adequacy' in terms of the new cycle of stories and consequences they generate (p. 272).

Stories lend themselves to a multitude of readings; in every story there are embedded a range of stories whose meanings shift according to kind of interpretation the reader wishes to make.[23] For example, divorce stories may be heard as commentaries on the social organisation of divorce, at one level, or as organisers of individual experience on another, or as expressions of psychological processes on yet another. All kinds of interpretive activities, however, involve struggles over the fixing of meaning. Social scientists too are storytellers (Potter *et al.*, 1984; Gergen and Gergen, 1986; Clegg, 1993); data have no singular or inherent meaning, and the sense that we make of it, and the narratives we construct around it, are shaped by our theoretical perspectives and methodological commitments.

Summary

In summary, the theoretical underpinnings of our study and the methodology we have adopted are closely linked. We begin from the recognition that neither language, nor language use, exist in either a social vacuum, a personal vacuum or an interpersonal vacuum. Language is organised in discourses, some of which are more dominant than others at any given time. At the same time, our engagements with social discourses are underpinned by emotional investments at different levels.

In divorce, two discourses currently predominate. First, the welfare discourse, which prioritises the needs of children, seeing children as the vulnerable 'victims' of divorce. It sets out powerful moral prescriptions for parenting, and leaves little room for any recognition of the psychology of the adults involved. Secondly, the discourse of 'harmony' idealises co-operative ongoing relations between the parents divorce on the basis that it is 'conflict' between them which renders children at most risk of harm. As we saw in chapter 1, the Family Law Act 1996 is built around these discourses, and mediation is being introduced in an attempt to prevent divorcing people from becoming involved in acrimonious battles with each other. These social discourses act as culturally available frameworks for understanding; in our study, we wanted to see how people drew upon them in making sense of their experiences.

We also wanted to uncover the range of narrative forms that divorcing people utilised in recounting their experiences, and to understand how these shaped, and were shaped by, discursive imperatives. Narratives are the means provided by a culture through which people translate 'knowing' into 'telling', they are a locus both for the articulation of experience and the fashioning of identities. A variety of narrative forms (or genres) feature as the socio-historical products of different cultures, but they are also informed by a range of discourses which are more or less dominant at any given time.

But making sense of experience is not just about choosing from among a range of socially available discourses or cultural narratives. When people talk about their experiences, they do so in the context of their own biographies, and part of what they reveal to us in speaking is something about their own habitual ways of coping with distressing or unforeseen events. In our study, we envisaged that the accounts people gave of their divorces would also reflect something about themselves, as social actors, with a personal history and an inner world of meanings. As we wished to understand these complex relationships between the subject and his or her world, it was imperative that we provided research participants with the opportunity, as far as possible, to articulate their own accounts. We wanted to avoid putting words into our subjects' mouths; we didn't just want them to supply us with crystallised answers to our sociological or psychological questions. We did not want subjects to feel that they were under any kind of obligation to supply us with the kinds of 'answers' they thought we wanted. We wanted to understand how *they* made sense of things, and to know about the personal meanings *they* created. We therefore collected personal narrative accounts of experience from each participant.

We used Davies & Harre's (1990) concept of 'subject positions' in discourse as a route into understanding the relations between the individual and the social, the inner and outer worlds of meaning. The concept has proved useful in understanding both why people tell the kinds of stories that they do, and the emotional investments they make in telling certain stories rather than others. Plummer's (1995) work reminds us that the stories people tell are rooted both in the material conditions of their existence, and in biography, passion and desire. Someone who takes up, negotiates or resists a discursive position is aligning her or himself with a particular range of cultural signifiers, which both facilitate and constrain actions, thoughts and feelings.

This leads us to the point that the emotional investments which people make in telling their stories has roots which go beyond rationality and conscious awareness. But it also leads to the recognition that repressions are not just psychological phenomena; they can, as Hollway

(1989) argues, arise as much from culturally problematic significations as they can from internally motivated ones. This is why we felt it important to include an analysis of discourse within a broader narrative approach.

We also wanted to be able to say something about the psychological aspects of subjective experiences beyond reporting on individual biographical accounts, and to draw out, if we could, commonalties of experiences. Rosenwald's (1988) 'multiple case study' approach, in which individual cases are brought 'into conversation' with one another, proved invaluable. The tasks of the analytic process therefore included identifying the genres into which individual narratives could be categorised, considering the range of discourses drawn upon in the stories, and theorising (using a psychodynamic framework) the psychological constellations that underlie narrative and discursive choices.

We have used the qualitative data both to qualify and enhance, as well as to challenge, the picture of divorce that emerges from the quantitative (GHQ) data. Interestingly, as we describe in chapter 5, the picture presented by the quantitative data was not straightforwardly confirmed by the qualitative data; the former presents a picture of divorce as a pathological experience, accompanied by a range of 'symptoms' of psychological distress. By contrast, the narrative accounts reveal a number of tensions and contradictions; divorce has positive aspects too, and perhaps is more accurately portrayed as an interpretative process, in which the subject seeks to resolve ambivalences and construct a new sense of self. Given the premium that continues to be placed on marriage and particular forms of 'family' in contemporary society, the narrative of divorce to which privileged status accrues is one of damage, disruption and regret.[24] As we shall see, however, our participants challenged this dominant narrative in a number of ways. The next two chapters discuss the findings.

Notes

[1]   See, however, the work of Johnston and Campbell (1988) on therapeutic family mediation.

[2]   There are, however, some notable exceptions to this general trend. Robinson (1991), for example, considers 'divorce as a private sorrow' from the perspective of a systemic approach which contextualises divorce transitions within a family life cycle framework. Some authors have drawn parallels between divorce and bereavement and have attempted to explain the former in terms of the theories and concepts of the latter (see Clulow (1990) for a discussion of the limitations of this approach). Others, particularly those involved directly in therapeutic work, have used psychodynamic

ideas to explain the psychological processes in divorce (see, for example, Vaughan (1987); Johnston and Campbell (1988)). In Britain, an important contribution to this line of work has been made by Christopher Clulow and his colleagues at the Tavistock Marital Studies Institute, London (see, for example, Clulow (1991; 1995)). Orbach (1992) offers a more 'popularised' version of the psychodynamic approach. Cantor (1982) advocates a specifically psychoanalytic orientation towards divorce, theorising the process as one of 'separation and individuation'. Despite these exceptions, however, the dominant paradigm has been based on a model of divorce as an 'adjustment' to loss and change (see, for example, Kitson and Holmes, (1992)) in which attempts are made to identify characteristics which distinguish those who adjust well from those who adjust poorly, with references to either individual characteristics, social circumstances, or some interaction between the two.

[3] The emphasis on experiences and feelings in our work, and the methodology we have employed to 'uncover' these hitherto hidden phenomena, can also be subjected to socio-historical analysis. Giddens (1991), for example, discusses current preoccupations with a 'project of the self' in late modernity; Lasch (1979) characterises contemporary Western industrialised societies in terms of a 'culture of narcissism', and Rose (1990) talks about 'subjectifying technologies'. There is therefore a sense in which our work itself is firmly located amongst the kinds of social and cultural trends we discussed in chapter 1; as such, our work not only responds to social change, but also helps to shape it. We am grateful to Mike Michael for reminding us about the benefits and *obligations* of reflexivity!

[4] The term 'discourse' has a range of meanings depending upon the theoretical framework in which it is employed. It is a term which, therefore, evades any general definition. In our work, we use the term to mean frameworks of understanding which organise the social world and make a difference to it. The concept of 'discourse' that we have employed in our work is perhaps closest to that of Laclau and Mouffe (1985). They see discourses as arresting the flow of differences, and as constructing centres around which certain kinds of social relations crystallise; in providing frameworks for understanding things, people and events, discourses constitute structures that provide for certain kinds of readings and constrain the possibilities for other readings. Discourses therefore function to partially fix meanings. Discursive structures act to legitimate and maintain particular power relations, but they are not ultimately determining, as they are always open to contest and change, and oppositional discourses do emerge that challenge the dominant and privileged ones. On this latter point, see Fairclough (1992).

[5] We are greatly endebted to Wendy Hollway for her comments on a much earlier version of this chapter and for her general encouragement and support as we worked on developing a 'psychosocial' approach to divorce.

[6] Our approach also departs from more recent social constructionist and discourse analytical accounts, insofar as it pursues specifically psychological questions and emphasises the interiority of discursive processes.

[7] See also Hollway (1989).

[8] This argument, however, overlooks the fact that subjectivity is always embodied; psychological subjects occupy both social spaces and physical spaces. Despite this limitation, we feel that the concept of 'discursive position' is a useful one for addressing the individual/social dichotomy in empirical work.

9   Although each particular discourse may represent such a 'closed' system, the existence of multiple, often competing, discourses suggests rather more openness in the process of positioning. We found, for example, considerable tensions in mothers' divorce stories between their positioning as 'good' parents within the welfare discourse, and their positioning as autonomous subjects within discourses of 'independence'. See further chapter 6, and Day Sclater and Yates (1999).

10 This is most likely to occur when the interviewer and interviewee are hierarchically positioned in relation to each other, but is not always the case. I am grateful to Mike Michael for this point.

11 See, for example, Fonow and Cook (1991). For a detailed exploration into the development of a 'psychosocial' approach based on narrative, see Andrews *et al.* (eds), (1999).

12 Whether narrative work constitutes a 'new paradigm' in the social sciences remains an open question. As Munby (1993) points out, narrative work has undoubtedly contributed significantly to the 'crisis in representation', a crisis founded in the challenging of realist epistemology. Involvement in narrative work is about making new kinds of knowledge claims, as Cartesian notions of 'truth', the foundational premises in which most knowledge generation is grounded, and the model of the individual as a rational being which has characterised Western thought since the Enlightenment, are challenged. See also Fisher (1985).

13 For a detailed exploration of these issues see Andrews *et al.* (1999).

14 Importantly, the subjectivity 'beyond' discourse is an embodied one. See Butler (1993); Grosz (1994); Gatens (1996); Shildrick (1997).

15 Kerby (1991) asks 'is there a subject who precedes expression in language?' (p. 74) and finds Lacan's concept of the mirror stage useful in exemplifying an I-identification that precedes language. On the foundations laid down in the mirror stage, the embodied subject is externalised in language and identifies with the externalisation (the projection). The mirror image is not experienced as separate from the child's identity and body image, but is a displacement from the immediacy of the tactile body. Herein, according to Lacan, lies the origin of self-consciousness, which is forever alienated. The mirror stage is indicative of the role that representation will play in relation to self throughout life. In narrative terms, the processes of the mirror stage in the imaginary belong to the 'prenarrative' past. Acts of meaning in the symbolic register refigure the prenarrative past in the light of present demands for sense and coherence.

16 This insight derives from the work of Foucault (1972). Departing from Hobbes' view that 'power' was something people had, Foucault argued that power was a discursive phenomenon that was manifested and realised in and through language. For Foucault, power was to be found in the continual play of discourses in the everyday exchanges and mundane activities of ordinary living. This conception of power is neither causal, mechanistic nor individualistic. See also Gordon (1980) and Sheridan (1980).

17 See Appendix 1.

18 There are two main journals in which papers discussing narrative approaches in the social sciences are often published: *Journal of Narrative and Life History* (USA) and *Auto/biography* (UK). See also successive volumes of *The Narrative Study of Lives*.

19 See chapter 1.

20 See, however, Polkinghorne (1988) and Kerby (1991).

21 See Hermans and Hermans-Jansen (1995) and McLeod (1997) on this issue.

22   See Brown and Day Sclater (1999) and Day Sclater and Yates (1999).

23   Kerby (1991, p. 88) argues that in psychoanalysis there is the possibility of at least five stories: (1) the presumed story, waiting to be told; the repressed story, belonging to the prenarrative level; (2) the story told by the patient, where facts are recounted in a certain manner, style or genre and for certain effects in the dialogical situation; (3) a further story that the patient constructs on the basis of her or his initial disclosure; this is the story of what the story actually means to the patient upon reflection; (4) the story heard by the analyst through the transference as the analyst's own feelings are evoked; (5) the underlying story which the analyst seeks behind what is told. The possibilities of these multiple stories around the same set of events illustrates the problematic nature of 'truth' amongst the proliferation of narratives.

24   Burck *et al.* (1996) point out that, in this climate, families may need to pathologise themselves in order to get help. These authors report on a 'non-pathologising' service for families which they have developed 'to help counter the prevailing political view in which divorce and one-parent families are viewed as damaging and "un-whole-some", thus adding to parents' distress' (pp. 163-164). They argue that it is possible to 'normalise' divorce as a common life cycle transition 'without denying the inevitable pain, disruption, upheaval and difficulties to be addressed' (p. 166).

5 Divorce: Symptoms and Feelings

Introduction

The next two chapters discuss the psychological aspects of divorce as these emerge from both the quantitative and qualitative data. Chapter 5 begins by discussing the range of 'symptoms' of psychological distress which commonly accompany separation and divorce; we set these in context, considering them, not in isolation, but in relation to the 'feelings' which the participants reported having experienced, and in relation to their narrative accounts. Importantly, no one-to-one relationship was found between the quantitative measures of psychological well-being and the qualitative data. The participants' scores on the General Health Questionnaires[1] reveal (as other quantitative studies have shown) that divorcing people report a range of symptoms indicative of acute psychological distress, which are worryingly severe in some cases. On the other hand, the qualitative data from the in depth interviews presents a somewhat different picture. If we consider what people say when they talk about their symptoms and feelings, it becomes clear that they make sense of them in ways that reduce their negative impact and that assist in the establishment and maintenance of their coping strategies.

Chapter 6 considers the divorce narratives in more detail, and we use an approach based on psychoanalytic object relations theory to offer a new perspective on the meanings of experiences, symptoms and feelings. However, divorce is not only a private experience which depends upon internal processes, conscious and unconscious. Rather, the stories that people tell to organise and make sense of their experiences bear also the hallmarks of culture; we show how the narrative genres which participants choose to provide frameworks for their stories, and the forms and structures of the accounts they give of their concerns, dilemmas and actions, both reflect and support their coping strategies, at the same time as they draw on wider cultural discourses. Thus we link the psychological processes involved in loving and losing to the culturally available 'scripts' for divorce. Throughout, and consistent with the aims of this project, we highlight the complex web of interactions among underlying psychological processes, the discourses participants invoke in making sense of their experiences, and the stories they tell about those experiences. The chapter concludes by emphasising the ambivalences of divorce, and argues for a better recognition of the painful emotions involved without resorting to pathologising the process; divorce is a deeply painful experience, but it has some positive aspects and usually has positive outcomes too.

The Psychological Aspects of Divorce

Chapter 3 reviewed the existing literature on the psychological aspects of divorce. From this review, it is apparent that divorce is often accompanied by acute psychological distress, which has most often been assessed by means of quantitative measures of psychological states. This general view was confirmed in this study by the quantitative (General Health Questionnaire) data collected but, as outlined in chapter 4, the need was felt to construct a more complete picture of divorce experiences by including a substantial qualitative element in this study. As argued in this section, the picture of divorce as accompanied by psychological difficulties, which emerges from the quantitative data, needs to be modified somewhat when the personal narratives are taken into account. It was not our aim to collect quantitative data from a sample large enough to permit statistical comparisons to be made; rather, we incorporated a quantitative element in this study in order to be able to compare the picture which emerged when employing a traditional research paradigm with that which emerged from the analysis of the personal narrative accounts. This section discusses the range of 'symptoms' of psychological distress which the participants experienced, as well as the variety of personal meanings they had for the individuals concerned.

Psychological Symptoms: The General Health Questionnaire Data

As outlined in chapter 4, participants were asked to complete the GHQ-28 three times at two-monthly intervals. Table Appdx. 2.1[2] shows the range of scores at Times 1, 2 and 3 from 11 people (2 men and 9 women) for whom we have full data at all three testing times. Using a threshold score of 4/5 (Goldberg and Hillier, 1979; Goldberg and Williams, 1988) as indicative of possible 'caseness', it can be seen that the average scores range from 12.9 at Time 1 to 11 at Time 3, indicating the severe drop in psychological well-being reported by our participants throughout the study period. These average scores are consistently very much higher than would be expected in the general population. Only one subject, Laura,[3] obtained a score at, or below, the threshold level at all three testing times.

There is also some indication from the GHQ scores that those who began dispute resolution by mediation fared less well psychologically than those who retained solicitors throughout, although the sample is too small to permit a statistical comparison to be made.[4] The average scores for those who mediated show an increase from 12.5 at Time 1 to 17 at Time 3, whereas the scores for those who did not mediate show instead a steady decrease.

Table Appdx. 2.2[5] shows the GHQ scores broken down by sub-scale. From this it can be seen that total scores on the 'anxiety' sub-scale are highest at all times, whilst those on the 'depression' sub-scale are consistently lowest. Table Appdx. 2.3[6] shows the average sub-scale scores. For those who mediated, the average scores on each sub-scale except 'anxiety' show an increase between Time 1 and Time 3, whereas the average scores for those who did not mediate show a decline on all four sub-scales. The difference is perhaps particularly marked on the 'depression' sub-scale, with the average at Time 3 being at 'threshold' level for those who mediated, and considerably lower in the non-mediation sample. The general pattern that emerges from the GHQ data is supported by the semi-structured interview data, collected at Time 4, eight months after the first interview. Participants were asked to look back over their experience and to comment upon the 'symptoms' they had experienced between separation and divorce, and their severity (0 = not at all, 5 = strongly).

Table Appdx. 2.4[7] summarises the results from the semi-structured interview data on the experience of symptoms. Symptoms of tension, irritability and anxiety predominate. Sleep disturbances, and problems with concentration and decision-making are also common. In addition, some participants spontaneously attributed the physical ill-health they had suffered to 'stress'. Others added symptoms of their own choosing to the list, including pains, tiredness, illness, depression, migraine and weariness. The semi-structured interview data do not, however, reveal the same trend towards a difference between those who mediated and those who did not, as emerged from the GHQ data.

Our quantitative GHQ data therefore present a picture that generally supports that which emerges from a range of empirical psychological studies which we reviewed in chapter 3. Divorce appears as a highly emotionally traumatic experience that has a major adverse impact on psychological well-being.

Psychological Symptoms: The Qualitative Data

The narratives collected in the unstructured interviews permit some insight into the personal meanings of these distressing symptoms. Thus, many participants told about how they felt themselves to be 'cracking up' or 'coming apart'; some told stories about having reached 'breaking point' and about having pulled themselves back from the brink. Others reported feeling at times that they had lost confidence in their ability to 'carry on any more'. Some sought relief from the pain in fantasies about 'running away from it all'. Reports of profound depression, an absence of energy and motivation to carry on, even a desire to 'give up and die' were not uncommon.

For example, at Time 1, Sheila reported profound feelings of loss, confusion, anger, emptiness and low self esteem. She said that she felt very vicious, often feeling that she wanted to kill Brian. Symptoms of anxiety, tension and feelings of panic overwhelmed her at times, and she reported that physical ill health had been brought on by the stress she had undergone since the separation. Sheila had contacted the Samaritans when she was at a particularly low ebb, and had received some psychotherapy. Sheila felt very unsupported, and considered that her solicitor was 'inaccessible'. Sheila described herself as like a small child lost in a crowd, frightened of the future, of losing her home, having no stability in life and nothing to live for. She said she felt utterly exhausted; she wanted to feel angry, but did not even have the energy for that most of the time. At Time 2, Sheila's GHQ score had fallen to almost threshold level; at interview, she was still obviously very distressed, but she was beginning to gain some strength from experiencing her own ability simply to survive. At Time 3 (although her GHQ score had increased again at this point), Sheila was beginning to see the light at the end of the tunnel; she had begun to feel that the divorce was 'making' rather than 'breaking' her, and had begun to look forward to the future and to 'getting her own life back' again. Here is how Sheila talked about the overwhelming distress she felt at Time 1:

I want to do something and yet, all the time this is holding me back, you know, what is happening at the moment, the emotional stress of it, makes me so *tired*, and emotionally tired, and physically tired. At the same time, I *have* to keep pushing myself, just to keep my mental stability. Erm, it's hard to sort of gallop along, because I suppose there's this awful feeling that all you want to do is to sort of go into a great depressed state and just sit in a heap and not do anything. But you know you can't do that...I mean, I-I-I wake up in the morning with that most terrible panic attack all the time, and I just feel total despair...The panic attacks, they get so bad that I can't hold on to my mind, you know, it's really that difficult...I've even felt like laying down in the road, just so that someone would notice me, because you feel, I don't know, just so utterly alone really, you know, this awful aloneness...You only need one extra thing which puts you over the edge...And there's this awful feeling that you are out of control...My lack of wanting to go on living is quite (pause), is like you have no, erm, I don't (pause), I think, 'well, what's it for?' What I'm doing now, whatever I do, I feel th-there's no purpose, erm, there's no purpose in getting up. I think, 'what for?' That's what it feels like.

However, the qualitative data reveal that the acutely distressing symptoms are only part of the story. There was no straightforward, one-to-one correspondence between the quantitative and the qualitative data, primarily because the unstructured interviews revealed a range of ambivalences and contradictions, as well as fluctuating emotions; at the same time as participants report a range of distressing symptoms, they also talk positively about finding their strengths to meet the challenge and to carry on. These positive attitudes and aspirations, which co-exist alongside symptoms of acute distress, are not discernible from the quantitative data alone, and they challenge the pathologised picture of divorce that emerges from many traditional studies. Alongside the painful scenarios, it was possible to ascertain, in most cases, a determination to survive, not to give in to or be beaten by circumstances, and many people explained their symptoms with reference to material and relational difficulties over which they felt they had no control. In order to explore these issues further, let us look closely at one of the case studies.

Laura and Peter

At the time of the first interview, Laura was 43 years old and had been separated from Peter for two years, following Peter's admission of adultery. They had been married for 18 years. Laura works part time, and receives Family Credit. She is the mother of two teenage children, both living with her. Laura's case illustrates the complexities of the psychological processes involved in divorce, in particular the co-existence of contradictory states of mind and fluctuating emotions. It also illustrates the interrelationship between feelings, coping strategies and divorce discourses; the prevailing idea that a 'harmonious' divorce is best for the children is something that Laura cites as presenting a barrier to the expression of her emotions. Laura's case also illustrates the complex relationship between the qualitative and the quantitative data; Laura is the participant with the lowest GHQ score, indicating a relative absence of symptoms but, in the interviews, she reported having experienced acute emotional turmoil from time to time. Indeed, as we shall see, she talked about having reached breaking point, and about having felt suicidal. A particularly difficult issue for Laura (as for other mothers in our study) was that of the children's contact with their father. Laura found the idea that her husband's girlfriend was forming a relationship with her children one of the most difficult things to bear; in her own words: 'I literally went to pieces'. But Laura also describes how she managed to recover her equanimity; she tells how she was saved by the re-emergence of her 'fighting spirit' which her mother encouraged; acknowledging her anger prevented her from reaching the depths of despair. Yet Laura, like others, had problems in accepting, let alone expressing her anger:

> It just hurt the whole time. Angry, I was really, really angry but, on the other hand, I knew I couldn't do anything because of the children.

Laura was not the only subject who positioned herself [8] as a 'responsible parent' in what we have called the 'welfare discourse' in this way. The welfare discourse can be seen as a framework for understanding upon which many divorcing people draw in making sense of their experience.[9] It is one which prioritises the needs of children in divorce, and which sees parental harmony as the surest way of meeting those needs. It contains also, by default, powerful moral prescriptions for parental behaviour. Laura's case shows the emotional difficulties which can arise as a result of positioning in the welfare discourse; in her case, her focus on the children's needs seemed to de-legitimise the anger she felt, and served as a barrier towards her expression of it. Laura sees the result of this as driving her to breaking point. However, it was acknowledging her anger, with the encouragement of her mother, which Laura saw as responsible for the re-surfacing of her will to survive, and her ability to repair her almost-defeated self. Here is the story Laura told about these events:

And one particular day, I rang up my mum. I'd had enough. It wasn't long after he left. I said I loved them dearly, the children were old enough, and they were fine. And mum must've heard something in my voice: 'What are you going to do?' Erm, and I never said a word. I was just sort of crying on the phone. 'Don't you do anything stupid.' I said, I can't take anything, I can't take any more. I said, I've had it. 'What about the children?' I said, they're fine, they're old enough now, they know what's happening, they're OK. 'Don't you do anything stupid.' I said, well I can't take any more. And she turned round and she said to me 'Do you want *her* looking after *your* children?' And that was the thing that done it. She said, 'good', she said, 'You're in fighting spirit again', she said, 'Now are you going to do anything stupid?' I said, no, I said, because I'm *damned* if I am going to let that bitch near my children.

Laura is talking here about the resurfacing of her will to survive, specifically in the context of allowing herself to feel angry, jealous and rivalrous. As time went by, Laura became more likely to express anger in the interviews, and less likely to talk about feeling low and depressed. The qualitative interviews show her dealing with her painful emotions by expressing opposition to her estranged husband Peter. She reports that she refused to allow the divorce (which Peter wanted, so that he could remarry) to proceed in the absence of any financial settlement, for example. By Time 3, Laura expresses an intense, though ambivalent, hatred for Peter.

If I see him, I hate him. My idea would be to have nothing more to do with him whatsoever. Then I could start getting on with my life. But I cannot do that because of the children.

The hatred may, in some ways, help Laura to cope but, in other ways it remains difficult to manage. Laura sees that what might be best for her is in conflict with what she perceives her children's needs to be; positioning in the welfare discourse is emotionally problematic for Laura who wants two contradictory things: both her 'own life', free of ties to Peter, and to do the best she can to be a 'responsible' parent. Many of Laura's anxieties, like those of other parents in our study, are located in the complexities of post-separation parenting, and she realises that there are tensions and contradictions. Here is Laura talking at Time 3:

But I mean, he no longer rings them up, he no longer sees them. You know, I was reading an article in a magazine some time ago now, about marriage break-ups, how fathers lose touch with the children within about two years, and I thought, that is exactly what is happening...In some ways I like it, because that means I will have nothing more to do with him. But then I put myself in their shoes, and I think well, how would I feel if I had nothing to do with my father?...But I know that if he has been in touch with the children, then I start tensing up again, wondering what the hell he is up to now. At the very beginning, and even now, I am terrified of losing the children to him.

Laura clearly feels herself being pulled in several ways at once, and there is also an element of competitiveness in relation to Peter; Peter is here constructed as a rival parent, and the competitiveness implies feelings of both vulnerability and jealousy. The central tension relates to the ways in which Laura perceives her children's needs (through the welfare discourse, they need their father) and her own needs (through a contradictory 'independence' discourse, she needs to be free of Peter).[10] This tension perhaps evidences Laura's negotiations around positioning herself in the welfare discourse; part of her wants to be the 'responsible parent', but another part of her pulls the other way: she also wants to be an independent woman, who has left a painful past behind her. Reconciling this tension proves to be difficult for Laura, and she vacillates, uncertain about what to do.

Laura's uncertainty, however, may reflect a deeper ambivalence which has psychological roots, and which relates to her negotiations around issues of attachment and loss. Paradoxically, perhaps, Laura's apparent need to be completely free of Peter may indicate that her attachment to him is not yet fully resolved; her ambivalences around post-divorce parenting, and around positioning in the welfare discourse, have an emotional subtext which relates to her own experience of loving and losing. The welfare discourse enables her to see her children as the vulnerable ones, the ones whose needs must come first, and in this way it would seem to militate against the achievement of the final separation from Peter which Laura apparently seeks. However, the welfare discourse perhaps also provides a repository where Laura's own vulnerabilities are located; in psychoanalytic terms, a culturally acceptable site for her to expel or project her own vulnerability, which is then perceived as belonging not to her, but to her children.[11]

Laura's positioning of herself in relation to the welfare discourse seems therefore to reflect her ambivalent needs for attachment and separation, to be both strong and vulnerable. There are considerable tensions between the 'text' of what Laura says and the emotional subtexts of the meanings she is constructing in her talk. We shall be returning to this point later in our discussion but, for the moment, Laura's case adequately illustrates the complex relationship between the qualitative and quantitative data, and the ambivalent emotions associated with divorce which are not detected by the quantitative data alone. It is all the more potent because her GHQ score was consistently comparatively low. It is, of course, possible that the GHQ, which seeks to identify changes 'in the last few weeks', fails to pick up on more chronic difficulties.

The GHQ measures a range of symptoms of potential psychiatric morbidity, but it tells us nothing about the meaning of these symptoms in the context of individual lives, or about the contradictory states of mind which co-exist with the symptoms of psychological distress and which, possibly, serve to defend the subject against their incapacitating effects. Laura's case illustrates the way in which the acknowledgement of anger can ward off symptoms of depression and despair; being angry provided her with a means to resist experiencing despair. We have seen, however, how the dominance of the welfare discourse seemed to pose a barrier to the unequivocal success of her survival strategy; she does not feel wholly at home with her anger, or her hatred of Peter, and she talks about this ambivalence in terms of her children's interests. Laura vacillates in her resistance to positioning in the welfare discourse which perhaps, in turn, affects the efficacy of her coping strategy.

Of course, few people are wholly at home with their own angry and destructive feelings all of the time. In psychoanalytic terms, ambivalence implies a 'depressive' position,[12] in which positive and negative feelings can co-exist in an integrated manner. Inability to tolerate ambivalence is a feature of the 'paranoid-schizoid' position[13] in which parts of the self which experience painful emotions are split off and expelled or projected outside the self. In Laura's case, however, we have seen how her anger is strategically useful to her, psychologically speaking; it remains connected to something real and is not wholly split off, as it would be if she allowed no doubts to creep in. As we discuss more fully in the next chapter, a return to paranoid-schizoid states of mind is common in the face of experiences of loss such as that involved in the breakdown of an intimate relationship;[14] the important point which emerges at this stage, through our examination of Laura's case, is that expressing angry feelings can serve positive functions in constructing and maintaining strategies for psychological survival.

Feelings and Emotions: The Semi-Structured Interviews

In the semi-structured interviews at Time 4, participants were also asked to reflect upon the range of feelings and emotions they had experienced in relation to separation and divorce. In asking about this, we hoped to enrich the strictly quantitative GHQ data on symptomatology we had collected. Table Appdx. 2.5[15] gives a summary of the semi-structured interview data on feelings and emotions, which participants provided in response to direct questions about them. Participants responded on a scale of 0-5 (0 = not at all, 5 = strongly). Loss, anger, upset and sadness were the feelings most strongly reported, closely followed by trauma, numbness and loneliness. Other feelings, such as guilt, hatred, viciousness, loss of trust, a desire for vengeance, self-pity and a sense of injustice, were also spontaneously mentioned.

Participants' responses indicate the wide range of negative and painful feelings associated with breaking up. Again, however, the qualitative data from the in-depth interviews helps to complete the picture and, to some extent, challenges the 'divorce as disaster' image which otherwise would emerge. The narratives indicated that divorce is an emotionally painful experience, but it is also one that can have a positive side.

At Time 4, participants were also asked to reflect on whether anything positive had come out of the experience of the break-up; only one was doubtful. Richard, for example, mentioned 'freedom, happy, content with myself, not living a lie anymore, healthier, more relaxed.' Molly talked about 'having discovered reserves of an ability to cope and make my own decisions, discovered more of myself, a freer person. I have blossomed as a person, made new friends, started new interests. I am getting better at saying 'no'.' Gina, too, said that the positive things included 'no more arguments, more peaceful at home, independence, developing my own friendship network, discovered more about myself, competence, liking myself more.'

But, reflecting on the positive did not mean that the pain had disappeared, or been forgotten. Helen, for example, talked about feelings of 'relief and freedom' which the divorce had brought her 'but they didn't last.' Fiona said that she felt both 'frustrated and relieved' when her divorce came through. Sheila mentioned, in the same breath, 'anger and anxiety over money, wanting to kill him, knowledge that I can survive.' Jill summed up these ambivalences in this way: 'I know it is a very painful process, but sometimes you do come out of it thinking, well, I have lost a lot, but I have gained a lot as well.'

The qualitative data therefore provide something of an antidote to the quantitative data and the semi-structured interviews; they illustrate the contradictory feelings associated with breaking up. Separation and loss invoke frightening feelings that are difficult to manage but, at the same time, separation also signifies something more positive: the opportunity for a new life, and a new 'self'.

Separation, Divorce and the Reconstruction of Self

In what has become a classical paper, sociologists Berger and Kellner (1966) discussed the pivotal role that marriage plays in the social construction of self. They argued that, on marriage, the new spouses participate in a joint construction of reality, whereby their individual biographies are reconstructed from the vantage point of the new partnership. They forge new identities within the relationship; the marriage becomes an anchor for a reconstructed self which perceives reality in new ways. Importantly, the sense of self of one partner becomes contingent upon the affirmation and regard of the other.[16] On separation or divorce, the joint reality is destroyed and one's sense of self is consequently threatened (Johnston and Campbell, 1988; Day Sclater and Richards, 1995). Divorcing people are therefore faced with the daunting task of rebuilding not only their lives but their very selves (Bohannon, 1971; Vaughan, 1987). In order to explore these issues further, let us look at another one of the case studies. Alison's case illustrates well the problems for the self when a marriage breaks down.

Alison and Ted

Alison was married for 20 years and had four children before filing for divorce on the basis of Ted's adultery. At the time of the first interview she had been separated for two and a half years. Her divorce brought severe financial problems in its wake, difficulties that were compounded by Ted's intermittent employment and a previous bankruptcy. At the time of the first interview, Alison and the children were struggling to manage on Income Support and their home was subject to a repossession order. Perhaps not surprisingly, Alison reported a range of difficult emotions including anger, a sense of failure and low self esteem. She also mentioned bitterness, hatred and a loss of trust. Alison reported that her initial abilities to cope waned over time rather than improved, and she was beset by symptoms of anxiety, irritability and depression.

Alison's difficulties were reflected in her high GHQ scores but these, in fact, decreased over time (see Tables Appdx. 2.1 and 2.2). At the final interview, Alison was still in difficulties, both materially and psychologically (her GHQ score at Time 3 was improving, but it was still 11, more than twice as high as the threshold level). At Time 4, she still felt anxious and depressed, and thought that she was smoking and drinking too much. At this stage, she described herself as 'in danger of losing it.' From the qualitative interviews, we can ascertain that her primary feeling was one of being trapped by both apparently insoluble material and financial problems, and by her own state of mind. Her material circumstances were such that she felt unable to do anything that made any difference. She felt worthless, and entertained frequent fantasies of running away from it all.

Alison's very real material difficulties were compounded by her fragile sense of self; she felt she had neither the energy nor the internal resources to work things out. She also had considerable difficulty in making sense of what had gone wrong with her marriage, a situation that proved to be crucial in relation to the necessity of rebuilding the self. Ted's admission of adultery and his leaving home came as a complete shock to Alison, leading her profoundly to question all her perceptions of the past and the value of her marriage. To Alison, Ted's adultery 'made the whole marriage seem like a sham.' This left her feeling that she had nothing to hold on to, not even the past, and with conflicting feelings of the pain of loss and betrayal, anger, fear and hatred.

Like Laura, Alison feared to experience or express her anger, though for different reasons. At the time of the first interview, the Building Society had already obtained a repossession order on Alison's home which, in any event, was in a negative equity situation. The Building Society was prevented from enforcing the repossession order by Ted's promise to the court to pay something off the mortgage arrears on a regular basis. But, as Alison later discovered, Ted failed to keep up the payments, and Alison lived daily with the knowledge that her home could be taken from her and the children at any moment. Because Alison relied on Income Support, she felt herself obliged to rely solely on Ted's goodwill to make the arrears payments. For this reason, she felt that she had to suppress her anger and to be at pains to remain amicable in her relations with Ted. This is Alison talking at Time 1:

But it was quite worrying, because I was never sure whether he was going to pay it or not. I always felt, and I still do feel, that whatever he gives me depends on, erm, how I am...If I was to be awkward in any way, then he would say, 'well, I'm not going to give you any money'...So I, I've I've felt that I haven't been able to speak my mind to him and tell him exactly what I thought of him because, if I did, he would stop the money...Erm, I sometimes feel cornered by him because I, I just feel I'm absolutely trapped.

At Time 1, Alison also described the psychological devastation she felt the separation had wreaked on her life and her self:

I was happy with me. I was extremely happy with me, and happy with what I'd got, and happy with being the person I was, with the things I did, with my husband, with my life, with my house. But all that has changed. I'm not happy with me any more. I'm not confident. I haven't the motivation to do anything. There's lots I want to do, there's lots that needs doing, but I just can't get up and do those things...I just haven't got the motivation and energy to get up and do it.

Alison also describes herself as having lost, along with her husband, a sense of her own self; she sees the separation as having changed her irrevocably, and she no longer has a sense of who she is. She articulates a divide between past and present, speaking about herself in the third person:

I don't know who I was now. I don't know who she was anyway. She must've been somebody quite different, 'cause whoever she was, she couldn't have been her anyway in the first place. So, who am I?

The brief extracts above illustrate a number of important points about the feelings involved in separation. First of all, it is clear that Alison is describing feeling acutely emotionally distressed; indeed, it pains the reader to empathise with the kinds of losses she describes. Alison clearly feels lost in a number of ways; within the marriage, she found an identity for herself about which she felt good but she sees the separation as having taken away her whole sense of who she was.

Two important points arise here. First, Alison's apparent loss of a coherent sense of who she is perhaps results from the ways in which Ted's adultery has had the effect of effacing their joint past; for Alison, the separation represents an abrupt discontinuity in her biography, and she has, as yet, no means of bridging the gap, or of providing for a coherent self which has continuity. Alison's memories of her marriage have all been disrupted by what she now knows and where she now is; she is deprived of a basis for constructing personal meanings and a sense of an enduring self. Alison is forced to rethink the past in radically new terms. The need to revisit the past to create a new sense of self, however, is common to all divorcing people; what is particularly difficult in Alison's case is that she has been so shocked by events, that she has little solid foundation in the history of her marriage upon which to build. This sentiment was echoed by other participants in our study, particularly those for whom the separation was unwelcome, or came as a shock. One woman felt that her husband had 'taken her past away' when he admitted his adultery and then left her. She felt she had no basis upon which to maintain any sense of self or to plan for the future.

Secondly, if Alison looks to the available divorce discourses and story genres for a place to begin to reconstruct her sense of self, she is faced with a plethora of negative, even pathologised, images. In her narrative, looking back over her life with Ted, Alison positions herself as Ted's wife within a discourse of romantic love, but Ted's adultery shatters that and Alison finds herself precipitated into a kind of no-man's-land where she finds no discourses in which to re-position herself in a positive way. On the contrary, the story genre to which Alison's narrative is closest at Time 1 is that of 'tragedy'.[17] She constructs herself in her story like King Lear, as betrayed, as wandering around in a wilderness, not knowing what to do or where to turn. The crucial point to make here is that divorce discourses generally are replete with negative images; Alison's experiences so easily find a home among them.

But this is not always the case. As we shall see, analysis of some of our other case studies reveals that some people are able to construct their divorce experience in a more positive way, working towards independence, looking towards the future, and looking back on the past of the marriage as negative and destructive. We will return to this point later. In Alison's case, there is little doubt that her non-initiator status in the divorce (she did not expect her marriage to end, and was shocked when the adultery came to light), as well as the very difficult material circumstances in which Alison found herself, played their part in predisposing her to talk about her experience in the terms that she did. But perhaps the lack of availability of positive genres for divorce stories is also important in structuring Alison's experience.

By Time 3, Alison's trauma has not yet abated, but her symptoms (as measured by the GHQ, see Table Appdx. 2.1) have lessened, and she is beginning to feel resentful that life seems to have nothing to offer her. Importantly, perhaps, she is beginning to feel angry:

> I think what happened was I got really down. I got so that I just didn't want to do anything any more...just sitting and staring and not even really thinking...I don't know what I am here for really sometimes, why I am here for, what's the point? What is the point of my being alive just to do things and be there for everybody else, not about me as a person? Where do I come into it? I wouldn't come into anywhere. I mean, I haven't done for months...At the moment, there doesn't seem to be any light at the end of the tunnel at all. And I just let things get really on top of me, and I just haven't got no fight left, nothing.

But Alison, at Time 3, at least has some vision of independence and freedom, because she talks about her fantasies of running away from it all:

> I think the best thing would be for me to pack up my car with my books and just clear off and leave them to it. Then Ted would have to come back here, and take over, and he could have the house and all its problems, and all the bills and everything else, and I could go off some place and be quite anonymous with my knife and my fork and my plate and my mug.

At Time 3, Alison also states how bitter she is now feeling:

> I am very bitter, I really am. And the longer it goes on, the more bitter I become.

But her bitterness seems to have its roots in the pain that she feels, particularly the pain of rejection:

> It is just like he is blowing away everything...I will never forgive him...not ever...And I suppose it will go on hurting until I am out of this town and I don't have to see him and I can put a space between us.

A further point which arises out of Alison's case is that the kinds of emotions she describes are common to most of our participants, even when they choose to initiate divorce; but not everyone deals with them, or narrativises their experience in the same way. These feelings seem to be related to the general psychology of attachment and loss, rather than to the precise mechanics of those processes. Further, it is also clear that although emotions are experienced individually, as our *own* feelings, they do not straightforwardly have their origins inside of us, but instead result from a complex process of interactions between the inner and the external worlds, and between ourselves and others.

Discussion

As has been seen, the GHQ data indicate that divorcing people can expect to experience a severe drop in emotional well-being which only gradually improves over time. This finding is consistent with those from a range of other quantitative studies.[18] But our qualitative data present a challenge to the image of divorce as a wholly negative, even 'pathologised', experience. The in-depth interviews not only reveal that distressing symptoms and negative feelings can co-exist with a positive will to survive and a constructive striving to create a better future, but also suggest that some of the feelings (such as anger) which we commonly regard as undesirable may actually serve positive psychological functions in supporting and sustaining effective coping strategies.

Whilst there has been some recognition on the part of researchers of the need for divorcing people to recreate a sense of self anew,[19] little attention has been paid to understanding the optimal conditions for this process, or the factors which might enhance the efficacy of individual strategies for survival. In the concluding section of this chapter, we would like to focus on the question of what might enhance the possibility of positive outcomes.

As emphasised in previous chapters, the traditional paradigm in psychology, as it has been employed in divorce research, has rested on an implicit dualism in which emotions and feelings are seen as internal properties of an individual who is fundamentally separate from the social and cultural world. On this view, the symptoms and feelings which divorcing people experience have been seen as reflections of their internal worlds. By contrast, the 'psychosocial' approach to divorce adopted here in this study led us to ask questions about the parts played by social discourses and cultural images in the constitution of personal psychological states. This approach to the analysis of the qualitative data has enabled us to regard participants' reported symptoms and feelings as deriving, not from within the individual, but as constituted within a complex web of interactions among individual biographies, coping strategies, material circumstances and social discourses.

It cannot be said, on the basis of our data, that divorce was unequivocally either a negative or a positive experience for any of our participants. Rather, divorce seems to be characterised by a profound emotional ambivalence that operates at a range of levels, both individually and socially. In the case studies discussed in this chapter, it is clear that attachments persist, but that they do so in tension with a need to rebuild an independent self, separate from the identity that was bound up with that of the partner in the marriage. Tensions also arise in the negotiations in which ideas about children's needs are formulated, at the same time as adults' own needs demand satisfaction. The dominant discourse of welfare shapes the expression of these emotional ambivalences, privileging the continuance of attachment and placing obstacles in the way of a final separation. The dominant discourse of harmony similarly places barriers in the way of expressions of anger and conflict. The result is that the negative side of ambivalence is stifled, and the emotional work of integrating, accepting and owning one's conflicting feelings is rendered all the more difficult.

It was mentioned earlier in this chapter that our participants who began dispute resolution by mediation seemed to fare less well psychologically (according to GHQ scores) than those who engaged solicitors from the beginning. This was a surprising finding, and it is one that warrants further investigation with a much larger sample.[20] Kelly *et al.* (1988) report a similar finding.[21] In their study, the mediation sample reported significantly higher levels of depression than their adversarial counterparts, and the authors suggest that this may reflect the personality attributes of the people who chose to mediate; they were less able to behave in a hostile and rejecting way. There may, however, be another explanation for these findings, namely that the barrier to the expression of hostile emotions, posed by the discourses of welfare and harmony, runs counter to ordinary coping strategies, thus militating against the achievement of psychological separation and emotional resolution. As clearly seen in Laura's case, it was getting back in touch with her anger, and the revitalisation of her 'fighting spirit', which served to ward off a debilitating depression.

The brief discussion of Alison's case indicated the emotional significance of being able to revisit and reinterpret the past as a route to reconstructing the self and imagining a future.[22] A crucially important, though neglected, aspect of the divorce process is the re-fashioning of the story of the past from the vantage point of the present. That telling one's story has a profound emotional significance is now beyond doubt (see, for example, McLeod, 1997); in the context of divorce, it is clear that making sense of experience by way of narrative accounting is an important part of psychological reconstruction, since personal narratives are one of the primary loci for the production of selves. Crucially, however, divorce dispute resolution practices (mediation, adversarial negotiation or litigation) provide opportunities for the telling of divorce stories in particular ways (Day Sclater, 1997a).

In some ways, the different dispute resolution practices have similar implications for the telling of divorce stories, but in other ways they diverge. The dominance of the welfare discourse in these different settings is what unites these diverse practices. The prioritising of particular constructions of children's 'needs' and the marginalising of those of adults,[23] the implications about the possibilities of risk and harm to children which both flow from and underpin the prescriptions for parenting implicit in the discourse,[24] and the positioning of children as vulnerable,[25] are common themes in all forms of divorce dispute resolution. On the other hand, the different practices of dispute resolution (mediation, adversarial negotiation or litigation) each uniquely presents an opportunity to tell a particular kind of story.[26]

In mediation, at least as it is practised in the UK, the focus is on the future and not the past; people who mediate are actively discouraged from dwelling on old hurts and wrongs and instead encouraged to articulate common values and make constructive plans for the future. The technique of 'reframing' plays an important role here; participants' narratives are literally reframed in the mediation process,[27] and it is the job of the mediator to ensure that this is done in as positive, co-operative and constructive a way as possible. Mediation thus denies people the opportunity to tell their own story in their own way; instead their stories (and, consequently, their selves) are re-fashioned in the mediation process according to the priorities of the dominant discourses of welfare and harmony.

In the adversarial process, people's stories are similarly fashioned; not by reframing, but ignoring, discounting and marginalising all those aspects of the story (including information about feelings and perceptions of injustices) which are deemed irrelevant to the legal process.

Looked at from a psychological point of view, divorce dispute resolution practices, insofar as they fashion the telling of divorce stories, participate, for better or worse, in the shaping of the self; for better or worse they affect psychological coping strategies as well as being affected by them.[28] The prevalent image of divorce in our society continues to be a negative one; divorcing people have few resources available to them to be able to construct positive stories or coping selves. This point shall be examined in more detail within the next chapter.

Notes

1. See Appendix 1.
2. See Appendix 2.
3. Throughout this study the participants' names and, where appropriate, both names and gender of their offspring, have been changed to ensure anonymity is preserved.
4. This finding warrants further investigation. It supports other findings, for example, those from the study of Kelly *et al.* (1988), discussed in chapter 2.
5. See Appendix 2.
6. See Appendix 2.
7. See Appendix 2.
8. Davies and Harre (1990) discuss how 'selves' are produced within discourses through a process of discursive 'positioning': see the discussion in chapter 4.
9. It is implicit, for example, in the Children Act 1989 and the Family Law Act 1996: see the discussion in chapter 1.
10. For a fuller discussion of the ways in which divorcing people manage these discursive tensions, see Day Sclater and Yates (1999).
11. For a fuller discussion of these psychological aspects of the welfare discourse, see Day Sclater (1998d) and Day Sclater and Piper (1999).
12. According to Hinshelwood (1991), 'The confluence of hatred and love towards the object gives rise to a particularly poignant sadness that Klein called depressive anxiety. This expresses the earliest and most anguished form of guilt due to ambivalent feelings towards an object. The infant [in the depressive position] is physically and emotionally mature enough to integrate his or her fragmented perceptions of mother, bringing together the separately good and bad versions that he or she has previously experienced' (p. 138).
13. See Hinshelwood (1991), pp. 156ff.
14. See also Brown and Day Sclater (1999).
15. See Appendix 2.
16. Jessica Benjamin in *Bonds of Love* refers to this phenomenon as 'recognition' and discusses it in psychodynamic terms. See Benjamin (1990).
17. 'Tragedy', a word of uncertain derivation, applied broadly to dramatic or other works in which events move to a fatal or disastrous conclusion (Drabble and Stringer, 1987, p. 570).
18. See the studies reviewed in chapter 3.
19. See, for example, Bohannon (1971); Johnston and Campbell (1988).
20. Our sample was too small to permit statistical comparisons because we wished to prioritise the qualitative aspect of the study.
21. This study is discussed in chapter 2.
22. This finding is entirely consistent with the theoretical work (discussed in chapter 4) on the relations between memory, narrative and identity.
23. For a fuller discussion of this point, see Day Sclater (1998d).
24. See Kaganas (1999).
25. See Piper (1996) and Day Sclater and Piper (1999).

26   See Day Sclater (1997b).
27   Discussed further in Day Sclater (1997a).
28   For an interesting commentary on these broader consequences of recent changes, see Nader (1992). She states that 'trading justice for harmony is one of the unrecognised fall-outs of the 1960s. So is trading law process for mind processing' (p. 468). She concludes that mandatory mediation compromises the basic freedoms of human citizens.

6   Stories, Genres, Psychologies

In this chapter, we explore the accounts that our participants gave of their divorce experiences; we discuss these in terms of narrative genre, and we offer a psychoanalytically-based perspective on the case studies brought 'into conversation' with each other (Rosenwald, 1988). We have already seen that the GHQ data produces a picture of divorce as an emotionally traumatic process. This picture, however, must be qualified with reference to the data from the semi-structured interviews and the narrative accounts. The former point to the positive feelings people have about divorce, feelings that co-exist (sometimes uncomfortably) with a range of symptoms of acute psychological distress. The narrative accounts offer us some insights into these tensions and complexities; they point to the deep ambivalences of divorce. The analytic perspective we have adopted enables us to examine the interactions among accounts of experience, cultural discourses, story genres and psychological processes.

Many commentators have asserted that divorce is not an event, but an ongoing process (see, for example, Kitson and Morgan, 1990). As we have seen, it is commonly characterised as a process of adjustment, as people adapt to the changes, gradually returning to normal. We reject this view, and instead we see divorcing people as being *changed* in the process,[1] as one of its central aspects (one that makes it simultaneously traumatic *and* positive) is a process of self-reconstruction. We have come to think, over the duration of our study, that divorce can best be characterised as an interpretive process,[2] in which individuals narrate experiences as a way of making sense of what has happened to them, and as a way of reconstructing the past and self identity.

That telling one's story matters and is an important part of human life which enables us to construct and maintain a sense of ourselves, is a premise which is rooted in therapeutic practice[3] (see, for example, Hermans and Hermans-Jansen, 1995; Burck *et al.*, 1996; McLeod, 1997) and which is gaining increasing acceptance in social scientific thought. Meaning-making is an essential and ongoing human enterprise which assumes an even greater significance in the context of biographical disruptions and dislocations of the sort divorce can bring. As we discussed in chapter 4, personal meanings are constructed, revised and negotiated in the process of narrative accounting. How people reinterpret the past has a bearing on how they deal with present concerns and how they prepare themselves for the future. As we shall see, narrative accounting also has a bearing upon how people negotiate the ambivalences of attachment and loss, and we see the narratives as expressing a range of survival strategies.

Narrative Genres in Divorce Stories

We have already touched on the question of the importance of narrative genre in our discussion of Alison's case in chapter 5. Whilst the notion of 'genre' has a multitude of meanings (Derrida, 1980), it refers fundamentally to a means of classifying story types according to their structures. Cohan and Shires (1988) put it this way:

> Texts belong to one genre as opposed to another when they share a similar narrative structure which paradigmatically projects, for a reader, a horizon of expectation and intelligibility based on conventions learned from prior knowledge of the genre (p. 77).

Thus the narrative structure organises events and actions into a signifying field according to familiar conventions of story and characterisation. According to Shafer (1980), 'common sense' is our storehouse of narrative structures, and it remains the source of intelligibility and certainty in human affairs. Importantly, however, story structures and genres are not fixed but, as signifying systems, they reflect historical and cultural conditions (Belsey, 1980; Cohan and Shires, 1988).

At a general level, then, the narrative genres available in a culture provide what may be thought of as outline story structures (or scripts) which people draw upon to make sense, order and meaning, out of their experiences. These scripts provide social templates for organising and mapping experience, but there are also psychological aspects to genre.

On the one hand, as we discussed in chapter 4, there is a range of cultural discourses upon which people may draw in giving accounts of their experiences. In divorce narratives, discourses of parenthood (motherhood, fatherhood) and the dominant discourses of child welfare and 'harmony' are commonly invoked. These discourses imply a limited range of subject positions (Davies and Harre, 1990) for tellers to take up, negotiate or actively challenge and resist. In this way, discourses may be said to have psychological 'effects' insofar as they provide frameworks for the structuring of subjectivities in the act of narrative accounting. Positioning in relation to discourse both predisposes and presupposes particular psychological constellations.[4] On the other hand, individuals bring their own biographies, their own ways of coping, their own passions, desires and aspirations for the future, to their divorce stories.

The narratives shape and are shaped by both cultural and psychological factors; they reflect both cultural preoccupations and psychological constellations and they impact reflexively upon both culture and psychology. The stories people tell each other are, or can become, part of a culture's stock of narratives which others may draw upon to make sense of their lives and, as Plummer (1995) puts it, all stories have their time, their place.[5] As we discussed in chapter 4, the stories people tell are capable of providing sites for the construction and transformation of subjectivities.[6] Divorce narratives therefore embody both culture and psychology, and a study of narrative form and content can actively resist the traditional boundaries that separate the individual from society, the subject from culture.

As Riessman (1990a) points out, divorce is almost always difficult, but interpretive work is one way through the hardship; telling one's story can have healing and empowering effects. In this chapter, we explore the interpretive work of meaning-making that divorcing people do in their narrative accounts.

In our study, two main genres of divorce stories were in evidence in the narratives: what may be called 'victim' stories and 'survivor' stories. Victim narratives can be of several types; most commonly they are those of 'tragedy' which place the participant on a trajectory from idealised past to devastating present and hopeless future. These stories are underpinned by an implicit appeal to a romantic, forever-after discourse of marriage;[7] the subject is positioned as a victim who has suffered, who has loved and lost through no fault of their own. We have already encountered an example of this genre in Alison's case.

The element of 'tragedy', however, is not always present, and some victim narratives challenge romanticised notions of marriage.[8] As we shall see, some of the stories told by Richard and James fell into this category. These are not stories of tragedy, because the idealisation of the past is absent, but they are stories that nevertheless provide victim positionings for the subject. Both Richard and James saw themselves as victims of the social organisation of marriage, which they talked about in gendered terms. There is also some variation among the victim narratives according to whether the subject constructs her or himself as the victim of circumstances or structural constraints, or the victim of the wrongdoing of the partner, or of more subjective forces, perceptions and feelings.

Survivor narratives comprise the second main genre into which the divorce stories fell. Like the victim narratives, they too can take several different forms. Hints of survivor stories can appear in tension with a predominantly victim genre. More commonly, however, survivor stories are produced in active resistance to victimhood; recognition of one's positioning as a victim can lead to a determination to survive, and the recounting of experience in a new narrative form (Day Sclater, 1998b). Just as elements of survivor stories can complicate victim narratives, so too can victim positionings appear in what are predominantly survivor stories. Participants may, for example, report experiencing guilt or a sense of injustice alongside an obvious determination to survive.

Arguably, survivor scripts are more readily available to women than they are to men in our culture.[9] There is a growing survival genre available to women which draws upon feminism, or upon the late Princess Diana's divorce story, or which is manifested in popular culture in such songs as Gloria Gaynor's 'I will survive', reputedly the most popular Karaoke song.

Whilst our participants' narratives fell, at a broad level, into these two genres, it is important also to emphasise that these genres take several forms and that they are not fixed. Based upon the same set of actual events, participants may, at one stage, story their experience in one genre, only later to tell it a different way. Meanings can alter as new biographical constructions are made; a participant once positioned as a 'victim' can be more optimistically placed as a 'survivor' in a new biographical construction (Day Sclater, 1998b). Let us now consider some of the case study data to illuminate our discussion of the complex relationships between story genre and psychological processes.

If we consider Laura's story, with which we already have some familiarity, we see Laura expressing a range of contradictory emotions and impulses; she seems to fluctuate in acting out her sadness and her anger, as she struggles to come to terms with the pain of loss. Parts of Laura's story are clearly within a 'victim' genre, and she even tells how she reached the point of considering suicide. It was Laura's acknowledgement of her anger which pulled her back from the brink. Laura's story of this transformation adheres much more clearly to a 'survivor' script; she talks about how the emergence of her 'fighting spirit' enabled her to carry on.

Perhaps what Laura is doing in this story is repositioning herself as a force to be reckoned with, as someone who had some chance of exerting control over her life. Importantly, however, Laura needed to acknowledge her anger to be able to position herself in this new way, but she found that there were barriers to sustaining it. The obstacles came from two sources. First, the welfare discourse which provides for an equation between a 'responsible' parent and a harmonious divorce. As we have seen, neither Laura's feelings nor her psychological needs sat easily with this. Laura talks about her needs in terms of a need to express anger, to separate, and to achieve independence. But, as we have seen, there is an emotional subtext to her words, a subtext which speaks of the emotional difficulties and ambivalences of separation, the irrational feelings about loss; there is a sense in which Laura's positioning of herself in the welfare discourse enables her to side-step these issues. Secondly, and relatedly, Laura was not able unequivocally to claim 'survivor' status for herself until the divorce, and the attendant financial matters, had been dealt with; the dispute resolution process, in which she perceived Peter as 'dragging his heels' presented an obstacle to the complete movement of Laura's story from the 'victim' to the 'survivor' genre. Here is Laura speaking at Time 3 about the difficulties of her current situation:

> Not knowing which way you are going, living on egg shells. I can't do anything, because if I do something with the house, or sort something out, he has only got to drive by here and say, 'Oh, she's done that!', off he goes to the solicitors, 'well, she has done this.' But I cannot talk to him and say, look, so-and-so needs doing, because I know full well that he is not going to agree to help pay for any of it, even though half of it is his house, he is not going to pay any more out on it...But I wish it was all over and done with.

In this brief extract we can see Laura positioning herself as 'victim' in a complex scenario in which she is not yet the mistress of her own life. An important point here is that the positions of 'victim' and 'survivor' are interdependent and relative, they are never final and complete, but have meaning in relation to each other and to the narrative as a whole. Laura's narrative is an account of someone trying to manage acute emotional turmoil within the limits set externally, in terms of legal necessities and material changes in her life. Laura may be a 'victim' in some ways, but we already know that she is a determined 'survivor' in others; the point is that she cannot consistently tell a story in the 'survivor' genre at the same time as she positions herself in the welfare discourse (which proscribes her anger) or is unable to exert much control over the financial side of the divorce.

Alison's case, which we also introduced earlier, is another example of a divorce story in the 'victim' genre. In her case, the demolition of the 'shared reality' of the marriage (Berger and Kellner, 1964), signified by Ted's adultery, left Alison feeling that she had lost everything important, including even a sense of who she was. Alison's initial positioning of herself as a 'victim' was partly sustained by her idealisation of the past and her marriage, and was accompanied by acute psychological distress. As in Laura's case, it was acknowledging her anger and bitter feelings (although Alison knew these to have roots in the pain of rejection), which begin to enable her to move, by Time 3, towards a narrative more in the survivor genre. This manifests itself in Alison's fantasy about running away to freedom.

A somewhat different scenario is presented in Richard's case. At Time 1, Richard's GHQ score was very low, but the first interview revealed him to be full of an intense anger and hatred which was still present at Time 4. In his story, Richard presented himself as someone who refused to allow himself to become a victim of circumstances; expressing his anger was what enabled him to avoid positioning himself as 'victim'. Yet, there was a sense in which Richard himself acknowledged that his angry feelings were serving to cover up an unbearable psychological pain. Richard thus adopted a coping strategy in which he storied himself as a survivor from the start.

Richard and Jennifer had agreed to go their separate ways when they reached the conclusion that there was no point in carrying on together. Richard blamed Jennifer for the failure of the marriage and, in particular, he was angry about the time and attention she had devoted to being a mother, perceiving himself as having been excluded and his needs ignored. Richard intended, on separation, to have nothing more to do with either Jennifer or Stacey (his daughter), and he wanted the divorce, and the attendant financial and property matters, settled as quickly as possible. To this end, he reverted (by his own admission) to threats and coercion, which enabled him to maintain a sense of being in control of what was happening. Richard's narrative was a 'survivor' story from the start, but we do not have to delve far below the surface to discover the underlying 'victim' story, and Richard's terror of it.

Whilst the majority of divorcing people express a degree of anger, hatred and resentment, Richard's feelings in this regard are worthy of comment because they are linked closely to his story of survival. Richard sometimes allowed his feelings to manifest themselves in murderous fantasies:

Someone should have told me how much cheaper it would have been to have killed or had them both [wife and daughter] killed.

Whilst it is clear that killing one's family is not a realistic option, the strength of the sentiment behind Richard's words cannot be ignored, and Richard was not alone in expressing murderous feelings.[10] The pain and anxiety which underlie such expressions are not always immediately visible on the face of the interview transcripts but Richard did retain an awareness that his survival depended on denying, or pushing out of existence, his sorrow and pain:

I understand a lot about pain and sorrow and all those things. But I look at it, and then I put it in a cupboard in my head, and get on with what has to be done.

That Richard's defensive strategy is reasonably effective is reflected in his low GHQ score at Time 1. Between Time 1 and Time 2, however, Jennifer left the house having found a new place to live, and Richard's score at Time 2 increased dramatically. At Time 2, a financial settlement had largely been agreed, but Richard remained unhappy with it, an unhappiness that translated into a more generalised sense of injustice. Still, however, Richard does not take up a position as a 'victim'; instead, he blames 'society' and 'gender relations' for the pain and the injustices he has suffered. Here is Richard talking at Time 2 about the biggest 'hurt' he feels he is reacting against:

The lies that society puts upon us. That tells your gender to play with little dolls, go out and have little girls, and tells my gender that they have got [to] be macho and hard and not cry. All those things. And then puts us together and lets us loose. And it doesn't work like that, and we wind up hurting each other. And anything I do to my wife, to my child, to your gender, is simply a cry of pain. When I told my wife that if she didn't get it [the financial settlement] sorted, and she took everything away from me, I was going to clump my daughter with a sledgehammer one day, that was the loudest cry of pain she would ever hear from me. There were no tears involved, no shouting. And she will never know it. She will never know it.

This brief extract illustrates the emotional pain and the profound psychological vulnerability which underlie the bitterness and anger which sustains Richard's 'survivor' story; only occasionally, as here, did this explicit acknowledgement of vulnerability break through the facade of coping and survival.

These brief illustrations from the case studies illustrate the complexities involved in imposing generic categories on divorce narratives, and reveal the fluidity of positions such as 'victim' and 'survivor', as well as the different psychological constellations which such stories can produce, sustain or support. In order further to develop our argument about the relations between story genre and psychological processes, we would like now to consider, in more detail, the question of psychological survival strategies, and how these are reflected in narrative. We saw, in relation to Richard's case, that the 'survivor' genre in which he told his story both reflected and sustained a range of conflicting feelings, primarily anger and vulnerability. Our argument now develops to show how particular divorce stories can be said to reflect particular survival strategies which help participants to weather the emotional storms of divorce.

Strategies for Survival

Personal narratives of divorce, whether those in which the participant is positioned as 'victim' or those which tell of survival, exhibit consistent tensions, the resolution (or attempted resolution) of which provide the motor for the story. Firstly, these are before-and-after narratives, where the 'after' (the breakdown of the marriage) is known, and the meaning of the 'before' is interpreted in the light of the already known conclusion; 'before' and 'after' are constructed in divorce narratives in tension with each other. Secondly, a further polarisation occurs between 'self' and 'other'; divorcing people commonly narratively construct a subjectivity that is everything the other (the departed partner) is not. We have found it useful to think of these tensions as indicative of survival strategies, which can be theorised in psychological terms, using Melanie Klein's idea of 'splitting'. This describes a process whereby, as a defensive manoeuvre, the subject introduces order and tolerability into a world otherwise felt as chaotic and intolerable, by imposing polarised perceptions on reality.[11] We will be discussing these ideas in more detail in a moment, but first we will examine the ways in which the 'splitting' Klein described is manifested in the divorce narratives.

A consistent theme in our participants' narratives was that of looking back over the marriage, of trying to make sense of what had gone wrong, and of trying to piece together a plausible account which rendered the participants' experiences and feelings comprehensible, and their actions justifiable to the listener.

As Freeman (1993) points out in relation to autobiography generally, the past is continually being reconstructed from the vantage point of the present.[12] In divorce, however, a crucial division occurs between past and present/future; the 'ending' of the story of the marriage is already known; the happy-ever-after till-death-us-do-part ending was never realised. Through narration, our participants confronted the ways in which, and explored the reasons for which, their marriages had departed from the promises of fairy tales but they did not find any readily available alternative genre in which to construct their experiences in anything like positive terms. Divorce is the antithesis of marriage, and is negatively valued by comparison, and this cultural fact is reflected in our participants' stories.

When polarisations occur, similar antitheses, with their differential valuations are set up. Thus, our participants commonly denigrated the past of the marriage, or questioned their previously positive perceptions whilst, even in the face of emotional difficulties and material obstacles, they idealised their present pursuit of 'independence' or 'freedom'. Some participants, at least initially, did the opposite, and idealised the marriage, talking in tragic terms and rendering themselves prey to a terrible sense of despair about the impending divorce.

The same processes of polarisation are in operation in both cases, however; both represent strategies for survival which assist in making sense of the present and in the work of mourning. From a psychological point of view, this revisiting of the past through narration probably plays a crucial role in the reconstructions of self which divorce renders necessary.[13]

Divorcing people do not only have to construct for themselves a new vision of the future, but also a new vision of the past, as the whole meaning of the past alters in the light of the marriage breakdown. Without a past, it is hard to maintain a sense of self. One woman in our study, whose marriage ended when she discovered that her husband was having a long-standing affair, said that one of the most difficult things for her had been that her husband had 'taken her past away'. In the light of her discovery, the whole meaning of the past of the marriage changed and she felt as though she had been cast adrift without an anchor.

Divorcing people do not narrate a history from a neutral position. Rather, their stories are infused with psychological investments and are driven by the need to survive. Making new sense of the past goes on against the backdrop of the survival strategy and the need to rebuild a sense of self.

'Splitting' as a defensive manoeuvre is also manifested in divorce stories as a polarisation between self and other, as destructive or painful parts of the self are expelled and perceived as belonging to the other. Sometimes it is guilt that is projected in this way, as the participant turns hostility inwards to attack the self, or adopts a victim status. Small wonder, perhaps, that divorcing people often report an enduring sense of persecution and injustice (Davis *et al.*, 1994).

These psychological manoeuvres manifest themselves in the 'victim' narratives that tell of wrongs done to the participant, in which the ex-partner is blamed for the breakdown of the marriage or for divorce conflict. They appear in survivor stories where survival depends upon getting even or getting revenge. They manifest themselves in stories of struggles within the confines of a dispute resolution procedure that is seen to favour the other. It seems likely that it is these psychological survival strategies that underlie the bitterness and conflict that is so often associated with divorce.

However, Laura's case, discussed earlier, alerts us to the possibility that it might be a mistake to regard such 'conflict' in purely negative terms; for Laura, it was the resurgence of her 'fighting spirit' which overrode a suicidal depression. For her, expressing opposition was a necessary part of survival, without which she was having considerable difficulty in rebuilding the self that she felt had been destroyed by Peter's abandonment of her. Alison, too, was to begin to rebuild herself in opposition to Ted, and Richard's was an extreme case where his opposition to Jennifer was almost a precondition for his continued existence.

James, on the other hand, was not so ready to polarise, but he found himself in an impasse, stuck with his 'head in the sand', unable to move forward and feeling an intense sadness. The process of rebuilding the self had hardly begun for James, though he had been separated for 9 months at the time of the first interview.

Jill, too, was depressed and 'stuck' (her declining GHQ score perhaps reflected the fact that she was prescribed medication by her GP between Time 2 and Time 3, and had started counselling); and this was reflected in both the form and content of her narrative. At Time 1 Jill, like other parents in our study, found the children's contact times particularly difficult:

Because I am finding it very difficult, you know, knowing that she [daughter] has got to go over there and his girlfriend is going to be dealing with her at some point. And I am finding it very hard to cope with. You know, I know at the end of the day I have got to put up with it, but I don't like it. You know, I haven't got to like it. I will never like it. You know, now I know how his first wife must have felt, you know how the resentment, you know the anger. I honestly, I really do feel for her, because I am in that position now.

Jill, however, feels unable to express her anger because she believes it would be detrimental to her daughter. When asked how she dealt with John when he upset her, she said:

Well I can't - I don't want to be - I don't think two wrongs make a right, you know...Um (pause) for the sake of my own - my daughter - you know I just sort of basically say to him, look, you talk to my solicitor, you know I don't want to argue with you. But he knows that he has got one over me all the time. He knows that he upsets me. I am sure of that. But for the sake of the baby, I don't say very much, or raise my voice in front of him. It's not going to do her any good.

By Time 3, however, Jill feels easier about making her anger more explicit, and she is ready to draw a line under the past. She is ready, too, to place herself and John on opposite sides of a divide:

I wish that he would just get out of my hair and leave me alone, but with her [daughter], I can't. He's always going to be there.

To be honest, sometimes the way he sort of comes in, I just wish he didn't have anything to do with her. I think it would be far better for her, because her life is always being disrupted. And if he said 'I don't want to see her', then you know, that certainly wouldn't - it probably would upset her if she were older, at the moment she is only a baby, so give it another couple of years, and if he turned round and said it, then I think it would have effects on her, but um (pause), it is like everything, they get used to it. Yes, I must admit deep down, if he turned round and said 'I don't want anything to do with her' I think it would be a good thing, you know, get out of my life completely.

Three important, and related, points emerge from our brief discussion of Jill's case. First, we can see evidence of a movement from a 'victim' towards a 'survivor' story between Time 1 and Time 3. Secondly, this movement is accompanied by an increased willingness to acknowledge her anger and, thirdly, it is also accompanied by a resistance to the welfare discourse. At Time 3, Jill no longer wholly accepts that her daughter's needs have to mitigate her own need to be free of John; Jill has recast her daughter's vulnerability in different terms. Together, these transitions mark the emergence of Jill's survival strategy; she is beginning to see things in before and after, self and other terms.

'Splitting' is also manifested in relation to perceptions about dispute resolution procedures. Helen was one of our participants who chose to try to resolve her divorce disputes by means of mediation rather than engaging solicitors from the start. She explained the reason for her choice at Time 1 as 'you know, to see if we could do it painlessly, because of the children.' One of the main reasons participants gave for choosing mediation was that it was seen to be 'best for the children'. Participants, generally, did not give explicit reasons why they thought mediation would be best for the children, but there was always an implicit reference to a child welfare discourse in which 'conflict' is seen as undesirable or even damaging to children. In this context, mediators and lawyers are put on opposite sides of a divide, with mediation seeming to promise an amicable (if not a painless) divorce, and the involvement of solicitors seeming to promise nothing more than protracted and costly conflict. As Helen said:

> I didn't want to go to a solicitor who would take it all over and be very sort of, um, well, I think they just go for the kill at times, and I didn't want that, because I didn't want to antagonise my ex-husband, um, because we don't want to have that sort of relationship as far as the kids are concerned.

It is as though, by avoiding solicitors, the negative and destructive feelings which divorce brings can be avoided. As Helen went on to say:

> And because as soon as I, I went to see a solicitor, um, you know, she was quite antagonistic and, er, I saw a couple before I decided which one to take because one in particular was going to go straight for the jugular, and I thought, well, that's not really what I want.

Helen's choice to attend mediation was therefore made partly because of the perceived positive aspects of mediation and partly because solicitors were perceived in negative terms, as fuelling conflict. These, of course, are exactly the polarised sentiments which underlie the provisions of the Family Law Act, 1996. The fear of conflict, here expressed by Helen, was felt by other participants in our study.[14] The choice of mediation can be seen as a way of addressing these fears, at both an individual and a social level. However, it could also be said that this is done at the expense of denying the psychological roots of 'conflict' in divorce.

This polarisation of dispute resolution procedures perhaps reflects a deeper psychological process, in which mediation is idealised and negative feelings and destructive impulses are projected instead onto the legal profession. Given the ambivalences which are part and parcel of the psychology of divorce, it is perhaps not surprising that this early idealisation of one and denigration of the other is unstable; participants find that it is extremely difficult always to be rational, amicable and harmonious, and that sentiments more appropriate to adversarial discourses emerge to disrupt harmonious fantasies.

Helen and Michael attended six mediation sessions to sort out the financial side of the divorce. They managed to reach an agreement which was embodied in a *Memorandum of Understanding* which was subsequently amended after scrutiny by and negotiation between their respective solicitors (the amendments took Michael's pension into account). At Time 2, Helen had stopped going to mediation, and had begun to think about it more critically, and about lawyers more positively:

> I think well, it [mediation] helped, um (pause), because it did throw up questions that I would probably have taken a lot longer to think about than if I hadn't gone...what I feel is, that because it is not the whole thing, it is simply mediation for the financial, that that there is nobody to deal with your emotions at the same time. And that is obviously not what those mediators are there for, but it is all so tied up, it is very difficult to separate, um, and I, you know, it seems better to have somebody to do it all for you...um, I think the emotions get in the way...I think it would be great if you could have a system where the solicitors were sort of on that site as well, you know, and you could sort it all out at the same time.

At Time 2, Helen's fantasy of a 'painless' divorce for the sake of the children is being put under severe strain:

> He wants to be a major part of the children's life without being a major part of the children's life. So, I don't know, in many ways I just, I wish I could be sort of a lot less in contact with him and a bit nasty to him when I do see him.

Helen realises that behaving amicably and 'putting the children first' is putting considerable strain on her:

And I suppose I just need something that is more for me, rather than constantly thinking about the children all the time.

By Time 3, the disruption of Helen's idealised view of mediation is even more pronounced, and the welfare discourse seems increasingly remote to the kinds of issues she is struggling with:

We no longer go to the mediation. Mediation, you know, well, you are together and somebody is directing you. It is all gone, you know, anything that is said between us, he just cuts it off...I really don't want to have any contact with him any more. I don't want to have to consider his needs...It would be much better if we could move completely to the other end of the country or something like that and never see him again.

Helen, at Time 3, also expresses misgivings about the effects of attending mediation on the children; far from seeing it as the route to a 'painless' divorce, or as best for the children, she is beginning to think in much more critical terms:

I think it is not really clear to the children why people, why the parents have split up and, um, you know, we went to mediation thinking that it would be, that what we were doing was best for the children...and to me now the answers just aren't very clear, because the children seem to have confused messages now about, um, you know, we both tend to have quite a good relationship in their eyes, so why can't we live together? They can't see it. And I don't feel any more satisfied than before I went to mediation. I think, you know, if we had had a very stormy break up, and just left it at that, the children might have been affected slightly differently, but I don't think they would be quite as confused as they are now...You know, I don't think it's very clear to them why our relationship didn't work...and I don't think mediation has made that clearer, and I don't know if doing what is considered to be best for the children is actually what is best for them. I think it's a very grey area.

This brief discussion of Helen's case illustrates a more general point: the idealisation of mediation, which is supported by positioning in discourses of welfare, perhaps serves a psychological function in containing a fear of conflict and of the destructive emotions which can be unleashed on divorce.

In Helen's case, her own experiences, and her increasing ability to tolerate her more negative emotions, resulted in her questioning the premises of the welfare discourse. She became less inclined to position herself unproblematically within it, and instead recast herself as a 'responsible' mother in a different way which challenged the traditional positioning of her children as vulnerable, at the same time as she was better able to integrate her own vulnerability and accept her own destructiveness. However, the welfare discourse continues to exert some hold over Helen; she cannot quite break free of it, or of Michael, except in fantasy, and asserting her own needs continues to be a source of anxiety and guilt. Helen's GHQ score increased by Time 3 to 24, and it seems not unreasonable to suppose that this perhaps reflects, at least in part, the inner turmoil occasioned by the increasing lack-of-fit between the co-operative values which Helen espoused so strongly and the hostile and destructive impulses of her inner world. Importantly, the welfare discourse is one which seems to suggest that, as adults, we ought to be able to control our feelings; this is partly why mediation can be idealised, it seems to suggest that it really is possible to put our feelings to one side, indeed, that the interests of our children demand this of us.

Helen's case illustrates the complexities and the mutualities of the interactions among psychological states, survival strategies, divorce discourses and dispute resolution practices. It also illustrates the difficulty of drawing a strict dividing line between mediation and other forms of divorce dispute resolution. Mediation continues 'in the shadow of the law' just as partisan negotiations inevitably draw, to some degree, on dominant welfare discourses. Helen's case illustrates the way in which there is an element of unconscious phantasy involved in imagining that the two occupy separate poles; how dispute resolution procedures are perceived, and the meanings attributed to them, derive at least in part from the inner world of the participant, at the same time as positioning in divorce discourses constrains the participant's activities and the personal meanings they produce. As internal conflicts take shape, are expressed and resolved, divorce discourses can serve changing psychological functions.

Dispute resolution is therefore connected to psychology in important ways which go beyond the mere 'effect' that psychological upset may have on the capacity to resolve divorce disputes. Rather, the disputes themselves are anchored in psychological processes, but participants deal with them in ways which reflect their survival strategies and the available discourses, in turn, constrain the psychological manoeuvrings which can be made.

Explaining the Psychology of Divorce

Coming to terms with divorce is a complex process of interactions among a personal biography, a biography of the marriage, social provisions and cultural scripts. Although, as we saw in Chapter 3, 'recovery' from divorce is most often characterised in terms of 'adjustment', often seen in terms of a linear model of 'progress', our work presents a rather different picture. In part, the different picture which we are able to draw of divorce depends upon the methodology which we chose to use (see chapter 4) and it depends, too, upon the theoretical framework which we have used to understand our participants' survival strategies.

As we have seen, allowing participants to tell their experiences in their own words, and to construct narrative accounts in forms of their own choosing, reveals separation and divorce as processes characterised by ambivalence, complexity and contradiction. Divorce does involve resolving attachments and coming to terms with loss, but it is more than that; it involves, too, the reconstruction of self, and these psychological processes take place in a context, over time, in which the matrices of the internal and external worlds collide and intersect in the stories people tell about their lives. Divorce discourses provide a powerful backdrop against which participants' survival strategies take shape, but neither they, nor psychology, are ultimately determining. It is the interactions which are important, and the unique ways in which each individual accepts, negotiates or resists positionings.

Any experience of 'loss' in adult life is apt to provoke what psychoanalyst Melanie Klein referred to as 'depressive anxiety' (Brown and Day Sclater, 1999), involving an unconscious anxiety that one has driven away, harmed or destroyed the person one loves. The experience of such anxiety can be particularly threatening because it recalls much earlier experiences of loving and losing. These early experiences are closely linked in the unconscious mind with one's own hatred, destructiveness and greed, and the phantasy that it is one's own destructive attacks which have threatened or harmed the loved one. Perhaps for the majority of divorcing people, depressive anxiety is not easy to tolerate; toleration of these feelings depends upon an ability to acknowledge and to accept one's own unconscious destructiveness and hostility, a capacity which is severely tested in the face of crises of loss such as divorce represents.

Few people will be likely to be able to maintain the modes of being and relating which characterise what Klein calls the 'depressive position'. These people are the few who can tolerate the mixture of guilt, sadness, remorse and loneliness and the other psychological burdens associated with loss, the few that can tolerate the deep ambivalences involved in recognising that the person one now hates is the same person whom one has loved and unconsciously still depends upon. As Ogden (1992) points out, coming to terms with loss in the depressive position means recognising that, even whilst one hates, the love that one has felt is still very real and present in the history of the relationship which one shares with the hated person; there is a profound sadness involved in the acknowledgement that history cannot be re-written and in the realisation that one cannot alter the fact that harm has been done. In the depressive position, the work of mourning gradually and painfully allows reparation to be made and recovery to occur.

But, perhaps the majority of divorcing people find the depressive anxiety difficult or impossible to tolerate. In the face of the real material privations and personal deprivations which most divorcing people suffer, in the face of the hostility, onslaught or even abuse from the other, it is perhaps not surprising that people resort to psychological manoeuvres and coping strategies in an attempt to ward off the psychological pain. Two such strategies tend to predominate.

First, the individual may respond by resorting to what Klein called a 'paranoid-schizoid' way of relating and organising experience, in which the integration of both love-object and self breaks down and fragments into polarised 'good' and 'bad', acceptable and unacceptable. As we have seen, Klein referred to this phenomenon as 'splitting' and saw it as a more 'primitive'[15] means whereby one is able to retain a sense of oneself as good and righteous by splitting off and projecting outwards the bad, destructive and hostile parts of oneself, which are then perceived as characteristics of the other. As Ogden (1992) puts it, the loving self is separated from the hating self, as the object is split into loved/hated.

A second line of defence available for the individual faced with intolerable depressive anxiety is that of 'manic defence'; this incorporates elements of both the depressive and paranoid-schizoid positions, and involves the denial of one's dependence on others,[16] which is reinforced by a phantasy of omnipotent control over the object. It protects against the anxiety of being abandoned by the object. Importantly, paranoid-schizoid ways of relating and organising experience, and manic defences, constitute components of the defensive repertoires of all individuals (Ogden, 1992). As such, they are 'normal' and not psycho-pathological ways of coping with loss in adult life.

The structures of the divorce narratives that we collected in our study exhibit themes that mirror these psychological processes. We have seen, for example, the ways in which divorce seems, at times, to present a threat to the very survival of oneself, and how coping strategies can depend upon disowning our own destructive feelings, blaming the other, retaliating and seeking revenge. Divorce stories are evaluative stories; they are stories which adopt a moral stance, and whose rhetoric persuades the listener that the subject's feelings are comprehensible, their actions justified. Acrimonious divorce disputes are unsurprising where paranoid-schizoid ways of coping predominate, or when manic defences are employed, compromising (or even negating) our capacities for love and trust, in an attempt simply to survive.[17]

As Brown and Day Sclater (1999) argue, a return to paranoid-schizoid ways of relating and perceiving is a common survival strategy in the face of the anxieties provoked by divorce. For this reason, divorce is a process that has an inherently conflictual dimension. 'Splitting', especially in relation to past/present and self/other, is a stance that facilitates psychological survival and may be a necessary means of reconstructing the sense of self that divorce so often threatens. However, it is clear that such survival strategies sit uneasily with the dominant discourses that emphasise co-operation and harmony, and they sit uneasily with dispute resolution practices that seek to focus on the future, burying the past. Most importantly, however, they sit uneasily with the profound neglect, in both mediation and adversarial practices, of emotional processes in divorce.

The personal narratives of divorcing people are, at once, painful stories of the loss and failure, and hopeful stories of reconstruction and survival; they capture the complexities and ambivalences of divorce. They represent sites for the revisiting of the past, and its creative appropriation in the service of building new visions of the self and of the future. The narratives are the products of both culture and psychology, structured by the discourses people invoke, at the same time as they interpret, negotiate, challenge and appropriate those discourses for their own ends. In the narratives, people make transitions between different subject positions; they cross and re-cross the territory between being a victim and being a survivor, as they traverse the uncertain terrain from past to present to future. These transitions embody both cultural imperatives and psychological needs, often in competition with each other. The internal demands of psychological survival strategies, which split the world into opposing camps, and contain anxiety by disowning feelings and separating good from bad, self from other, are managed in the narratives, often in conflict with the external demands of divorce dispute resolution.

The transformations of 'victims' of divorce into 'survivors' involves the interpretive activities of subjects who come face to face with their deepest vulnerabilities and can countenance ways of living with them. Women perhaps make these transitions more easily than men do, partly because there is less of a cultural premium for them on hiding or displacing vulnerability, and partly because the burdens they face are largely material and practical ones, which can be addressed at that level; for them, the pursuit of autonomy is a challenge they face with a lot to gain.[18] For men, by contrast, vulnerability is even more difficult to hold and contain; where there is no woman to carry it, survival is often bought at the cost of displacement or denial.[19] The discourses of welfare and harmony place demands and physical and psychological burdens on both fathers and mothers, demands that often clash with the effective operation of psychological strategies for survival. Becoming a survivor often means a willingness and an ability actively to resist the demands of the dominant discourses.

Notes

[1]   Vaughan (1987) argues that 'uncoupling' is more than leave-taking; it is a transition into a different life.

[2]   Riessman (1990) argues that 'interpretive work' is one of the ways through the hardships of divorce. Similarly, bereavement is commonly characterised as a search for meaning.

[3]   Kerby (1991, p. 86) characterises psychoanalysis as a clinical discipline whose purpose it is to construct the life stories of individuals, and to make available the implied subject of the story for the teller to claim for themselves.

[4]   For example, the discourse of welfare positions children as vulnerable and, as such, provides a repository for the projected vulnerabilities of adults (Day Sclater, 1998d; Day Sclater and Piper, 1999), and the discourse of harmony operates to de-legitimise the expression of conflict and hostility, thus facilitating psychological denial.

[5]   For example, widespread media coverage and popular discussion of the late Princess Diana's experiences of marriage and divorce have undoubtedly contributed to the legitimising of experiential 'confessions' and has lent an increased visibility to a particular genre of divorce story.

[6]   See Day Sclater (1998b) for further discussion of this point, in the context of a detailed analysis of one woman's divorce story.

[7]   Similarly, Riessman (1990) found that the major cultural theme that both men and women used to create their divorce accounts was the ideology of the companionate marriage.

[8]   Interestingly, Riessman (1990) reports that none of her sample of 104 people challenged the ideology of the companionate marriage; most dealt with the inherent tension within the ideology by seeing the partner (or themselves in some cases) to have failed to live up to expectations.

[9]   We are grateful to Candida Yates for this observation.

[10]   Walker (1994), for example, cites a father who said of his ex-wife, 'I could cheerfully chop her head off if she wasn't my daughter's mother', and a woman who said, 'I could cheerfully kill him'. Divorce can rouse extreme feelings.

[11]   In psychoanalytic terms, this involves both a splitting of the object and of the ego. See Hinshelwood (1989, pp. 433-435). He says, '[O]bjects are not objectively perceived...in fact they are frequently given unnaturally good natures or unnaturally bad ones. Children split their objects so that parental imagos are separately endowed in their child's imaginative play with wholly good and benign qualities and intentions, or else with wholly bad ones. As a result, splitting became a term employed to describe the way in which objects come to be separated into their good aspects and their bad ones.' In the splitting of the ego, aspects of the self are split off and projected into others; they are then perceived as aspects of the other. As Ogden (1992) argues, a degree of splitting is a feature of ordinary psychological functioning. Klein (1946), however, also described a splitting of objects that brought with it a fragmentation of the ego, giving rise to fears of annihilation. See also Laplanche and Pontalis (1988, p. 427-431).

[12]   Novelist Charles Powers states that memory has a future as well as a past. See Powers (1997).

[13]   See Bohannon (1971). See also Vaughan (1987) who argues that denigration of the marriage and of the other are common strategies employed in the process of self reconstruction following 'uncoupling'.

[14]   The same split was present in the debates leading up to the passing of the Family Law Act 1996; mediation was idealised and the adversarial process simultaneously denigrated.

[15]   'Primitive' here refers to an earlier level of organising experience; Klein's paranoid-schizoid position is characteristic of the first few months of life. The infant has the capacity to move into the depressive position at around six months of age.

[16]   It is sometimes referred to as 'counter-dependence'. See, e.g., Johnston and Campbell, 1988.

[17]   For further discussion, see Brown and Day Sclater, 1999.

[18]   In Riessman's study (1990a), women invoked a 'liberation' discourse, citing freedom from subordination and devaluation as the positive outcomes of divorce. Men were less positive (although less depressed on a quantitative measure), finding the loss of family and social ties hard to replace. They expressed relief at the freedom from obligation which divorce brought but, as in our study, were prone to regarding themselves in 'victim' terms, feeling that they had lost more than they had gained. Riessman concludes that divorce creates expressive hardships for men, in ways that it does not for women. These different and gendered experiences of divorce warrant further study, as they seem likely to have their roots in both the gendered experience of marriage and in the psychological aspects of gendered identity. See further Day Sclater and Yates (1999).

[19]   For a full discussion of masculine and feminine gendered identities, from a psychoanalytic perspective, see, for example, Maguire (1995) and Minsky (1996,

1998). For a discussion of this issue in the context of divorce, see Day Sclater and Yates (1999).

7   Conclusions

If marriage is central to the construction of both a shared reality and a personal identity (Berger and Kellner, 1964), then divorce represents a process in which the old certainties are dismantled, and the subject is confronted with a mammoth task of rebuilding the world and the self. When a marriage breaks down, important anchors break loose and we are cast adrift; continuity is lost, of the world and of the biographical self. Who and what we are, and what the world is like, are all called into question. We can no longer unproblematically look to the past, to our memories, to feel safe in the knowledge that things are as they always have been; the past has irrevocably changed and has to be read in new ways. Established biographical patterns are dislocated, and we are faced with the task of reconstructing new meanings for the past, a new sense of self and a new vision for the future. These tasks have to be faced against the backdrop of the deep emotional and psychological investments we have made in our intimate relationships, investments which hark back to our earliest experiences in infancy and which continue to live on in the unconscious mind. In our endeavours to reconstruct our lives and our selves, we are faced with a culture replete with, on the one hand, negative images of divorce as chaos and disaster[1] and, on the other hand, idealised images of post-divorce families. Neither of these images bears much relation to the perceptions and lived experiences of divorcing people.

As Riessman (1990a) has argued, divorce strikes at the roots of identity. This is what makes it such a traumatic and painful process. But herein also lie the possibilities for positive outcomes; rebuilding a sense of self is a creative and constructive process. Coming through divorce is about overcoming our sense of failure to pursue new developmental pathways, it is about meeting challenges and finding new strengths to cope with adversity, it is about creating new hopes to carry us through the pain towards a better future. Coming through divorce involves creating new meanings to replace the old. In this final chapter, we would like to draw together the threads of our arguments and consider some of the factors that facilitate survival and those that militate against it.

We have characterised divorce as an interpretive process, a process that is essentially one of meaning-making which has both social and psychological aspects. Social discourses and narratives about divorce pervade our culture, providing resources for us to draw upon in constructing our own life stories. These social scripts provide templates for our own efforts at meaning-making but, as we have seen, they can be constricting as well as facilitating. The dominant image of divorce as destructive and damaging persists, linked closely to the social anxieties occasioned by the changing family patterns we discussed in chapter 1. Alongside this, however, exist contradictory idealised images of post-divorce families, constructed in discourses of welfare and harmony, representing a variation on the theme of the 'happy ever after' of fairy tales. Psychoanalytic theory helps us to understand how our personal and social ambivalences, which are deeply rooted in our early experiences, manifest themselves in the signifying power we accord to 'family', such that divorce carries with it overtones of threat and overwhelming anxiety. We manage these, at both personal and social levels, by splitting: 'family' is good, divorce is bad. Casting divorce in this light is what enables us to maintain our sense that 'family' represents all that is good, safe and comfortable.

But, as seen in chapter 1, families are changing, whether we like it or not, and divorce rates have increased to the extent that it has become a commonplace occurrence. As we argued in chapter 1, currently we are perhaps witnessing new measures aimed at 'normalising' divorce in terms of a family transition, creating the possibility for a more positive narrative of divorce to emerge. These developments however, bring new problems of their own, and traditional investments in familial ideologies show a remarkable persistence. It would seem that we are in a transitory stage; 'the family' has changed almost beyond recognition, but we have not yet left old ideas and values behind. In this context, not only do we split 'family' and divorce and put them on opposite sides of a value-laden divide, but we also split divorce, characterising some as 'good' and others as 'bad'.[2] This dual process of idealisation and denigration, which is occurring at the level of social discourse and political rhetoric, mirrors a psychological defence for coping with overwhelming anxiety.

The 'bad' divorce is conflict-ridden, accusatory, adversarial, costly (in both financial and emotional terms) and associated with the legal process. Families are torn asunder by it, children suffer at the hands of selfish and irresponsible parents who pursue their rights, linked to their retributive agendas. Fathers disappear out of children's lives and fail to keep up payments. People are intent on dwelling on past wrongs and on obtaining justice at all costs. The 'good' divorce is the opposite. It is harmonious and characterised by rational appraisal and behaviour which plans properly for the future. Responsible parents put their own feelings to one side for the sake of the children, and build constructive relationships with each other, of a sort they were unable to do whilst married. The 'good' divorce keeps families together, and is associated with mediation. This polarisation is clearly reflected in the Government Green and White Papers (Lord Chancellor's Department, 1993, 1995), in the Parliamentary debates which led to the Family Law Act 1996, and in the Act itself. Not all divorces are 'bad' any longer; where marriages really are incapable of being saved, divorce can be a solution, but we are exhorted to choose the 'civilised' kind. The 'good' divorce, constructed within discourses of harmony and welfare, has become the ideal to strive for.

As we have seen, the dominant discourses of welfare and harmony are invoked by people in telling their divorce stories. But they are not accepted unquestioningly. Rather, they are interpreted and reinterpreted, negotiated, challenged and resisted as people struggle to rebuild their lives. But the prescriptions of the dominant discourses, and the 'positions' they provide, can conflict with survival strategies and present obstacles to the rebuilding process. Ideals of harmony sit uneasily with psychological needs to separate and with the angry and destructive feelings that surface in that process. Encouragement to focus on the future sits uneasily with the need to revisit and reinterpret the past that is essential for biographical repair and the integration of experience. Thus, although the discourses of welfare and harmony do, in some sense, mark the possibility for more positive images of divorce to emerge, divorcing people do not seem to find them particularly helpful and they may, in fact, mitigate the efficacy of commonly employed ways of coping. Further, the discourses of the 'good' divorce represent the 'idealised' pole of a binary divide, with the shadow of the 'bad' divorce continually present.

One of the main obstacles to the construction of positive divorce stories seems to be the dearth of alternative narratives available in our culture. For women, alternative genres have been generated by feminism; here women can aspire to autonomy and independence, and can construct stories in which they claim survivor status for themselves. But they can only do so at a cost. The financial hardships and the burdens of lone parenting loom large, and the discourses of the 'good' divorce mean that true independence can only be achieved at a cost of being positioned as a selfish or irresponsible mother who is prepared to put her own needs before those of her children.[3] Divorcing mothers are caught in an impossible double bind, as the discourses of harmony and independence pull in opposite directions.[4]

For men, alternative genres have been developed within the 'men's rights' movement but, as Collier (1999) argues, in the context of the so-called 'crisis in masculinity', the characters in these scenarios are most often positioned as the new 'victims' of divorce. The 'new man' is neither supported by family policy, nor is his presence wholly welcomed by his ex-partner as she pursues her own agenda for an independent life. Whilst recent changes in family law have given fathers a greater stake in children's lives,[5] the legal changes have not been accompanied by the necessary practical, cultural and psychic changes for parenting to become a truly gender-neutral activity. As Collier (1999) argues, the sex war rages on in a new form in the area of post-divorce parenting. Thus, attempts by both women and men to re-cast their divorce experiences in positive terms by drawing on these alternative genres, are in danger of proceeding in the face of the other's deep resistance. Despite the prevalence of the ideology of harmony, new conflicts are being generated, new battlegrounds staked out.[6]

Conflicts about the story to be told undoubtedly enter into the formation of divorce disputes.[7] But it is perhaps too easy to forget that divorce disputes do not take place between two gender-neutral individuals; men and women are gendered beings, and gender is an important dimension of experience in both marriage and divorce. In this context, it is naïve to overplay the gender-neutrality of law and to overlook the important links between contemporary divorce and gender relations. 'Parental responsibility' is a gender-neutral concept in law[8] and, in the practices of dispute resolution, it is discursively constructed in relation to 'child welfare' and 'harmony' but, importantly, it has meaning for individual mothers and fathers in relation to broader discourses and practices of parenting which remain profoundly gendered. As long ago as 1973, Jessie Bernard talked about the differences between 'his' and 'her' marriage; these differences are also reflected in divorce experiences.

Riessman (1990a),[9] for example, identified gender differences in the ways in which divorcing women and men recreated emotional intimacy in their memories of the marriage. She found that the women identified a lack of reciprocity in the relationship that brought about disappointment, and that they felt let down by a lack of emotional closeness with their husbands. Men, by contrast, did not focus much on the disappointments of emotional intimacy, but were rather more concerned about their wives' physical availability; what caused disappointment for the men was their apparent lack of centrality in their wives' lives, and many resented the attention their wives gave to others (including children). Riessman concludes that men and women, from the vantage point of divorce, construct very different accounts of the marriage which are linked in important ways to prevailing ideologies and practices of gender. Riessman also found that men and women were exposed to different kinds of hardships on divorce, and that they have particular ways of coping with those hardships. The burdens for women include the daily care of children, lack of money, worry about child support payments and lack of help. The main burden for men was the 'loss' of family and diminishing social networks. Many of the women in Riessman's study responded to the stress by becoming depressed, whereas the men dealt with their distress in different ways, including constant activity and drinking. Riessman concludes that men and women have different vocabularies of distress, and the findings from our study would support this, although our sample is much smaller.

That men and women have different concerns and sources of stress and that they deal with them in different ways is undoubtedly a factor in the conflict that ensues as they attempt to fashion positive divorce stories for themselves. As others have argued (see, for example, Collier (1995, 1999); Fineman (1991, 1995); Smart (1989)), we have perhaps been premature to wipe gender off the divorce agenda. Issues of gender politics remain live ones which continually threaten to subvert the explicit gender-neutrality of law; men and women interpret the discourses of welfare and harmony through gendered lenses, and do not automatically align themselves with the 'neutral' positions for parents that the discourses offer.[10]

Divorce dispute resolution practices help to shape the stories that are told (Day Sclater, 1997a). The main difference between the adversarial process and mediation, in this respect, is that the former permits two separate, perhaps competing, stories to be told; ultimately, it is up to the judge to decide which story he thinks has the greater merits.[11] Mediation, on the other hand, is concerned to find common ground between the disputants and, to this end, seeks out concerns and values that are amenable to being re-cast as shared ones; this process can be regarded as one of facilitating the construction of a joint story.

But difficult emotions are notable for their absence in both kinds of stories. Expressions of anger and hostility are actively discouraged[12] and are said to be the cause of harm to children. A parent who feels angry and hostile towards the other is likely also to feel guilty about what effect their feelings are likely to have on the children. Some of the mothers in our study felt unable to express their anger for this reason. The suppression of anger, as we saw in the case studies, however, is not necessarily to be considered a 'healthy' response from a psychological point of view; it can pose barriers to the acceptance (and therefore to the healthy integration) of hostile and destructive impulses. If we are unable to 'own' our own anger (or any other part of ourselves for that matter), we must not assume that it will simply go away. Rather, we will be likely to deal with it either by splitting and projection (attributing our own destructive impulses to others, and thereby maintaining a holier-than-thou image of ourselves) or by 'acting out' our unprocessed emotions, thereby causing pain and destruction to others. The 'good' divorce has no place for anger and hostility; because of this, it may encourage projections and so impede the building of both constructive relationships and a new, integrated, sense of self.

We cannot discount the possibility that the dominant discourses themselves foster conflict; insofar as they deny gender difference, they are apt to provoke defensive reactions. As Day Sclater and Yates (1999) argue, men and women construct different meanings for the welfare discourse. Women can feel constrained by its emphasis on the needs of children and the apparent necessity for continued and harmonious relationships with their departed partners. Men often interpret it in terms of justice, and use it as a basis from which to pursue their perceived 'rights' in relation to children. Both readings depend upon a phantasy that the other has a power that they do not, in reality, possess. The gender-neutrality of law is subverted by the psychological survival strategies that men and women are obliged to adopt in the face of a legal system that permits neither gender difference nor the owning of hostile emotions. The gender-neutrality of law is reformulated through the eyes and experiences of gendered social actors who bring to it their own concerns, feelings and ways of coping; their attempts at meaning-making do not exclude considerations of gender in the way that the law does.

As has been argued elsewhere (Day Sclater, 1998d; Day Sclater and Piper, 1999), the deployment of the welfare discourse, in practice, may also do children a disservice insofar as it facilitates the projection of adult vulnerabilities onto children. If divorcing parents cannot be allowed to 'own' their own vulnerable feelings and parts of themselves, it should come as no surprise to find these being projected onto children; parents then fight 'to protect children's interests' with an energy and a tenacity underpinned by their own emotional investments. The emotional energy with which some parents fight about their children is indicative of the profound vulnerabilities of their own which they are obliged to hide. It is our view that this denial of emotion does not lend itself to the achievement of healthy, positive outcomes.

Our dispute resolution practices will remain ill-suited to the needs of divorcing people if we continue to pathologise the associated emotions, on the one hand, or minimise and sanitise them on the other. As Craib (1998) argues, there is a tendency, in our culture either to pathologise powerful emotions or to recast them as everyday experiences; both are opposite sides of the same coin, and that coin signifies our deep-set inability to cope with powerful, ambivalent or ambiguous emotion at a social level. Craib argues that the task that faces us, as a society, is one of learning to tolerate the multiple ambiguities and ambivalences that simply being human presents us with. In relation to divorce, this means better acceptance of the associated emotional processes. It means lifting the taboo on the expression of feeling to discourage denial, unhealthy projections and 'acting out'. It means creating a space for the revisiting and reinterpretation of the past, the polarisation of past and present, self and other (often along gender lines) as necessary psychological processes without which it is impossible to establish and maintain the sense of self which is so important in divorce. It means creating the conditions for the construction of positive stories that can provide the starting blocks for the construction of a new identity quite different from that which existed during the marriage.

Is Harmony Possible?

In this context, it becomes necessary to re-examine the premium currently placed on 'harmony' in divorce. Our foregoing discussion suggests not only that the harmonious divorces will be rare, but also that they cannot simply be imposed by new legal regulations or procedures. On the contrary, if harmony is sought at the expense of a denial of destructiveness and hostility, the tasks of psychological resolution may be impaired. Psychoanalyst Thomas Ogden (1992) argues that 'splitting' can, in some circumstances, serve positive psychological functions. He goes as far as to say that it is an inability adequately to employ such defensive manoeuvres which leads to severe psychopathology. If the primary anxiety of the 'paranoid-schizoid' position is the annihilation of self and one's valued objects, it is splitting that protects the individual by safeguarding her or his needs to both love and hate; by splitting, one is able to both love and hate safely. As Ogden puts it:

> Splitting allows the infant to feed safely and to love, and to desire and hate safely, without developing an overwhelming anxiety that he is being destroyed by, or destroying that which he loves (Ogden, 1992, p. 57).

Thus, according to Ogden, the achievement of adequate splitting is a precondition for healthy integration and a continuous sense of self. The reason for this is that it is only when the subject has achieved relative freedom from the anxiety that loving and hating experiences will 'contaminate' each other, that these different facets of experience can be more closely integrated, as they are in the depressive position.

Sociologist and group psychotherapist Ian Craib (1994) talks about the ways in which we, as a society, seek to manage grief, but his points are relevant too to any discussion of divorce. Craib argues that it is the unbearability of the feelings of panic involved in loss which lead us to imagine that grief is a predictable and controllable process, that it involves the expression (and resolution) of a particular series of emotions, through which a bereaved person will pass on their developmental road to recovery. However, he argues that the experience of loss will almost always go deeper than our social formulae allow; they way each of us will grieve depends very much on our own personal histories and our habitual coping strategies.

Craib further argues that our theories and rituals about grief represent an effort which reflects deep difficulties in accepting our own ambivalences about loss as well as the uncomfortable fact of our mortality. Thus, we pathologise grief by placing it in the hands of experts, a process that permits us to maintain the fantasy that our feelings can be managed. For Craib, losses of various kinds are things we have to live with every day of our lives; experiencing disappointments is part and parcel of being human. His argument, therefore, is one which seeks to de-pathologise grief whilst not denying the depth of ambivalent, chaotic, destructive and painful emotion which accompanies it as a matter of course.

There are obvious parallels in divorce. The Family Law Act explicitly addresses itself to minimising the messy emotions associated with divorce. It seems highly likely that co-operative dispute resolution procedures cannot deal with loss and grief any better than the old adversarial ones could, but they can be seen as a way, typical in late modernity, of imposing prescriptions for behaviours which foreground our rationality at the expense of our emotions. The discourse of the 'good' divorce serves to sever the chaotic and destructive feelings and parts of ourselves from the rational and manageable parts of ourselves, with the former being driven underground. In the process, the natural disappointments that attend loss become sanitised and only with difficulty can find expression. Insofar as the dominant discourses embody behavioural prescriptions, their *modus operandi* is one of bringing moral pressure to bear, of inducing feelings of guilt and inadequacy in those who have difficulty in managing the darker sides of themselves. Some participants in our study experienced exhortations to co-operation, not as encouragement towards more constructive ways of relating, but as persecution. It is indeed ironic that the psychological hold which these new discourses seem to have over us has its roots in a fantasy that our emotional lives can be rendered smooth and predictable, that the pain of divorce can be minimised, if not obliterated altogether. As long as co-operation in divorce is idealised, it is unlikely that the destructive feelings that underlie conflict can be properly owned.

The theme of polarisation which characterised our participants' narratives, we think, is what underlies divorce conflict as a psychological phenomenon. This narrative theme, as we have seen, reflects a deeper splitting which is best understood with reference to the Object Relations tradition in psychoanalysis. The divorce narratives we collected were primarily stories of a self precipitated by the experience of loss into defensive and regressive modes of behaviour (which we called 'survival strategies') that have the effect of putting dangerous emotions at one step removed.

We are, at this point, forced towards the conclusion that the dominant discourses of the 'good' divorce may, in some cases, be detrimental to divorcing people and to their children. We are reminded of the findings of D'Errico and Elwork (1991), Walker (1993, 1994) and Kelly *et al.* (1988), discussed in chapter 2, as well as our own tentative findings that people who begin dispute resolution by mediation seemed to fare less well psychologically[13] than those who employed solicitors throughout, mentioned in chapter 5. These studies raise serious questions not only about the difficulties of implementing ideals of co-operation, but also about the psychological impact of dispute resolution discourses and practices. Adherence to a harmonious ideal may stand in the way of healthy integration. The psychological processes of divorce may impact upon dispute resolution processes but, equally, our study has shown that this interaction is a two-way process. At each stage, the prescriptions of the dominant discourses are read and re-read in the light of the demands of emotional expression and the integrity of selfhood. At each stage, the dominant discourses acquire new meanings that are played out in different ways. At the same time, the discourses of welfare and harmony pose constraints upon survival strategies, rendering some feelings unmanageable, some conduct deplorable.

Our findings suggest three main things of importance to family policy. They present a challenge to those solicitors, mediators and court welfare officers whose task it is to manage divorce dispute resolution, and they present a challenge too to the premises that underlie the Family Law Act.

First, divorce can be emotionally very traumatic, but the coping strategies which many people adopt to enable them to weather the emotional storms of divorce often involve a 'splitting', at a psychological level, a defence strategy which places husband and wife on the opposite sides of a divide and which provides a psychological basis for conflict and bitterness.

Secondly, despite the emotional trauma which divorce can bring, the story is not altogether a pessimistic one; rather, divorce is not only about coming to terms with loss, but it is also about the positive rebuilding of a new post-divorce sense of self. This rebuilding process, however, involves revisiting and reinterpreting the past of the marriage from the vantage point of the present; this making sense of the past may be a pre-requisite for letting go and moving on.

Thirdly, we would suggest that the time has come to set aside pathologised images of the divorce process, and to recognise that the future psychological health of our society rests upon an acceptance of the reality of the darker side of human nature, of its hostile and destructive aspects, which co-exist with its finer and more 'civilised' parts. As Craib (1994) argues, we need to overcome our fears about emotional expression, and to learn to tolerate life's ambivalences and ambiguities, and to own those aspects of ourselves that we are forever tempted to deny. Divorcing people pay a high price for the premium that our society places on rationality; as Richards (1989) argues, we may always be 'reluctant mourners'; we find it hard to let go of our unconscious wishes and desires, and the ambivalent feelings will continue to surface and subvert our conscious lives in a multitude of ways. The task facing those who create policy or manage divorce processes is one of permitting us to own our feelings, however intolerable they might be.

As Brown and Day Sclater (1999) argue, dispute resolution practices can serve as forums for the 'containment' of some of the raw and unprocessed emotions and anxieties that surface when a significant relationship breaks down. These emotions can lose some of their destructive power, as they are metabolised and transformed in a contained setting. As Price (1998) argues, drawing on the work of psychoanalyst Bion, 'containment' facilitates the transition from emotional experience into thought-full experience, as emotional comprehension enables thinking to begin. In such a context, the 'acting out' of unprocessed emotions can be replaced by the creative production of positive divorce stories that facilitate the emergence of a new sense of self. Divorce dispute resolution clearly is not, and should not be, 'therapy', but this does not prevent it from being potentially therapeutic in its effects. These insights raise new questions about the conditions that are necessary for dispute resolution practices to act in the service of 'containment'. It may be that, from this perspective, the formal legal process has rather more to offer than is currently thought.

Cooper (1999) argues, in the context of a discussion of the complexities of the phenomenon of child abuse and law's response to it, that law can operate as a kind of social 'reality principle'; law, he says, should be capable, like a mature adult, of coping with emotions, ambivalences, uncertainty and complexity. Should family courts become more 'therapeutic' in their approach? This would certainly be one way of addressing the kinds of problems we have been discussing. In the USA, 'therapeutic' forms of mediation have taken a hold in a way that continues to be resisted in Britain. But the 'triumph of the therapeutic' (Rieff, 1966; Lasch, 1980), or the 'tyranny of experts' (King and Piper, 1995), would not be a development welcomed by everyone. Lasch is not alone in seeing the proliferation of therapeutic practices as providing the liberal state with a new system of indirect controls that threaten true participatory democracy.

The acknowledgement of emotional complexity need not imply the need for therapeutic interventions, much less the need for law to become a therapeutic practice of sorts. In any event, as King and Piper (1995) convincingly argue, not only is law ill-equipped to deal with human problems in all their complexity, but the very nature of law *as law* precludes any fundamental changes; new discourses may evolve, and will impact on law but, importantly, they will themselves be altered as law adopts, transforms and reconstitutes them according to its own premises and classifications. 'Law enslaves', they say (p. 136) and it necessarily does so; anything else would compromise law's boundaries, its authority and its functions.

It does not follow, however, that law must remain unresponsive to the vicissitudes and complexities of human predicaments. Law can, and should, respond and adapt to human need as well as organise, manage and prescribe. Law connotes authority, and its boundaries could more effectively be put in the service of 'containment', without compromising its integrity *as law*. The signifying power law commands could facilitate an important shift in the dominant discourses, better to address the needs and concerns of divorcing people. There is, of course, a sense in which it might be said that family law is already showing signs of change in this direction. The recent move away from formal legal procedures to more informal modes of divorce dispute resolution (Family Law Act 1996) does represent an accession of law's territory to mediation, and this shift has been rationalised as a better way of addressing the needs of divorcing families. But, as we have shown, these reforms are predicated on a model of divorce as 'dysfunctional'[14] and on a denial of emotional complexity and gender difference. As we argued in chapter 1, the reforms may have gone some way towards alleviating social anxieties about changing family patterns, but they have not addressed a deeper problem and the dominance of discourses of welfare and harmony looks set to produce new sets of anxieties for divorcing men and women.

It is important that we move away from models of the divorce process that pathologise it or which regard conflict as 'dysfunctional' and equally important that we do not minimise or sanitise difficult emotions. As Craib (1998) puts it, there is a current tendency to turn the 'tigers' of powerful emotions into the 'pussycats' of everyday feelings. We should also beware of any slide into fantasies that therapies of various sorts can best address the problems that confront us. In our analysis, we have drawn heavily on psychotherapeutic discourses but these highlight, not the need for therapy for divorce as a pathological process, but rather point to the need for a reformulation of the ways in which our society is prone either to pathologise or to sanitise emotions; poor substitutes for accepting that they are an integral part of the human condition. Psychoanalysis is a discourse that is rooted, foremost, in therapeutic practice, but it is also a way of thinking about politics, culture and our contemporary way of organising society and managing people (Rustin, 1991; Minsky, 1998). Crucially, it points to the necessity for us, as individuals and as a society, to be able to tolerate paradox, ambiguity, contradiction and conflict. From this perspective, the denial of these dimensions in the discourse of harmony may be read as a retrograde and defensive step. The recent transition from formal to informal modes of divorce dispute resolution is a step that accords with the cultural paradigms of late modernity; to continue with Craib's metaphor, we seek to manage those things that seem to threaten social stability and cohesion by recasting angry tigers as docile pussycats (Craib, 1998). Without adequate 'containment', the pussycats may start to purr in the dispute resolution process, but the roar of the tiger will continue to be heard in the jungle of human experience.

Notes

1 As Abelsohn (1992) says, perhaps what is truly remarkable is that divorcing families are not more disturbed than they actually are, given society's focus on risk, dysfunction and disaster and the continued stigmatisation of divorce. Despite the vast amount of research work that has been carried out, the complex upheavals of divorce remain largely uncharted territory; we still lack a positive normative frame for divorce.

2 Constance Ahrons wrote a book in 1994 entitled *The Good Divorce*, and subtitled *Keeping Your Family Together When Your Marriage Falls Apart.*

3 See Neale and Smart (1999); Kaganas (1999).

4 See Day Sclater and Yates (1999).

5 For a discussion of this in historical context, see Day Sclater *et al.* (1999).

6 See Bailey-Harris *et al.* (1998). These authors have monitored applications under the Children Act 1989 and have found that, contrary to the intentions of the Act and to the ideology of harmony, disputed cases are increasing in frequency and are taking longer to resolve. The issue of 'implacable hostility' in contact cases has also been the subject of much recent discussion in the legal press, as courts attempt to manage these apparently intractable cases. See Kaganas (1999).

7 Mediator Ann Milne (1988) offers a 'taxonomy' of divorce disputes. She identifies four main types of conflicts: psychological conflicts, communication conflicts, substantive conflicts and systemic conflicts. Conflicts in relation to the 'divorce account' are included in the category of 'psychological conflicts'. She argues that mediation can assist by helping to fashion new accounts that focus on 'less provocative' aspects of the marital discord: 'An account that includes a validation of the good intentions of each spouse and avoids blame and finger pointing lessens defensiveness and moves the couple from an antagonistic posture of individual enhancement to a more co-operative posture of shared understanding' (p. 31).

8 Children Act, 1989.

9 See also Arendell (1986, 1995); Arditti and Allen (1993); Fineman (1995); Simpson *et al.* (1995); Neale and Smart (1999).

10 Our findings on the question of gender are discussed in Day Sclater and Yates (1999).

11 See Jackson (1990, 1995, 1996) and Papke (1991) for a full discussion of the functions of narrative in relation to law.

12   In mediation, such expressions can be tackled by 're-framing'. This does not, of course, eliminate the emotions, but simply introduces a context in which their expression is rendered unacceptable.

13   According, at least, to GHQ scores.

14   See, for example, Kaslow (1988).

Bibliography

Abbott, P. and Wallace, C. (1992), *The Family and the New Right*, Pluto Press, London.

Abelsohn, D. (1992), 'A Good Enough Separation: Some Characteristic Operations and Tasks', *Family Process*, vol. 31, pp. 61-83.

Ahier, B. (1986), *Conciliation, Divorce and the Probation Service*, UEA, Social Work Monographs, No. 2.

Ahrons, C. (1994), *The Good Divorce: Keeping Your Family Together When Your Marriage Comes Apart*, Bloomsbury, London.

Alexander, I.E. (1988), 'Personality, Psychological Assessment and Psychobiography', *Journal of Personality*, vol. 56, pp. 265-294, Special Issue on Psychobiography and Life Narratives.

Althusser, L. (1971), *Lenin and Philosophy*, New Left Books, London.

Amato, P.R. (1994), 'The Impact of Divorce on Men and Women in India and the United States', *Journal of Comparative Family Studies*, vol. 25, pp. 207-221.

Amato, P.R. and Booth, A. (1991), 'The Consequences of Divorce for Attitudes towards Divorce and Gender Roles', *Journal of Family Issues*, vol. 9, pp. 306-322.

Ambrose, P., Harper, J. and Pemberton, R. (1993), *Surviving Divorce: Men Beyond Marriage*, Rowman & Allanheld, Totowa, New York.

Andrews, M., Day Sclater, S., Squire, C. and Treacher, A. (eds) (1999), *Lines of Narrative*, Routledge, London (forthcoming).

Apter, T. (1993), 'Altered Views: Fathers' Closeness to Teenage Daughters', in R. Josselson and A. Lieblich (eds), *The Narrative Study of Lives*, vol. 1, Sage, London.

Arditti, J.A. and Allen, K.R. (1993), 'Distressed Fathers' Perceptions of Legal and Relational Inequities Post-Divorce', *Family and Conciliation Courts Review*, vol. 31, pp. 461-476.

Arditti, J.A. and Keith, T.Z. (1993), 'Visitation Frequency, Child Support Payment, and the Father-Child Relationship Post-Divorce, *Journal of Marriage and the Family*, vol. 55, pp. 699-712.

Arditti, J.A. and Madden-Dedrich, D. (1995), 'No Regrets: Custodial Mothers' Accounts of Difficulties and Benefits of Divorce', *Contemporary Family Therapy*, vol. 17, pp. 229-248.

Arditti, J.A. and Madden-Dedrich, D. (1997), 'Joint and Sole Custody Mothers: Implications for Research and Practice', *Families in Society: The Journal of Contemporary Human Services*, vol. 78, pp. 36-45.

190   *Divorce: A Psychosocial Study*

202

Arendell, T. (1986), *Mothers and Divorce*, University of California Press, London.

Arendell, T. (1995), *Fathers and Divorce*, Sage, London.

Aseltine, R.H. and Kessler, R.C. (1993), 'Marital Disruption and Depression in a Community Sample', *Journal of Health and Social Behaviour*, vol. 34, pp. 237-251.

Ashford, S. (1987), 'Family Matters', *British Social Attitudes*, vol. 4, pp. 121-152.

Astor, H. (1995), 'Review of *The Responsible Parent: A Study in Divorce Mediation*, by C. Piper', *Social and Legal Studies*, vol. 4, pp. 544-545.

Babb, P. (1995), 'A Review of 1993', *Population Trends* 79, Spring 1995, pp. 1-9.

Babb, P. and Bethune, A. (1995), 'Trends in Births Outside Marriage, *Population Trends* 81, Autumn 1995, pp. 17-22.

Bahr, S.J. (1996), 'Review of *Family Mediation: Contemporary Issues*, by H.H. Irving and M. Benjamin', *Family and Conciliation Courts Review*, vol. 58, p. 805.

Bailey-Harris, R., Davis, G., Barron, J. and Pearce, J. (1998), *Monitoring Private Law Applications Under the Children Act: A Research Report to the Nuffield Foundation*, University of Bristol.

Bainham, A., Day Sclater, S. and Richards, M. (eds) (1999), *What is a Parent? A Socio-Legal Analysis*, Hart, Oxford.

Baker, A. and Townsend, P. (1996), 'Post-Divorce Parenting: Rethinking Shared Residence', *Child and Family Law Quarterly*, vol. 8, pp. 217-227.

Bakhurst, D. and Sypnowich, C. (eds) (1995), *The Social Self*, Sage, London.

Banks, M., Clegg, C., Jackson, P., Kemp, N., Stafford, E. and Wall, T. (1980). 'The Use of the General Health Questionnaire as an Indicator of Mental Health in Occupational Studies', *Journal of Occupational Psychology*, vol. 53, pp. 187-194.

Barthes, R. (1977), 'The Death of the Author', reprinted from *Image, Music, Text*, in D. Lodge (ed) *Modern Criticism and Theory: A Reader*, Longman, London, (1988), pp. 167-172.

Barthes, R. (1990), *The Pleasure of the Text*, Blackwell, Oxford, (trans. R. Miller)

Bastard, B. and Cardia-Voneche, L. (1995), 'Inter-Professional Tensions in the Divorce Process in France', *International Journal of Law and the Family*, vol. 9, pp. 275.

Beck, U. (1992), *Risk Society: Towards a New Modernity*, Sage, London.

Beck, U. and Beck-Gernsheim, E. (1995), *The Normal Chaos of Love*, Polity, Cambridge.

Bell, S.E. (1988), 'Becoming a Political Woman: The Reconstruction and Interpretation of Experience Through Stories', in A.D. Todd and S. Fisher (eds), *Gender and Discourse: The Power of Talk*, Ablex, New Jersey.

Bell, S.E. (1991), 'Commentary on *Perspectives of Embodiment: The Uses of Narrativity in Ethnographic Writing*', *Journal of Narrative and Life History*, vol. 1, pp. 245-254.

Belsey, C. (1980), *Critical Practice*, Methuen, London.

Belsey, C. (1994), *Desire: Love Stories in Western Culture*, Blackwell, Oxford.

Benjamin, J. (1990), *The Bonds of Love: Psychoanalysis, Feminism and the Problem of Domination*, Virago, London.

Benstock, S. (1988), *The Private Self: Theory and Practice of Women's Autobiographical Writings*, Routledge, London.

Berger, P.L. and Kellner, H. (1964), 'Marriage and the Construction of Reality', in M. Anderson (ed), *Sociology of the Family*, Penguin, London, (1971), (2nd edn 1980).

Berman, W.H. (1985), 'Continued Attachment After Legal Divorce', *Journal of Family Issues*, vol. 6, pp. 375-392.

Bernard, J. (1973), *The Future of Marriage*, Souvenir Press, New York.

Bertaux, D. (ed), (1981), *Biography and Society*, Sage, London.

Bertaux, D. and Kohl, M. (1984), 'The Life Story Approach: A Continental View', *Annual Review of Sociology*, vol. 10, pp. 215-37.

Betchen, S.J. (1992), 'Short-term Psychodynamic Therapy with a Divorced Mother', *Families in Society*, vol. 73, pp. 116-121.

Bird, R. and Cretney, S. (1996), *Divorce: The New Law: The Family Law Act, 1996*, Jordans, Family Law, Bristol.

Bisagni, G.M. and Eckenrode, J. (1995), 'The Role of Work Identity in Women's Adjustment to Divorce', *American Journal of Orthopsychiatry*, vol. 65, pp. 574-583.

Bishop, G., Hodson, D., Raeside, D., Robinson, S. and Smallacombe, R. (1996), *Divorce Reform: A Guide for Lawyers and Mediators*, FT Law and Tax, London.

Black, A.E. and Pedrocarroll, J. (1993), 'Role of Parent-Child Relationships in Mediating the Effects of Marital Disruption', *Journal of the American Academy of Child and Adolescent Psychiatry*, vol. 32, pp.1019-1027.

Blankenhorn, D. (1995), *Fatherless America: Confronting Our Most Urgent Social Problem*, Basic Books, New York.

Boardman, A.P. (1987), 'The General Health Questionnaire and the Detection of Emotional Disorder by General Practitioners: A Replicated Study', *British Journal of Psychiatry*, vol. 151, pp. 373-381.

Bogolub, E. (1991), 'Women and Mid-life Divorce: Some Practice Issues', *Social Work*, vol. 36, pp. 428-433.

Bohannon, P. (ed) (1971), *Divorce and After*, Doubleday, New York.

Booth, A. and Amato, P. (1991), 'Divorce and Psychological Stress', *Journal of Health and Social Behaviour*, vol. 32, pp. 396-407.

Booth, A., Edwards, N. and Johnson, D. (1991), 'Social Integration and Divorce', *Social Forces*, vol. 70, pp. 207-224.

Booth Committee, (1985), *Report of the Matrimonial Causes Procedure Committee*, Chair Mrs Justice Booth, DBE, HMSO, London.

Borden, W. (1992), 'Narrative Perspectives in Psychosocial Intervention Following Adverse Life Events', *Social Work*, vol. 37, pp. 135-141.

Bordow, S. and Gibson, J. (1994), *Evaluation of the Family Court Mediation Service*, Family Court of Australia, Research and Evaluation Unit, Research Report No. 12.

Bottomley, A. (1984), 'Resolving Family Disputes: A Critical View', in M. Freeman (ed) *State, Law and the Family*, Tavistock, London.

Bottomley, A. (1985), 'What is Happening to Family Law? A Feminist Critique of Conciliation', in J. Brophy and C. Smart (eds.), *Women in Law: Explorations in Law, Family and Sexuality*, RKP, London.

Bowen, M.L. (1987), *The Legal Context of Family Conciliation: A Guide for Solicitors and the Divorce Court Welfare Service*, Further Education Unit, Teeside Polytechnic.

Bowers, J. (1988), 'Review Essay: *Discourse and Social Psychology* by J Potter & M Wetherell', *British Journal of Social Psychology*, vol. 27, pp. 185-192.

Bowman, P.J. (1993), 'The Impact of Economic Marginality Among African American Husbands and Fathers', in H. McAdoo, (ed), *Family Ethnicity*, Sage, London.

Bracher, M. (1993), *Lacan, Discourse and Social Change: A Psychoanalytic Cultural Criticism*, Cornell University Press, London.

Brannen, J. (1988), 'Research Note: The Study of Sensitive Subjects. Notes on Interviewing', *Sociological Review*, vol. 36, pp. 552-563.

Brannen, J. (1993), 'The Effects of Research on Participants: Findings From a Study of Mothers and Employment', *Sociological Review*, vol. 41, pp. 328-346.

British Psychological Society, (1989), Psychotherapy Section Newsletter, No.7 (December 1989).

Britton, B.K. and Pellegrini, A. (eds) (1990), *Narrative Thought and Narrative Language*, Lawrence Erlbaum, Hillsdale, NJ.

Brooks, P. (1994), *Psychoanalysis and Storytelling*, Blackwell, Oxford.

Brophy, J. (1985), 'Child Care and the Growth of Power', in J. Brophy and C. Smart (eds), *Women In Law*, RKP, London.

Brophy, J. (1989), 'Custody Law, Child Care and Inequality in Britain', in C. Smart and S. Sevenhuijsen (eds), *Child Custody and the Politics of Gender*, Routledge, London.

Brown, G. and Harris, T. (1978), *Social Origins of Depression*, Tavistock, London.

Brown, J. and Day-Sclater, S. (1999), 'Divorce: A Psychodynamic Perspective', in S. Day Sclater and C. Piper (eds), *Undercurrents of Divorce*, Ashgate, Aldershot.

Bruch, C.S. (1992), 'And How are the Children?' *Family and Conciliation Courts Review*, vol. 30, pp. 112-134.

Bruch, C. (1993), 'When to Use and When to Avoid Mediation: A Lawyer's Guide', *Family and Conciliation Courts Review*, vol. 31, pp. 101-107.

Bruner, J. (1986), *Actual Minds, Possible Worlds*, Harvard University Press, Cambridge, MA.

Bruner, J. (1987), 'Life as Narrative', *Social Research*, vol. 54, pp. 11-32.

Bruner, J. (1990), *Acts of Meaning*, Harvard University Press, Cambridge MA.

Bryan, P. (1992), 'Killing Us Softly: Divorce Mediation and the Politics of Power', *Buffalo Law Review*, vol. 40, pp. 441-523.

Bucher, C. (1990), *Three Models on a Rocking Horse: A Comparative Study in Narratology*, Narr, Tubingen.

Buehler, C. and Legg, B.H. (1993), 'Mothers' Receipt of Social Support and Their Psychological Well-Being Following Marital Separation', *Journal of Social and Personal Relations*, vol. 10, pp. 21-38.

Burck, C., Hildebrand, J. and Mann, J. (1996), 'Women's Tales: Systemic Groupwork With Mothers Post-Separation', *Journal of Family Therapy,* vol. 18, pp. 163-182.

Burman, E. (1994), *Deconstructing Developmental Psychology*, Routledge, London.

Burman, E. and Parker, I. (1993), 'Discourse Analysis: The Turn to the Text', in E. Burman and I. Parker (eds), *Discourse Analytic Research*, Routledge, London.

Burr, V. (1995), *An Introduction to Social Constructionism*, Routledge, London.

Bursik, K. (1991a), 'Adaptation to Divorce and Ego Development in Adult Women', *Journal of Personality and Social Psychology*, vol. 60, pp. 300-306.

Bursik, K. (1991b), 'Correlates of Women's Adjustment During the Separation and Divorce Process', *Journal of Divorce and Remarriage*, vol. 14, pp. 137-162.

Burton, S., Regan, L. and Kelly, L. (1988), *Supporting Women and Challenging Men: Lessons from the Domestic Violence Intervention Project*, The Policy Press, Bristol.

Butler, J. (1993), *Bodies That Matter: On the Discursive Limits of Sex*, Routledge, London.

Cantor, D.W. (1982), 'Divorce: Separation or Separation-Individualtion?', *American Journal of Psychoanalysis*, vol. 42, pp. 307-313.

Carbone, J. (1996), 'Feminism, Gender and the Consequences of Divorce', in M. Freeman (ed), *Divorce: Where Next?*, Dartmouth, Aldershot.

Carbonneau, T.E. (1986), 'A Consideration of Alternatives to Divorce Litigation', *University of Illinois Law Review*, vol. 4, pp. 1119-1192.

Carlson, R. (1988), 'Exemplary Lives: The Uses of Psychobiography for Theory Development', *Journal of Personality*, Vol 56, pp.105-138, Special Issue on Psychobiography and Life Narratives.

Cartwright, R. and Krantiz, H. (1991), 'REM Latency and the Recovery from Depression: Getting Over Divorce', *American Journal of Psychiatry*, vol. 148, pp. 1530-1535.

Chandler, J. (1991), *Women Without Husbands: An Exploration of the Margins of Marriage*, Macmillan, London.

Charon, R. (1986), 'To Render the Lives of Patients', *Literature and Medicine*, vol. 5, pp. 58-74.

Chase, S. (1995), 'Taking Narrative Seriously: Consequences for Theory and Method in Interview Studies', in R, Josselson and A. Lieblich (eds), *The Narratuive Study of Lives*, Vol. 3, Sage, London.

Chase, S.E. and Bell C.S. (1991), 'Interpreting the Complexity of Women's Subjectivity', in K. Rogers and E. McMahan (eds), *Interactive Oral Interviewing*. Erlbaum, Hillsdale, NJ.

Cherlin, A.J. (1992), *Marriage, Divorce, Remarriage*, (2nd edn), Harvard University Press, Cambridge, MA.

Chiriboga, D.A., Catron, L.S. and Associates (1991), *Divorce: Crisis, Challenge or Relief?*, New York University Press, New York.

Chodorow, N. (1978), *The Reproduction of Mothering: Psychoanalysis and the Sociology of Gender*, University of California Press, Berkeley, CA.

Christensen, A. and Shenk, J. (1991), 'Communication, Conflict and Psychological Distance in Non-Distressed, Clinical and Divorcing Couples', *Journal of Consulting and Clinical Psychology*, vol. 59, pp. 458-463.

Clark, J.A. and Mishler E.G. (1992), 'Attending to Patients' Stories: Reframing the Clinical Task', *Sociology of Health and Illness*, vol. 14, pp. 344-372.

Clegg, S.R. (1993), 'Narrative, Power and Social Theory', in D.K. Munby (ed), *Narrative and Social Control: Critical Perspectives, Annual Review of Communication Research*, vol. 21, pp.15-45, Sage, London.

Clifford, J. and Marcus G.E. (eds), (1986), *Writing Culture: The Poetics and Politics of Ethnography*, University of California Press, Berkeley, CA.

Clulow, C.F. (1990), 'Divorce as Bereavement: Similarities and Differences', *Family and Conciliation Courts Review*, vol. 28, pp. 19-22.

Clulow, C. (1991), 'Impasses of Divorce: Which Way Forward?', *Family and Conciliation Courts Review*, vol. 31, pp. 244-248.

Clulow, C. (1995), 'Psychological Processes in Divorce', notes from a lecture presented at the Tavistock Institute of Marital Studies (personal communication).

Clulow, C. and Mattinson, J. (1995), *Marriage Inside Out: Understanding Problems of Intimacy*, Penguin, Harmnodsworth.

Cockett, M. and Tripp, J. (1994), *The Exeter Family Study: Family Breakdown and its Impact on Children*, University of Exeter Press, Exeter.

Cohan, S. and Shires, L. (1988), *Telling Stories: A Theoretical Analysis of Narrative Fiction*, Routledge, London.

Cohen, O. (1995), 'Divorced Fathers Raise Their Children by Themselves', *Journal of Divorce and Remarriage*, vol. 23, pp. 55-73.

Cohen, O. (1996), 'The Personal Well-being of Single-Parent Family Heads Rearing their Children by Themselves: A Comparative Study', *Contemporary Family Therapy*, vol. 18, pp.129-146.

Cohen, O. and Savaya, R. (1997), ' "Broken Glass": The Divorced Woman in Moslem Arab Society in Israel', *Family Process*, vol. 36, pp. 225-245.

Cohler, B.J. (1982), 'Personal Narrative and Life Course', *Life-Span Development and Behaviour*, vol. 4, pp. 205-241.

Colburn, K., Lin, P.L. and Moore, M.C. (1992), 'Gender and the Divorce Experience', *Journal of Divorce and Remarriage*, vol. 17, pp. 87-108.

Collier, R. (1995), *Masculinity, Law and the Family*, Routledge, London.

Collier, R. (1999), 'From Women's Emancipation to Sex War? Heterosexuality and the Politics of Divorce', in S. Day Sclater and C. Piper (eds), *Undercurrents of Divorce*, Ashgate, Aldershot (in press).

Collins, P. (1997), 'Negotiating a Life', paper presented at the BSA Auto/biography Study Group Conference, Manchester.

Coogler, O.J. (1978), *Structured Mediation in Divorce Settlement*, Lexington Books, Lexington, MA.

Coontz, S. (1992), *The Way We Never Were: American Families and the Nostalgia Trap*, Basic Books, New York.

Cooper, A. (1999). 'With Justice in Mind', in M. King (ed), *Moral Agendas For Children's Welfare*, Routledge, London.

Coote, A., Harman, H. and Hewitt, H. (1990/1994), 'Changing Patterns of Family Life', in J. Eekelaar and M. Maclean (eds.), *A Reader on Family Law*, Oxford University Press, Oxford.

Corlyon, J. (1993), 'Violent Allegations', *Family Mediation*, vol. 3, pp. 14-15.

Cornell, D., Rosenfeld, M. and Carlson, D. (1992), *Deconstruction and the Possibility of Justice*, Routledge, London.

Corser, C. and Philip, A. (1978), 'Emotional Disturbance in Newly Registered General Practice Patients', *British Journal of Psychiatry*, vol. 132, pp. 172-176.

Cortazzi, M. (1993), *Narrative Analysis*, Falmer, London.

Coulter, J. (1979), *The Social Construction of Mind*, Macmillan, London.

Coulthard, M. (1977/1986), *An Introduction to Discourse Analysis*, Longman, London.

Cox, B., Blaxter, M., Buckle, A., Fenner, N., Golding, J., Gore, M., Huppert, F., Nickson, J., Roth, M., Stark, J., Wadsworth, M. and Wichelow, M. (1987), *The Health and Lifestyle Survey*, Health Promotion Trust, Cambridge.

Craib, I. (1994), *The Importance of Disappointment*, Routledge, London.

Craib, I. (1998), 'Thinking About Feeling', Paper presented at the Modern Feelings Symposium, University of East London.

Craig, J. (1997), 'Population Review', *Population Trends* 88 (Summer 1997), pp. 5-12.

Craig, Y. (1993), 'Learned Helplessness and Learned Resistance in Family Mediation and Conciliation', *Family Mediation*, vol. 3, pp. 17-18.

Davies, B. and Harre, R. (1990), 'Positioning: The Discursive Production of Selves', *Journal for the Theory of Social Behaviour*, vol. 20, pp. 43-63.

Davis, G. (1988), *Partisans and Mediators: The Resolution of Divorce Disputes*, Clarendon Press, Oxford.

Davis, G., Cretney, S. and Collins, J. (1994), *Simple Quarrels*, Clarendon Press, Oxford.

Davis, G. and Roberts, M. (1988), *Access to Agreement*, Open University Press, Milton Keynes.

Day Sclater, S. (1995a), 'The Limits of Mediation, *Family Law*, vol. 25, pp. 494-497.

Day Sclater, S. (1995b), 'Theory and Method for a Psychosocial Approach to Divorce', East London Papers, No. 2, University of East London.

Day Sclater, S. (1996a), 'Children and Divorce: An Overview of Research in Context', address delivered at the AGM of the Milton Keynes Family Mediation Service, November 1996.

Day Sclater, S. (1996b), 'Divorce Reform and the Reconstruction of Family', unpublished paper, Centre for Family Research, University of Cambridge.

Day Sclater, S. (1996c), 'Dilemmas in Feminist Responses to Law', unpublished paper, Centre for Family Research, University of Cambridge.

Day Sclater, S. (1997a), 'Narratives of Divorce', *Journal of Social Welfare and Family Law*, vol. 19, pp. 423-441.

Day Sclater, S. (1997b), 'Narrating Subjects-in-Culture: Rethinking Reflexivity', Paper presented to the Culture and Psychology Symposium, 5th European Congress on Psychology, Dublin, 1997.

Day Sclater, S. (1998a), 'Review of *Mediating and Negotiating Marital Conflicts* by D. Ellis and N. Stuckless', *International Journal of Law, Policy and the Family*, vol. 12, pp. 247-251.

Day Sclater, S. (1998b), 'Nina's Story: An Exploration into the Construction and Transformation of Subjectivities in Narrative Accounting', *Auto/biography*, vol. 6, pp. 67-77.

Day Sclater, S. (1998c), 'Creating the Self: Stories as Transitional Phenomena', *Auto/biography*, vol. 6, pp. 85-92.

Day Sclater, S. (1998d), 'Children and Divorce: Hidden Agendas?', paper presented at the Children and Social Exclusion Conference, Hull, March 1998.

Day Sclater, S. (1999a), 'The Bubble That Burst: Jane's Divorce Story', *Self, Agency and Society*, (forthcoming)

Day Sclater, S. (1999b). 'Experiences of Divorce', in S. Day Sclater and C. Piper (eds), *Undercurrents of Divorce*, Ashgate, Aldershot (in press).

Day Sclater, S. and Richards, M. (1995), 'How Adults Cope With Divorce: Strategies for Survival', *Family Law*, vol. 25, pp. 143-147.

Day Sclater, S., Bainham, A. and Richards, M. (1999), 'Introduction', in A. Bainham, S. Day Sclater and M. Richards (eds), *What is a Parent? A Socio-Legal Analysis*, Hart, Oxford (forthcoming).

Day Sclater, S. and Piper, C. (1999), 'The Family Law Act 1996 in Context', in S. Day Sclater and C. Piper (eds), *Undercurrents of Divorce*, Ashgate, Aldershot (in press).

Day Sclater, S. and Piper, C. (eds) (1999), *Undercurrents of Divorce*, Ashgate, Aldershot (in press).

Day Sclater, S. and Yates, C. (1999), 'The Psycho-Politics of Divorce', in A. Bainham, S. Day Sclater and M. Richards (eds), *What is a Parent? A Socio-Legal Analysis*, Hart, Oxford (forthcoming).

Dennis, N. and Erdos, G. (1992), *Families Without Fatherhood*, IEA Health and Welfare Unit, London.

Denny, J. (1997), 'Review of *The Divorce Mediation Handbook* by P. James', *Library Journal*, vol. 122, p. 105.

Denzin, N. (1989a), *Interpetive Biography*, Sage, London.

Denzin, N. (1989b), *The Research Act*, Prentice Hall, New Jersey.

Denzin, N. (1990), 'Harold and Agnes: a Feminist Narrative Undoing', *Sociological Theory*, vol. 8, pp. 198-216.

Denzin, N. (1992), *Symbolic Interactionism and Cultural Studies*, Blackwell, Oxford.

Denzin, N. and Lincoln, Y.S. (eds) (1994), *Handbook of Qualitative Research*, Sage, London.

D'Errico, M.G. and Elwork, A. (1991), 'Are Self-Determined Divorce and Child Custody Agreements Really Better?', *Family and Conciliation Courts Review*, vol. 29, pp. 104-113.

Derrida, J. (1978a), 'Structure, Sign and Play in the Discourse of the Human Sciences', reprinted in D. Lodge (ed) *Modern Criticism and Theory: A Reader*, (1988), Longman, London.

Derrida, J. (1978b), *Writing and Difference*, Routledge, London, (trans. A. Bass).

Derrida, J. (1980), 'The Law of Genre', in W.J.T. Mitchell (ed), *On Narrative*, University of Chicago Press, London.

Derrida, J. (1992), *Acts of Literature*, (Trans. A. Attridge), Routledge, London.

Diduck, A. (1999), 'Dividing the Family Assets', in S. Day Sclater and C. Piper (eds), *Undercurrents of Divorce*, Ashgate, Aldershot (in press).

Diedrick, P. (1991), 'Gender Differences in Divorce Adjustment', *Journal of Divorce and Remarriage*, vol. 14, pp. 33-45.

van Dijk, T.A. (1985), *Handbook of Discourse Analysis*, Academic Press, London.

Dillon, P. A. and Emery, R. E. (1996), 'Divorce Mediation and the Resolution of Child Custody Disputes: Long Term Effects', *American Journal of Orthopsychiatry*, vol. 66, pp. 131-140.

Dinerstein, R.D. (1992), 'A Meditation on the Theories of Practice', *Hastings Law Journal*, vol. 43, pp. 971-989.

Dingwall, R. (1988), 'Empowerment or Enforcement: Some Questions About Power and Control in Divorce Mediation', in R. Dingwall and J. Eekelaar (eds), *Divorce Mediation and the Legal Process*, Clarendon Press, Oxford.

Dingwall, R. and Eekelaar, J. (1986), 'Judgements of Solomon: Psychology and Family Law', in M. Richards and P. Light (eds), *Children of Social Worlds*, Polity, Cambridge.

Dingwall, R. and Eekelaar, J. (eds) (1988), *Divorce Mediation and the Legal Process*, Clarendon Press, Oxford.

Dingwall, R. and Greatbatch, D. (1991), 'Behind Closed Doors: A Preliminary Report on Mediator/Client Interaction in England', *Family and Conciliation Courts Review*, vo. 29, pp. 291-303.

198   *Divorce: A Psychosocial Study*

Dingwall, R. and Greatbatch, D. (1993), 'Who is in Charge? Rhetoric and Evidence in the Study of Mediation', *Journal of Social Welfare and Family Law*, vol. 15, pp. 367-385.

Dingwall, R. and Greatbatch, D. (1994), 'Divorce Mediation: The Virtues of Formality?', in J. Eekelaar and M. Maclean (eds), *A Reader on Family Law*, Oxford University Press, Oxford.

Dingwall, R. and Greatbatch, D. (1995), 'Family Mediation Researchers and Practitioners in the Shadow of the Green Paper: A Rejoinder to Marian Roberts', *Journal of Social Welfare and Family Law*, vol. 17, pp. 199-206.

Donzelot, J. (1980), *The Policing of Families*, Huchinson, London.

Drabble, M. and Stringer, J. (eds) (1987), *The Concise Oxford Companion to English Literature*, Oxford University Press, Oxford.

Duffy, M.E. (1995), 'Factors Influencing the Health Behaviours of Divorced Women with Children', *Journal of Divorce and Remarriage*, vol. 22, pp. 1-12.

Duncan, S. (1994), 'Disrupting the Surface of Order and Innocence: Towards a Theory of Sexuality and the Law', *Feminist Legal Studies*, vol. 2, pp. 3-28.

Duncan-Jones, P. (1979), 'Validity and the Uses of the GHQ', *British Journal of Psychiatry*, vol. 135, p. 382.

Dunne, J. and Hedrick, M. (1994), 'The Parental Alienation Syndrome: An Analysis of 16 Selected Cases', *Journal of Divorce and Remarriage*, vol. 21, pp. 21-38.

Duryee, M.A. (1992), 'Mandatory Mediation: Myth and Reality', *Family and Conciliation Courts Review*, vol. 30, pp. 507-518.

Duryee, M.A. (1995), 'Guidelines for Family Court Services Intervention When There Are Allegations of Domestic Violence', *Family and Conciliation Courts Review*, vol. 33, pp. 79-86.

Edwards, D. and Potter, J. (1992), *Discursive Psychology*, Sage, London.

Eekelaar, J. (1991), 'Parental Responsibility: State of Nature or Nature of the State?', *Journal of Social Welfare and Family Law*, vol. 13, pp. 37-50.

Eekelaar, J. and Dingwall, R. (1988), 'The Development of Conciliation in England', in R. Dingwall and J. Eekelaar (eds), *Divorce Mediation and the Legal Process*, Clarendon Press, Oxford.

Elliott, B.J. (1993), 'Divorce and Well-being: Causes and Effects?', in *Targeting Health Promotion*, Health Promotion Trust, London.

Elliott, F.R. (1986), *The Family: Change or Continuity?*, Macmillan, Basingstoke.

Elliott, F.R. (1996), *Gender, Family and Society*, Macmillan, Basingstoke.

Elliott, J., Richards, M. and Warwick, H. (1992), 'The Consequences of Divorce for the Health and Well-being of Adults and Children', Final Report for the Health Promotion Research Trust, London.

Ellis, C. and Flaherty, M.J. (eds), (1992), *Investigating Subjectivity: Research on Lived Experience*, Sage, London.

Ellis, D. and Stuckless, N. (1996), *Mediating and Negotiating Marital Conflicts*, Sage, London.

Ellman, M. (ed), (1994), *Psychoanalytic Literary Criticism*, Longman, London.

Elwork, A. (1992), 'Psycholegal Treatment and Intervention: The Next Challenge', *Law and Human Behaviour*, vol. 16, pp. 175-183.

Emery, R.E. and Dillon, P. (1994), 'Conceptualising the Divorce Process: Renegotiating Boundaries of Intimacy and Power in the Divorced Family System', *Family Relations*, vol. 43, pp.374-379.

Emery, R.E., Matthews, S.G. and Kitzmann, K.M. (1994), 'Child Custody Mediation and Litigation: Parents' Satisfaction and Functioning One-Year After Settlement', *Journal of Consulting and Clinical Psychology*, vol. 62, pp. 124-129.

Fairclough, N. (1989), *Language and Power*, Longman, London.

Fairclough, N. (1992), *Discourse and Social Change*, Polity, Cambridge.

Farmer, R. and Harvey, P. (1975), 'Minor Psychiatric Disturbance in Young Adults: The Use of the General Health Questionnaire in the Estimation of the Prevalence of Non-Psychotic Disturbance in Different Groups', *Social Science and Medicine*, vol. 9, pp. 467-474.

Felstiner, W.L.F. and Sarat, A. (1988), 'Negotiation Between Lawyer and Client in an American Divorce', in R. Dingwall and J. Eekelaar (eds), *Divorce Mediation and the Legal Process*, Clarendon Press, Oxford.

Fernquist, R.M. and Cutright, P. (1998), 'Societal Integration and Age-Standardized Suicide Rates in 21 Developed Countries, 1955-1989', *Social Science Research*, vol. 27, issue 2, pp.109-127.

Finch, J. and Summerfield, P. (1991), 'Social Reconstruction and the Emergence of the Companionate Marriage, 1945-59', in D. Clark (ed), *Marriage, Domestic Life and Social Change*, Routledge, London.

Fine, M.A., McKenry, P.C. and Chung, H. (1992), 'Postdivorce Adjustment of Black and White Single Parents', *Journal of Divorce and Remarriage*, vol. 17, pp. 121-134.

Fineman, M.A. (1991), *The Illusion of Equality: The Rhetoric and Reality of Divorce Reform*, University of Chicago Press, Chicago.

Fineman, M.A. (1995), *The Neutered Mother, The Sexual Family and Other Twentieth Century Tragedies*, Routledge, London.

Fineman, M.A. and Karpin, I. (eds) (1995), *Mothers in Law: Feminist Theory and the Legal Regulation of Motherhood*, Columbia University Press, New York.

Finer Report (1974), *Report of the Committee on One Parent Families*, Cmnd 5629, HMSO, London.

Finlay-Jones, R.A. and Burvill, P.W. (1977), 'The Prevalence of Minor Psychiatric Morbidity in the Community', *Psychological Medicine*, vol. 7, pp. 475-489.

Fisher, T. (ed.) (1990/1992), *Family Conciliation Within the UK: Policy and Practice*, Jordans, Bristol.

Fisher, T. (1993), 'The Incidence of Domestic Violence in a Family Mediation Service', *Family Mediation*, vol. 3, p. 16.

Fisher, T. (1994), 'Dr Joan B. Kelly's Visit: November 93', *Family Mediation*, vol. 3, pp.13-15.

Fisher, W. (1985), 'The Narrative Paradigm: An Elaboration', *Communication Monoraphs*, vol. 52, pp.347-367.

Folberg, J. and Milne, A. (eds) (1988), *Divorce Mediation: Theory and Practice*, Guilford, New York.

Folkenflik, R. (ed), (1993), *The Culture of Autobiography: Constructions and Self Representation*, Stanford University Press.

Fonow, M.M. and Cook, J.A. (eds) (1991), *Beyond Methodology: Feminist Scholarship as Lived Research*, Indiana University Press, Bloomington.

Forster, J. (1982), *Divorce Conciliation: A Study of Services in England and Abroad with Implications for Scotland*, Scottish Council for Single Parents, Edinburgh.

Foucault, M. (1972/1974), *The Archaeology of Knowledge*, Tavistock, London, (trans. A.M. Sheridan Smith).

Fowler, R. (1981), *Literature as Social Discourse: The Practice of Linguistic Criticism*, Batsford, London.

Fowler, R., Hodge, R., Kress, G. and Trew, T. (eds) (1979), *Language and Control*, RKP, London.

Fox, D. and Prilleltensky, I. (eds) (1997), *Critical Psychology: An Introduction*, Sage, London.

Fox Harding, L. (1996), *Family, State and Social Policy*, Macmillan, Basingstoke.

Freedman, S. and Taylor, C. (1983), *Roland Barthes: A Bibliographical Readers' Guide*, Garland, New York.

Freeman, M. (1993), *Rewriting the Self: History, Memory, Narrative*, Routledge, London.

Freeman, M.D.A. (ed) (1984), *The State, Law and the Family*, Sweet and Maxwell/Tavistock, London.

Freeman, M.D.A. (ed) (1996), *Divorce: Where Next?* Dartmouth, Aldershot.

Friedman, G.J. (1993), *A Guide to Divorce Mediation: How to Reach a Fair, Legal Settlement at a Fraction of the Cost*, Workman Publishing, New York.

Funkenstein, A. (1993), 'The Incomprehensible Catastrophe: Memory and Narrative', in R. Josselson and A. Lieblich (eds), (1993), *The Narrative Study of Lives*, vol. 1, Sage, London.

Furstenberg, F.F. and Cherlin, A.J. (1991), *Divided Families*, Harvard University Press, Cambridge, MA.

Galanter, M. and Cahill, M. (1994), ' "Most Cases Settle": Judicial Promotion and Regulation of Settlements', *Stanford Law Review*, vol. 46, pp. 1339-1391.

Gale, D. (1994), 'The Impact of Culture on the Work of Family Mediators', *Family Mediation*, vol. 4, p. 4.

Gander, A.M. (1991), 'After the Divorce: Familial Factors that Predict Well-Being for Older and Younger Persons', *Journal of Divorce and Remarriage*, vol. 15, pp. 175-192.

Garcia, A. (1995), 'The Problematics of Representation in Community Mediation Hearings: Implications for Mediation Practice', *Journal of Sociology and Social Welfare*, vol. 22, pp. 23-46.

Garvin, V., Kalter, N. and Hansell, J. (1993), 'Divorced Women: Individual Differences in Stressors, Mediating Factors, and Adjustment Outcome', *American Journal of Orthopsychiatry*, vol. 63, pp. 232-240.

Garvin, V., Kalter, N. and Hansell, J. (1993), 'Divorced Women: Factors Contributing to Resiliency and Vulnerability', *Journal of Divorce and Remarriage*, vol. 21, pp. 21-39.

Gately, D.W. and Schwebel, A.I. (1991), 'The Challenge Model of Children's Adjustment to Parental Divorce: Explaining Favourable Post-Divorce Outcomes in Children', *Journal of Family Psychology*, vol. 5, pp. 60-81.

Gatens, M. (1996), *Imaginary Bodies: Ethics, Power and Corporeality*, Routledge, London.

Gavey, N. (1989), 'Feminist Poststructuralism and Discourse Analysis: Contributions to Feminist Psychology', *Psychology of Women Quarterly*, vol. 13, pp. 459-475.

Gee, J.P. (1986), 'Units in the Production of Narrative Discourse', *Discourse Processes*, vol. 9, pp. 391-422.

Gee, J.P. (1991), 'A Linguistic Approach to Narrative', *Journal of Narrative and Life History*, vol. 1, pp. 15-39.

Geiger, S.N. (1986), 'Women's Life Histories: Method and Content', *Signs*, vol. 11, pp. 334-351.

Gelles, R. (1995), *Contemporary Families: A Sociological View*, Sage, London.

Gergen, K. (1993), *Refiguring Self and Psychology*, Dartmouth, Aldershot.

Gergen, K. and Gergen, M. (1983), 'Narratives of the Self', in T. Sarbin and K. Sheibe (eds), *Studies in Social Identity*, Praeger, New York.

Gergen, K and Gergen, M. (1984), 'The Social Construction of Narrative Accounts', in K. Gergen and M. Gergen (eds), *Historical Social Psychology*, Erlbaum, Hillside N.J.

Gergen, K. and Gergen, M. (1986), 'Narrative Form and the Construction of Psychological Science', in T. Sarbin (ed), *Narrative Psychology: The Storied Nature of Human Conduct*, Praeger, New York.

Gergen, K. and Gergen, M.(1993), 'Narratives of the Gendered Body in Popular Autobiography', in R. Josselson and A. Lieblich (eds), *The Narrative Study of Lives*, vol 1, Sage, London.

Gergen, M. (1994), 'The Social Construction of Personal Histories: Gendered Lives in Popular Autobiographies', in T. Sarbin and J. Kitsuse (eds), *Constructing the Social*, Sage, London.

Giddens, A. (1991), *Modernity and Self Identity*, Polity, Cambridge.

Giddens, A. (1992), *The Transformation of Intimacy*, Polity, Cambridge.

Giddens, A. (1996) *In Defence of Sociology*, Polity, Cambridge.

Gigy, L. and Kelly, J.B. (1992), 'Reasons for Divorce: Perspectives on Divorcing Men and Women', *Journal of Divorce and Remarriage*, vol. 18, pp. 169-187.

Gleason, F.S. (1994), 'Review of G. Kitson and W. Holmes *Portrait of Divorce: Adjustment to Marital Breakdown*', *Family and Conciliation Courts Review*, vol. 32, pp. 249-250.

Globe, R., Gowers, J., Morgan, D. and Kline, P. (1979), 'Artificial Pacemaker Patients: Treatment Outcome and Goldberg's General Health Questionnaire', *Journal of Psychosomatic Research*, vol. 23, pp. 175-179.

Goldberg, D. (1978), *Manual of the General Health Questionnaire*, NFER Nelson, Windsor.

Goldberg, D. (1985), 'Identifying Psychiatric Illness Among General Medical Patients', *British Medical Journal*, vol. 291, pp. 161-163.

Goldberg, D. (1986), 'Use of the General Health Questionnaire in Clinical Work', *British Medical Journal*, vol. 293, pp. 1188-1189.

Goldberg, D. and Blackwell, B. (1970), 'Psychiatric Illness in General Practice: A Detailed Study Using a New Method of Case Investigation', *British Medical Journal*, vol. 2, pp. 439-443.

Goldberg, D. and Hillier, V. (1979), 'A Scaled Version of the General Health Questionnaire', *Psychological Medicine*, vol. 9, pp. 139-145.

Goldberg, D. and Williams, P. (1988), *A User's Guide to the General Health Questionnaire*, NFER Nelson, The Basingstoke Press, Basingstoke.

Goldscheider, F.K. (1994), 'Divorce and Remarriage: Effects on the Elderly Population', *Review in Clinical Gerenotology*, vol. 4, pp. 253-259.

Goode, W.J. (1993), *World Changes in Divorce Patterns*, Yale University Press, London.

Goodman, C.C. (1993), 'Divorce After Long-term Marriages: Former Spouse Relationships', *Journal of Divorce and Remarriage*, vol. 20, pp. 43-61.

Gordon, C. (ed) (1980), *Michel Foucault: Power/Knowledge, Selected Interviews and Other Writings 1972-1977 by Michel Foucault*, Harvester, Brighton.

Gorelick, S. (1991), 'Contradictions of Feminist Methodology',*Gender & Society*, vol. 5, pp. 459-477.

Gottman, J.M. (1998), 'Psychology and the Study of Marital Processes', *Annual Review of Psychology*, vol. 49, pp.169-197.

Gove, W.R. and Sin, H.C. (1989), 'The Psychological Well-Being of Divorced and Widowed Men and Women', *Journal of Family Issues*, vol. 10, pp. 122-144.

Granvold, D.K. (1994), 'Cognitive-Behavioral Divorce Therapy', in D.K. Granvold, (ed), *Cognitive and Behavioral Treatment: Methods and Applications*, Brooks/Cole Publishing Co: Pacific Grove, CA.

Gray, C.A. and Shields, J.J. (1992), 'The Development of an Instrument to Measure the Psychological Response to Separation and Divorce', *Journal of Divorce and Remarriage*, vol. 17, pp. 43-56.

Gray, J.D. and Silver, R.C. (1990), 'Opposite Sides of the Same Coin: Former Spouses' Divergent Perspectives in Coping with Divorce', *Journal of Personality and Social Psychology*, vol. 59, pp. 1180-1191.

Greatbatch, D. and Dingwall, R. (1997), 'Argumentative Talk in Divorce Mediation Sessions', *American Sociological Review*, vol. 62, pp. 151-170.

Green, D. (1989), 'Tales of Discovery: Narrative Approaches to Training Clinical Psychologists', in *British Psychological Society, Psychotherapy Section Newsletter*, No 7, December 1989, pp.28-36.

Greenwood, J. (1992), 'Discursive Practices and Psychological Science', *American Behavioural Science*, vol. 36, pp. 114-123.

Grillo, T. (1991), 'The Mediation Alternative: Process Dangers for Women', *Yale Law Journal*, vol. 100, pp. 1545-1610.

Grosz, E. (1994), *Volatile Bodies: Towards a Corporeal Feminism*, Routledge, London.

Guttmann, J. (1993), *Divorce in Psychosocial Perspective: Theory and Research*, Lawrence Erlbaum, Hillsdale, NJ.

Haberland, K.F. (1992), 'Narrative Thought and Narrative Language', *Contemporary Psychology*, vol. 37, pp. 324-325.

Haffey, M. and Cohen, P.M. (1992), 'Treatment Issues for Divorcing Women', *Families in Society*, vol. 73, pp. 142-148.

Hale, The Right Hon. Mrs Justice (1997), *Public Lives and Private Duties: What is Family Law For?*, 8th ESRC Annual Lecture.

Hall, L. (1987), 'Review of *The Process of Divorce*, by K. Kressel, and *Divorce Mediation*, by J.M. Haynes, and *Family Mediation Practice*, by J.A. Lemmon', *Negotiation Journal*, vol. 3, pp. 147-154.

Hammen, C. (1992), 'Life Events and Despression: The Plot Thickens', *American Journal of Comparative Psychiatry*, vol. 20, pp. 179-193.

Hammond, R.J. and Muller, G. O. (1992), 'The Late-Life Divorced: Another Look', *Journal of Divorce and Remarriage*, vol. 17, pp. 135-150.

Harding, S. (1989), 'Interim Report: The Changing Family', *British Social Attitudes,* vol. 6, pp. 143-155.

Harne, L. and Radford, J. (1994), 'Reinstating Patriarchy: The Politics of the Family and the New Legislation', in A. Mullender and R. Morley (eds), *Children Living with Domestic Violence*, Whiting and Birch, London.

Haskey, J. (1994), 'Stepfamilies and Stepchildren in Great Britain', *Population Trends* 76 (Summer 1994), pp. 17-28.

Haskey, J. (1995), 'Trends in Marriage and Cohabitation: The Decline in Marriage and the Changing Pattern of Living in Partnerships', *Population Trends* 80 (Summer 1995), pp. 5-15.

Haskey, J. (1996a), 'The Proportion of Married Couples who Divorce: Past Patterns and Current Prospects', *Population Trends* 83 (Spring 1996), pp. 25-36.

Haskey, J. (1996b), 'Divorce and Children: Fact Proven and Interval Between Petition and Decree', *Population Trends* 84 (Summer 1996), pp. 28-32.

Haskey, J. (1996c), 'Population Review: Families and Households in Great Britain', *Population Trends* 85 (Autumn 1996), pp. 7-24.

Haskey, J. (1997), 'Spouses with Identical Residential Addresses Before Marriage: An Indicator of Pre-Marital Cohabitation', *Population Trends* 89 (Autumn 1997), pp. 13-23.

Hauser-Dann, J. (1988), 'Divorce Mediation: A Growing Field?', *Arbitration Journal*, vol. 43, pp. 15-22.

Haynes, J. (1981), *Divorce Mediation: A Practical Guide for Therapists and Counselors*, Springer, New York.

Haynes, J. (1988), 'Power Balancing', in J. Folberg and A. Milne (eds), *Divorce Mediation: Theory and Practice*, Guilford Press, London.

Haynes, J. (1993), *Alternative Dispute Resolution: The Fundamentals of Family Mediation*, Old Bailey Press, Kent.

Heath, S. and Dale, A. (1994), 'Household and Family Formation in Great Britain: The Ethnic Dimension', *Population Trends* 77 (Autumn 1994), pp. 5-13.

Helm, B., Boyd, L.W. and Longwill, C.K. (1992), 'Professional Interdependence in Divorce Practices: The Psychotherapist and the Mediator', *Family and Conciliation Courts Review*, vol. 30, pp. 385-396.

Hemstrom, O. (1996), 'Is Marriage Dissolution Linked to Differences in Mortality Risks for Men and Women?' *Journal of Marriage and the Family*, vol. 58, pp. 366-378.

Henriques, J., Hollway, W., Urwin, C., Venn, C. and Walkerdine, V. (1998), *Changing the Subject: Psychology, Social Regulation and Subjectivity*, 2nd edn, Routledge, London (1st edn 1984, Methuen).

Herman, M.S. (1982), 'Review of *Divorce Mediation: A Rational Alternative to the Adversarial System*, by H.H. Irving and M. Benjamin, and *Divorce Mediation: A Practical Guide for Therapists and Counsellors*, by J.M. Haynes, *Journal of Marriage and the Family*, vol. 44, pp. 505-506.

Hermans, H.J.M. and Hermans-Jansen, E. (1995), *Self-Narratives: The Construction of Meaning in Psychotherapy*, Guilford Press, New York.

Hester, M. and Pearson, C. (1993), 'Domestic Violence, Mediation and Child Contact Arrangements: Issues from Current Research', *Family Mediation*, vol. 3, pp. 3-6.

Hildago, P. (1992), 'Are You Writing Fact or Fiction?', in T. Iles (ed), *All Sides of the Subject: Women and Biography*, Teachers College Press, Columbia University, New York.

Hinshelwood, R.D. (1991), *A Dictionary of Kleinian Thought*, Free Association Books, London.

Hochschild, A. (1989), *The Second Shift*, Piatkus, London, U.K.

Hoggett, B. (1992), 'Ten Years of Family Law Reform', *Newsletter of the Socio-Legal Studies Association*, Winter 1992, pp. 2-3.

Holland, T.P. and Kilpatrick, A.C. (1993), 'Using Narrative Techniques to Enhance Multicultural Practice', *Journal of Social Work Education*, vol. 29, pp. 302-308.

Hollway, W. (1989), *Subjectivity and Method in Psychology*, Sage, London.

Hollway, W. and Jefferson, T. (1997), 'Eliciting Narrative Through the In-Depth Interview', *Qualitative Inquiry*, vol. 3, pp.53-70.

Hooper, C.A. (1994), 'Do Families Need Fathers? The Impact of Divorce on Children', in A. Mullender and R. Morley (eds), *Children Living with Domestic Violence*, Whiting and Birch, London.

Horton, M. (1996), *Family Homes and Domestic Violence: The New Legislation*, FT Law and Tax, London.

Horwitz, A.V., White, H.R. and Howell-White, S. (1996), 'The Use of Multiple Outcomes in Stress Research: A Case Study of Gender Differences in Responses to Marital Dissolution', *Journal of Health and Social Behaviour*, vol. 37, pp. 278-291.

Hu, Y. and Goldman, N. (1990), 'Mortality Differentials by Marital Status: An International Comparison', *Demography*, vol. 27, pp. 233-268.

Hughes, R., Good, E.S. and Candell, K. (1993), 'A Longitudinal Study of the Effects of Social Support on the Psychological Adjustment of Divorced Mothers', *Journal of Divorce and Remarriage*, vol. 19, pp. 37-56.

Hutter, M. (ed) (1991), *The Family Experience: A Reader in Cultural Diversity*, Macmillan, New York.

Ibanez, T. and Iniguez, L. (eds) (1997), *Critical Social Psychology*, Sage, London.

Iles, T. (ed) (1992), *All Sides of the Subject: Women and Biography*, Teachers College Press, University of Columbia, New York.

Ingleby, D. (1986), 'Development in Social Context', in M. Richards and P. Light (eds), *Children of Social Worlds*, Polity, Cambridge.

Ingleby, R. (1988), 'The Solicitor as Intermediary', in R. Dingwall and J. Eekelaar (eds), *Divorce Mediation and the Legal Process*, Clarendon Press, Oxford.

Ingleby, R. (1992), *Solicitors and Divorce*, Clarendon Press, Oxford.

Irving, H.H. and Benjamin, M. (1981), *Divorce Mediation: A Rational Alternatiuve to the Adversarial System*, Universe Books, New York.

Irving, H.H. and Benjamin, M. (1987), *Family Mediation: Theory and Practice of Dispute Resolution*, Carswell, Toronto.

Irving, H.H. and Benjamin, M. (1995), *Family Mediation: Contemporary Issues*, Sage, London.

Jackson, B. (1990), 'Narrative Theories and Legal Discourse', in C. Nash (ed), *Narrative In Culture: The Uses of Storytelling in the Sciences, Philosophy and Literature*, Routledge, London.

Jackson, B. (1995), *Making Sense in Law*, Deborah Charles Publications, Liverpool.

Jackson, B. (1996), *Making Sense in Jurisprudence*, Deborah Charles Publications, Liverpool.

Jackson, E. (1993), 'Contradictions and Coherence in Feminist Responses to Law', *Journal of Law and Society*, vol. 20, pp. 398-407.

James, A. and Richards, M. (1999), 'Sociological Perspectives, Family Policy, Family Law and Children: Adult Thinking and Sociological Tinkering', in *Journal of Social Welfare and Family Law,* (forthcoming).

Johnston, J. (1993), 'Gender, Violent Conflict and Mediation', *Family Mediation*, vol. 3, pp. 9-13.

Johnston, J. and Campbell, L. (1988), *Impasses of Divorce: The Dynamics and Resolution of Family Conflict*, Free Press, New York.

Josselson, R. (1995), 'Imagining the Real: Empathy, Narrative and the Dialogic Self', in R. Josselson and A. Lieblich (eds), *The Narrative Study of Lives*, vol. 3, Sage, London.

Josselson, R and Lieblich, A. (eds), (1993), *The Narrative Study of Lives*, vol. 1, Sage, London.

Kaganas, F. (1999), 'Contact, Conflict and Risk', in S. Day Sclater and C. Piper (eds), *Undercurrents of Divorce*, Ashgate, Aldershot (in press).

Kaganas, F. and Piper, C. (1993), 'Towards a Definition of Abuse', *Family Mediation*, vol. 3, pp. 7-8.

Kaganas, F. and Piper C. (1994a), 'The Divorce Consultation Paper and Domestic Violence', *Family Law*, vol. 24, pp. 143-145.

Kaganas, F. and Piper, C. (1994b), 'Domestic Violence and Divorce Mediation', *Journal of Social Welfare and Family Law*, vol. 16, pp. 265-278.

Kaganas, F. and Piper, C. (1999), 'Divorce and Domestic Violence', in S. Day Sclater and C. Piper (eds), *Undercurrents of Divorce*, Ashgate, Aldershot (in press).

Kahn, S. (1990), *The Ex-Wife Syndrome: Cutting the Cord and Breaking Free After Marriage Ends*, Edbury Press, London.

Kaplan, E. A. (1983), *Women and Film*, Methuen, London.

Kaslow, F.W. (1988), 'The Psychological Dimension of Divorce Mediation', in J. Folberg and A, Milne (eds), *Divorce Mediation: Theory and Practice*, Guilford, New York.

Keitner, G.I. and Muller, I.W. (1990), 'Family Functioning and Depression: An Overview', *American Journal of Psychiatry*, vol. 147, pp. 1128-1137.

Kelly, J. (1980), 'Divorce: The Adult Expperience', in B. Wolman and G. Stricker (eds), *Handbook of Developmental Psychology*, Prentice Hall, New Jersey.

Kelly, J., Gigy, L. and Hausman, S. (1988), 'Mediated and Adversarial Divorce: Initial Findings from a Longitudinal Study', in J. Folberg and A. Milne (eds), *Divorce Mediation: Theory and Practice*, Guilford, New York.

Kelly, J. (1991), 'Mediated and Adversarial Divorce Resolution Processes: A Comparison of Post-Divorce Outcomes', *Family Law*, vol. 21, pp. 382-388.

Kemper, T.D. (ed) (1990), *Research Agendas in the Sociology of Emotions*, State University of New York Press, New York.

Kerby, A.P. (1991), *Narrative and the Self*, Indiana University Press, Bloomington, Illinois.

Kiernan, K. (1992), 'Men and Women at Work and at Home', *British Social Attitudes*, vol. 9, pp. 89-111.

Kiernan, K. and Wicks, M. (1990), *Family Change and Future Policy*, Family Policy Studies Centre, London.

Kincaid, S.B. and Caldwell, R.A. (1995), 'Marital Separation: Causes, Coping and Consequences', *Journal of Divorce and Remarriage*, vol. 22, pp. 109-128.

King, M. (1991), 'Child Welfare Within Law: The Emergence of a Hybrid Discourse', *Journal of Law and Society*, vol. 18, pp. 303-322.

King, M. and Piper, C. (1995), *How the Law Thinks About Children*, Arena, Aldershot.

Kitson, G.C. and Morgan, L.A. (1990), 'The Multiple Consequences of Divorce: A Decade Review', *Journal of Marriage and the Family*, vol. 52, pp. 913-924.

Kitson, G.C. and Morgan, L.A. (1991), 'The Multiple Consequences of Divorce', in A. Booth (ed), *Contemporary Families: Looking Forward, Looking Back*, National Council on Family Relations, Minneapolis.

Kitson, G.C. (with Holmes, W.M.) (1992), *Portrait of Divorce: Adjustment to Marital Breakdown*, Guilford, New York.

Klein, M. (1946), 'Notes on Some Schizoid Mechanisms', *International Journal of Psychoanalysis*, vol. 27, pp. 99-110.

Koopman, E.J., Hunt, E.J. and Stafford, V. (1984), 'Child-Related Agreements in Mediated and Non-Mediated Divorce Settlements: A Preliminary Examination and Discussion of Implications', *Conciliation Courts Review*, vol. 22, pp. 19-25.

Kressel, K. (1985), *The Process of Divorce*, Basic Books, New York.

Kressel, K. (1997), 'Practice-Relevant Research in Mediation: Toward a Reflective Research Paradigm', *Negotiation Journal*, vol. 13, pp. 143-160.

Kressel, K., Fronter, E.A., Forlenza, S., Butler, F. and Fish, L. (1994), 'The Settlement-Orientation vs. the Problem-Solving Style in Custody Mediation', *Journal of Social Issues*, vol. 50, pp. 67-84.

Kroger, J. (1993), 'Identity and Context', in R. Josselson and A. Lieblich (eds), *The Narrative Study of Lives*, Vol. 1, Sage, London.

Kruk, E. (1992), 'Psychological and Structural Factors Contribution to the Disengagement of Non-Custodial Fathers after Divorce', *Family and Conciliation Courts Review*, vol. 30, pp. 81-107.

Kruk, E. (1993), 'Promoting Co-operative Parenting After Separation: A Therapeutic/Interventionist Model of Family Mediation', *Journal of Family Therapy*, vol. 15, pp. 235-261.

Kumar, R. and Robson, K.M. (1984), 'A Prospective Study of Emotional Disorders in Childbearing Women', *British Journal of Psychiatry*, vol. 144, pp. 35-47.

Kurdek, L.A. (1991), 'The Relations Between Reported Well-Being and Divorce History, Availability of a Proximate Adult, and Gender', *Journal of Marriage and the Family*, vol. 53, pp. 71-78.

Labov, W. (1972), *Language in the Inner City*, University of Pennsylvania Press, Philadelphia.

Labov, W. (1982), 'Speech Actions and Reactions in Personal Narrative', in D. Tannen (ed), *Analysing Discourse: Text and Talk*, Georgetown University Press, Washington, D C.

Lacan, J. (1957/1966), 'The Insistence of the Letter in the Unconscious', reprinted in D. Lodge (ed), *Modern Criticism and Theory: A Reader*, Longman, London, (1988).

Lacan, J. (1966/1977), *Ecrits: A Selection*, Routledge, London, (trans. A. Sheridan).

Lacey, N. (1998), *Unspeakable Subjects: Feminist Essays in Legal and Social Theory*, Hart, Oxford.

Laclau, E. and Mouffe, C. (1985), *Hegemony and Socialist Strategy: Towards a Radical Democratic Politics,* Verso, London.

Laird, J. (1988), 'Women and Stories: Restorying Women's Self Constructions', in M. McGoldrick, C. Anderson and F. Walsh (eds), *Women in Families: A Framework for Family Therapy*, Norton, New York.

Lamb, M.E. (1996), 'Review of *Fatherless America: Confronting Our Most Urgent Social Problem* by D. Blankenhorn', *Journal of Marriage and the Family*, vol. 58, pp. 526-527.

Lamb, M.E. and Sagi, A. (eds), (1983), *Fatherhood and Family Policy*, Lawrence Erlbaum, Hillsdale, New Jersey.

Landau, B. (1995), 'The Toronto Forum on Women Abuse: The Process and the Outcome', *Family and Conciliation Courts Review*, vol. 33, pp. 63-78.

Langellier, K.M. and Peterson, E.E. (1993), 'Family Storytelling as a Strategy of Social Control', in D.K. Munby (ed), *Narrative and Social Control: Critical Perspectives*, *Annual Review of Communication Research*, vol. 21, pp.49-76, Sage, London.

Laplanche, J. and Pontalis, J.B. (1988), *The Language of Psychoanalysis*, Karnac, London.

Lapsley, R. and Westlake, M. (1988), *Film Theory: An Introduction*, Manchester University Press, Manchester.

Lasch, C. (1979), *The Culture of Narcissism*, Norton, New York.

Lasch, C. (1980), 'Life in the Therapeutic State', *The New York Review*, 12 June, pp. 24-32.

Law Commission (1988), *Facing the Future: A Discussion Paper on the Grounds for Divorce*, Law Com, No. 170, HMSO, London.

Law Commission (1990), *Family Law: The Ground for Divorce*, Law Com, No. 192, HMSO, London.

Lee, C.M., Picard, M. and Blain, M.D. (1994), 'A Methodological and Substantive Review of Intervention Outcome Studies for Families Undergoing Divorce', *Journal of Family Psychology*, vol. 8, pp. 3-15.

Leenaars, A.A., Yang, B.J. and Lester, D. (1993), 'The Effect of Domestic and Economic Stress on Suicide Rates in Canada and the USA', *Journal of Clinical Psychology*, vol. 49, pp. 918-921.

Lemmon, J.A. (1985), *Family Mediation Practice*, Free Press, New York.

Lester, D. (1997a), 'Domestic Integration and Suicide Rates in the Provinces of Canada', *Psychological Reports*, vol. 81, (Part 2), p.1114.

Lester, D. (1997b), 'Domestic Social Integration and Suicide in Israel', *Israel Journal of Psychiatry and Related Sciences*, vol. 34, issue 2, pp.157-161.

Leudar, I. and Antaki, C. (1996), 'Discourse Participation, Reported Speech and Research Practices in Social Psychology', *Theory and Psychology*, vol. 6, pp. 5-29.

Lieblich, A. (1993), 'Looking at Change', in R. Josselson and A. Lieblich, (eds) (1993), *The Narrative Study of Lives*, Vol 1, Sage, London.

Lieblich, A. and Josselson, R. (eds) (1994), *The Narrative Study of Lives*, Vol. 2, *Exploring Identity and Gender*, Sage, London.

Livingston Bruce, M. and Kim, L.M. (1992), 'Differences in the Effects of Divorce on Major Depression in Men and Women', *American Journal of Psychiatry*, vol. 149, pp. 914-917.

Lord Chancellor's Department (1983) *Report of the Inter-Departmental Committee on Conciliation*, HMSO, London.

Lord Chancellor's Department (1993), *Looking to the Future: Mediation and the Ground for Divorce: A Consultation Paper*, (Green Paper), Cm 2424, HMSO, London.

Lord Chancellor's Deptartment (1995), *Looking to the Future: Mediation and the Ground for Divorce: The Government's Proposals*, (White Paper), Cm 2799, HMSO, London.

Lorenz, F.O., Simons, R.L., Conger, R.D., Elder, G.H., Johnson, C. and Chao, W. (1997), "Married and recently Divorced Mothers", *Journal of Marriage and the Family*, vol. 59, pp. 219-232.

MacAdams, D. (1985), *Power, Intimacy and the Life Story*, Guilford.Press, New York.

MacCannell, J.F. (1986), *Figuring Lacan: Criticism and the Cultural Unconscious*, University of Nebraska Press, Lincoln.

Maccoby, E.E. and Mnookin, R.H. (1992), *Dividing the Child: Social and Legal Dilemmas of Custody*, Harvard University Press, London.

Maclean, M. (1991), *Surviving Divorce: Women's Resources After Separation*, Macmillan, London.

Macmillan, A. (1989), 'Developmental Narratives: The Construction of Life Stories in Therapy', in *British Psychological Society, Psychotherapy Section Newsletter*, No 7, December 1989, pp. 19-27.

Magana, H. and Taylor, N. (1993), 'Child Custody Mediation and Spouse Abuse: A Descriptive Study of a Protocol', *Family and Conciliation Courts Review*, vol. 31, pp. 50-64.

Magnus, S.M. (1997), 'For Better or for Worse', *Guardian*, 10 September, pp. 10-11.

Maguire, M. (1995), *Men and Women, Passion and Power*, Routledge, London.

Maines, D.R. (1993), 'Narrative's Moment and Sociology's Phenomena: Towards a Narrative Sociology', *Sociological Quarterly*, vol. 34, pp. 17-38.

Mair, M. (1989), 'Psychology as a Discipline of Discourse', in *British Psychological Society, Psychotherapy Section Newsletter*, No 7, December 1989, pp. 2-12.

210   *Divorce: A Psychosocial Study*

Manning, P. and Cullum-Swann, B. (1994), 'Narrative, Content and Semiotic Analysis', in N. Denzin and D.Y. Lincoln (eds), *Handbook of Qualitative Research*, Sage, London.
Mansfield, P. and Collard, J. (1988), *The Beginning of the Rest of Your Life: A Portrait of Newly-Wed Marriage*, Macmillan, Basingstoke.
Margulies, S. and Luchow, A. (1992), 'Litigation, Mediation and the Psychology of Divorce', *Journal of Psychiatry and Law*, vol. 20, pp. 483-504.
Marsiglio, W. (1991), 'Paternal Engagement Activities with Minor Children', *Journal of Marriage and the Family*, vol. 53, pp. 973-986.
Masheter, C. (1990), 'Postdivorce Relationship Between Ex-Spouses: A Literature Review', *Journal of Divorce and Remarriage*, vol. 14, pp. 97-122.
Masheter, C. (1991), 'Postdivorce Relationships Between Ex-spouses: The Role of Attachment and Interpersonal Conflict', *Journal of Marriage and the Family*, vol. 53, pp. 103-110.
Mastekaasa, A. (1994a), 'Psychological Well-Being and Marital Dissolution: Selection Effects', *Journal of Family Issues*, vol. 15, pp. 208-228.
Mastekaasa, A. (1994b), 'Marital Status, Distress, and Well-Being: An International Comparison', *Journal of Comparative Family Studies*, vol. 25, pp. 183-201.
McAdams, D.P. (1988), 'Biography, Narrative and Lives: An Introduction', *Journal of Personality*, vol. 56, issue 1, pp. 1-18, Special Issue on Psychobiography and Life Narratives.
McAdams, D.P. and Ochberg, R.L. (eds) (1988), *Journal of Personality*, vol 56, Special Issue on Psychobiography and Life Narratives.
McAllister, F. (ed) (1995), *Marital Breakdown and the Health of the Nation*, 2nd edn, One Plus One, U.K.
McCall, M. (1990), 'The Significance of Storytelling', *Studies in Symbolic Interactionism*, vol. 11, pp. 145-161.
McCarthy, P. and Walker, J. (1996), *The Longer Term Impact of Family Mediation*, Joseph Rowntree Foundation, Social Policy Research Findings, No. 103.
McEwen, C.A., Maiman, R.J. and Mather, L. (1994), 'Lawyers, Mediation and the Management of Divorce Practice', *Law and Society Review*, vol. 28, pp. 149-187.
McEwan, H. (1992), 'Stories Lives Tell: Narrative and Dialogue in Education', *American Journal of Education*, vol. 100, pp. 396-399.
McGlone, F., Park, A. and Roberts, C. (1996), 'Relative Values: Kinship and Friendship', in R. Jowell, J. Curtice, A. Park, L. Brook and K. Thomson (eds), *British Social Attitudes: The 13th Report*, Dartmouth, Aldershot.
McIsaac, H. (1992), ' "Mediation Alternative: Process Dangers for Women" summarised by Hugh McIsaac', *Family and Conciliation Courts Review*, vol. 30, pp. 415-421.
McIsaac, H. (1995), 'Preface', in H.H. Irving and M. Benjamin, *Family Mediation: Contemporary Issues*, Sage, London.

McLeod, J. (1997), *Narrative and Psychotherapy*, Sage, London.
Metts, S. and Cupach, W.R. (1995), 'Postdivorce Relations', in M.A. Fitzpatrick and A.L. Vangelisti (eds), *Explaining Family Interactions*, Sage, California.
Merrell, F. (1985), *A Semiotic Theory of Texts*, Mouton, New York.
Miall, D. (1990), 'Changing the Self: The Affective Plot in Literary Narratives', in *British Psychological Society, Psychotherapy Section Newsletter*, No. 8, pp. 30-39.
Mies, M. (1993), 'Towards a Methodology for Feminist Research', in M. Hammersley (ed), *Social Research: Philosophy, Politics and Practice*, Sage, London.
Miller, N.B., Smerglia, V.L., Guadet, D.S. and Kitson, G.C. (1998), 'Stressful Life Events, Social Support, and the Distress of Widowed and Divorced Women - A Counteractive Model, *Journal of Family Issues*, vol. 19, pp. 181-203.
Milne, A. (1988), 'The Nature of Divorce Disputes', in J. Folberg and A. Milne (eds), *Divorce Mediation: Theory and Practice*, Guilford, New York.
Milroy, L. (1987), *Observing and Analysing Natural Language*, Blackwell, Oxford.
Minsky, R. (ed) (1996), *Psychoanalysis and Gender*, Routledge, London.
Minsky, R. (1998), *Psychoanalysis and Culture: Contemporary States of Mind*, Polity, Cambridge.
Mishler, E.G. (1986), *Research Interviewing: Context and Narrative*, Harvard University Press, London.
Mishler, E.G. (1991), 'Representing Discourse: The Rhetoric of Transcription', *Journal of Narrative and Life History,* vol. 1, pp. 255-280.
Mishler, E.G. (1992), 'Work, Identity and Narrative: An Artist-Craftsman's Story', in G.C. Rosenwald and R. Ochberg (eds) *Storied Lives: The Cultural Politics of Self Understanding*, Yale University Press, London.
Mitchell, W.J.T. (ed) (1980), *On Narrative*, University of Chicago Press, Chicago.
Mitchellflynn, C. and Hutchinson, R.L. (1993), 'A Longitudinal Study of the Problems and Concerns of Urban Divorced Men', *Journal of Divorce and Remarriage*, vol. 19, pp. 161-182.
Mnookin, R. and Kornhauser, L. (1979), 'Bargaining in the Shadow of the Law: The Case of Divorce', *Yale Law Journal*, vol. 88, pp. 950-997.
Moi, T. (1985), *Sexual Textual Politics; Feminist Literary Theory*, Routledge, London.
Morgan, L.A. (1991), *After Marriage Ends: Economic Consequences for Midlife Women*, Sage, California.
Morgan, P. (1996), 'Family Crisis Affects Us All', in C. Donnellan (ed), *Marriage and Divorce: Issues for the Nineties*, Independence Educational Publishers, Cambridge.
Morkham, T. (1993), 'Close Encounters of the Unpleasant Kind', *Family Mediation*, vol. 3, pp. 19-20.
Morrison, A.S. (1987), 'Is Divorce Mediation the Practice of Law? A Matter of Perspective', *California Law Review,* vol. 75, pp. 1093-1155.

Morss, J. (1995), *Growing Critical*, Routledge, London.

Mullender, A. and Morley, R. (eds) (1994), *Children Living With Domestic Violence*, Whiting and Birch, London.

Munby, D.K (1993), 'Introduction', in D.K. Munby (ed), *Narrative and Social Control: Critical Perspectives, Annual Review of Communication Research*, vol. 21, Sage, London.

Murch, M. (1980), *Justice and Welfare in Divorce*, Sweet and Maxwell, London.

Murphy, M. and Berrington, A. (1993), 'Household Change in the 1980s: A Review', *Population Trends*, 73 (Autumn 1993), pp. 18-26.

Nader, N. (1992), 'From Legal Process to Mind Processing', *Family and Conciliation Courts Review*, vol. 30, pp. 468-473.

Naffine, N. (1990), *Law and the Sexes: Explorations in Feminist Jurisprudence*, Allen and Unwin, London.

Nash, C. (ed) (1990), *Narrative in Culture: The Uses of Storytelling in the Sciences, Philosophy and Literature*, Routledge, London.

Nathanson, I.G. (1995), 'Divorce and Women's Spirituality', *Journal of Divorce and Remarriage*, vol. 22, pp.179-188.

Nazarro, R. (1992), 'Analysis of a Narrative', *International Journal of Psychology*, vol. 27, pp. 191-198.

Neale, B. and Smart, C. (1997), 'Experiments with Parenthood?', *Sociology*, vol. 31, pp.201-219.

Neale, B. and Smart, C. (1999), 'In Whose Best Interests? Theorising Family Life After Separation and Divorce', in S. Day Sclater and C. Piper (eds), *Undercurrents of Divorce*, Ashgate, Aldershot (in press).

Neff, J.A. and Schulter, T.D. (1993), 'Marital Status and Depressive Symptoms: The Role of Race, Ethnicity and Sex', *Journal of Divorce and Remarriage*, vol. 20, pp. 137-160.

Nelson, G. (1994), 'Emotional Well-being of Separated and Married Women: Long Term Follow-up Study', *American Journal of Orthopsychiatry*, vol. 64, pp. 150-160.

Neuman, S. (ed) (1991), *Autobiography and Questions of Gender*, Frank Cass & Co Ltd, London.

Newmark, L., Harrell, A. and Salem, P. (1995), 'Domestic Violence and Empowerment in Custody and Visitation Cases', *Family and Conciliation Courts Review*, vol. 33, pp. 30-62.

O'Brien, M. (1992), 'Changing Conceptions of Fatherhood', In U. Bjornberg (ed), *European Parents in the 1990s: Contradictions and Comparisons*, Transaction Publishers: New Brunswick, New Jersey.

Ochberg, R.L. (1988), 'Life Stories and the Psychosocial Construction of Careers', *Journal of Personality*, vol. 56, pp.173-204, Special Issue on Psychobiography and Life Narratives.

Ochberg, R.L. (1994), 'Life Stories and Storied Lives', in A. Lieblich and R. Josselson (eds) (1994), *The Narrative Study of Lives*, Volume 2, Exploring Identity and Gender, Sage, London.

O'Donovan, K. (1993), *Family Law Matters*, Pluto, London.

Office for National Statistics, (1997), 'Marriage and Divorce Statistics: Review of the Registrar General on Marriages and Divorces in England and Wales, 1994', Series FM2, no.22, The Stationery Office, London.

Ogden, T. (1992), *The Matrix of the Mind: Object Relations and the Psychoanalytic Dialogue*, Maresfield Library, London.

Ogus, A., Walker, J. and Jones-Lee, M. (1989), *The Costs and Effectiveness of Conciliation in England and Wales, Report of the Conciliation Project Unit, University of Newcastle upon Tyne, to the Lord Chancellor*, University of Newcastle.

Okin, S. M. (1989), *Justice, Gender and The Family*, New York, Basic Books.

Olney, J. (ed) (1980), *Autobiography: Essays, Theoretical and Critical*, Princeton University Press, Princeton, New Jersey.

Orbach, S. (1992), 'The Well of Solitude', *Guardian*, 21-22 March, p.12.

Papke, D.R. (ed), *Narrative and the Legal Discourse*, Deborah Charles Publications, Liverpool.

Parker, I. (1992), *Discourse Dymanics: Critical Analysis for Social and Individual Psychology*, Routledge, London.

Parker, I. (1989), *The Crisis in Social Psychology and How to End It*, Routledge, London.

Parker, I. and Spears, R. (eds) (1996), *Psychology and Society: Radical Theory and Practice*, Pluto, London.

Parkinson, L. (1986), *Conciliation in Separation and Divorce: Finding Common Ground*, Croom Helm, London.

Parsons, T.(1955), 'The Isolated Conjugal Family', reprinted in M. Anderson (ed), *Sociology of the Family*, 2nd edition, Penguin, Harmondsworth, 1980, pp. 178-198.

Parton, N. (1991), *Governing the Family: Child Care, Child protection and the State*, Macmillan, Basingstoke.

Pearson, J. (1991), 'The Equity of Mediated Divorce Settlements', *Mediation Quarterly*, vol. 9, pp. 179-197.

Pearson, J. and Thoennes, N. (1985), 'Divorce Mediation: An Overview of Research Results', *Columbia Journal of Law and Social Problems*, vol. 19, pp. 451-484.

Pearson, J. and Thoennes, N. (1988), 'Divorce Mediation Research Results', in J. Folberg and A. Milne (eds), *Divorce Mediation: Theory and Practice*, Guilford Press, London.

Personal Narratives Group (eds) (1989), *Interpreting Women's Lives: Feminist Theory and Personal Narratives*, Indiana University Press, Bloomington.

Pett, M.A., Vaughancole, B. and Wampold, B.E. (1994), 'Maternal Employment and Perceived Stress: Their Impact on Children's Adjustment and Mother-Child Interaction in Young Divorced and Married Families', *Family Relations*, vol. 43, pp. 151-158.

Piper, C. (1993), *The Responsible Parent: A Study in Divorce Mediation*, Harvester/ Wheatsheaf, London.

Piper, C. (1996), 'Divorce Reform and the Image of the Child', *Journal of Law and Society*, vol. 23, pp. 364-382.

Piper, C. and Kaganas, F. (1997), 'The Family Law Act 1996 Section 1D: How Will 'They' Know if There is a Risk of Violence?', *Child and Family Law Quarterly*, vol. 9, pp. 269-279.

Piper, C. and Day Sclater, S. (1999), 'Changing Divorce', in S. Day Sclater and C. Piper (eds), *Undercurrents of Divorce*, Ashgate, Aldershot (in press).

Pledge, D.S. (1992), 'Marital Separation and Divorce: A Review of Individual-Responses to a Major Life Stressor', *Journal of Divorce and Remarriage*, vol. 17, pp. 151-181.

Plummer, K. (1983), *Documents of Life: An Introduction to the Problems and Literature of a Humanistic Method*, Allen & Unwin, London.

Plummer, K. (1995), *Telling Sexual Stories*, Routledge, London.

Polkinghorne, D.E. (1988), *Narrative Knowing and the Human Sciences*, State University of New York Press, Albany.

Popenoe, D. (1993), 'American Family Decline, 1960-1990: A Review and Appraisal', *Journal of Marriage and the Family*, vol. 55, pp. 527-542.

Potter, J., Stringer, P. and Wetherell, M. (1984), *Social Texts and Context: Literature and Social Psychology*, RKP, London.

Potter, J. and Wetherell, M. (1987), *Discourse and Social Psychology: Beyond Attitudes and Behaviour*, Sage, London.

Potter, J. and Wetherell, M. (1994), 'Analysing Discourse', in A. Bryman and R. G. Burgess (eds), *Analysing Qualitative Data*, Routledge, London.

Powers, C.T. (1997), *In the Memory of the Forest*, Anchor, London.

Price, H.S. (1998), 'Being in the Story, Being in the Picture: A Psychoanalytic Perspective on a Child's Storytelling', Paper presented at the Biography in Social Policy Conference, Tavistock Centre, London, September 1998.

Raitt, F. (1996), 'Domestic Violence and Divorce Mediation: A Rejoinder to Kaganas and Piper and a Proposal that the Mediation Process Should Always Serve the Best Interests of the Child', *Journal of Social Welfare and Family Law*, vol. 18, pp. 11-20.

Reinharz, S. (1994), 'Feminist Biography', in A. Lieblich and R. Josselson (eds), *The Narrative Study of Lives*, Volume 2, Exploring Identity and Gender, Sage, London.

Rice, J.K. (1994), 'Reconsidering Research on Divorce, Family Life Cycle, and the Meaning of Family', *Psychology of Women Quarterly*, vol. 18, pp. 559-584.

Rice, P. and Waugh, P. (eds) (1989), *Modern Literary Theory: A Reader*, Edward Arnold, London.

Richards, B. (1989), *Images of Freud: Cultural Responses to Psychoanalysis*, Dent, London.

Richards, M., Hardy, R. and Wadsworth, M. (1997), 'The Effects of Divorce and Separation on Mental Health in a National UK Birth Cohort', *Psychological Medicine*, vol. 27, pp.1121-1128.

Richardson, L. (1990), 'Narrative and Sociology', *Journal of Contemporary. Ethnography*, vol. 9, pp. 116-135.

Richardson, L. (1992), 'Resisting Resistance Narratives: A Representation for Communication', *Studies in Symbolic Interaction*, vol. 13, pp. 77-82.

Richardson, L. (1992), 'The Consequences of Poetic Representation: Writing the Other, Rewriting the Self', in C. Ellis and M.J. Flaherty, (eds), *Investigating Subjectivity: Research on Lived Experience*, Sage, London.

Ricoeur, P. (1981), *Hermeneutics and the Human Sciences: Essays on Language, Action and Interpretation*, Cambridge University Press, Cambridge, (trans. J Thompson).

Rieff, P. (1973), *The Triumph of the Therapeutic*, Penguin, Harmondswoth.

Riessman, C.K. (1987), 'When Gender is Not Enough: Women Interviewing Women', *Gender & Society*, vol. 1, pp. 172-207.

Riessman, C.K. (1990a), *Divorce Talk: Women and Men Make Sense of Personal Relationships*, Rutgers University Press, London.

Riessman, C.K. (1990b), 'Strategic Uses of Narrative in the Presentation of Self and Illness', *Social Science and Medicine*, vol. 30, pp. 1195-1200.

Riessman, C.K. (1991), 'Beyond Reductionism: Narrative Genres in Divorce Accounts', *Journal of Narrative and Life History*, vol. 1, pp. 41-68.

Riessman, C.K. (1992), 'Making Sense of Marital Violence: One Woman's Narrative', in G.C. Rosenwald and R.L. Ochberg, (eds) *Storied Lives: The Cultural Politics of Self Understanding*, Yale University Press, London.

Riessman, C.K. (1993), *Narrative Analysis*, Sage, London.

Roberts, M. (1990), 'The Essentials of Conciliation', in T. Fisher, (ed) *Family Conciliation Within the UK: Policy and Practice*, Jordans, Family Law, Bristol.

Roberts, M. (1992), 'Who is in Charge? Reflections on Recent Research on the Role of the Mediator', *Journal of Social Welfare and Family Law*, vol. 14, pp. 372-387.

Roberts, M. (1994), 'Who is in Charge? Effecting a Productive Exchange between Researchers and Practitioners in the Field of Family Mediation', *Journal of Social Welfare and Family Law*, vol. 16, pp. 439-454.

Roberts, M. (1996), 'Family Mediation and the Interests of Women', *Family Mediation*, vol. 6, pp. 8-10.

Roberts, M. (1997), *Mediation in Family Disputes*, 2nd edn, Arena, Aldershot.

Roberts, S. (1988), 'Three Models of Family Mediation', in R. Dingwall and J. Eekelaar, (eds) *Divorce Mediation and the Legal Process*, Clarendon Press, Oxford.

Robinson, M. (1991), *Family Transformation Through Divorce and Remarriage*, Routledge, London.

Roche, J. (1995), 'The Politics of Children's Rights', in J. Brannen and M. O'Brien, (eds) *Children in Families*, Falmer Press, London.

Roche, J. (1999), 'Children and Divorce: A Private Affair?', in S. Day Sclater and C. Piper (eds), *Undercurrents of Divorce*, Ashgate, Aldershot (in press).

Rodgers, B. and Pryor, J. (1998), *Divorce and Separation: The Outcomes for Children*, The Joseph Rowntree Foundation, York.

Rose, N. (1987), 'Beyond the Public/Private Division: Law, Power and the Family', *Journal of Law and Society*, vol. 14, pp. 61-76.

Rose, N. (1990), *Governing the Soul*, Routledge, London.

Rosenberg, J. (1992), 'In Defense of Mediation', *Family and Conciliation Courts Review*, vol. 30, pp. 422-467.

Rosenwald, G.C. (1988), 'A Theory of Multiple Case Research', *Journal of Personality*, vol. 56, pp. 239-264.

Rosenwald, G.C. (1992), 'Conclusion: Refelctions on Narrative Self-Understanding', in G.C. Rosenwald and R.L. Ochberg (eds), *Storied Lives: The Cultural Politics of Self Understanding*, Yale University Press, London.

Rosenwald, G.C. and Ochberg, R.L. (eds) (1992), *Storied Lives: The Cultural Politics of Self Understanding*, Yale University Press, London.

Rossiter, A.B. (1991), 'Initiator Status and Separation Adjustment', *Journal of Divorce and Remarriage*, vol. 15, pp. 141-155.

Runyan, W.M. (1982), *Life Histories and Psychobiography: Explorations in Theory and Method*, Oxford University Press, Oxford.

Runyan, W.M. (1988), 'Progress in Psychobiography', *Journal of Personality*, vol. 56, pp. 295-326, Special Issue on Psychobiography and Life Narratives.

Rustin, M. (1991), *The Good Society and the Inner World: Psychoanalysis, Politics and Culture*, Verso, London.

Rustin, M. (1997), 'Concluding Remarks', Paper delivered at the *Subjectivity Revisited Symposium* (Centre for Biography in Social Policy, University of East London), Birkbeck College, 1997.

Saleby, D. (1994), 'Culture, Theory and Narrative: The Intersection of Meanings in Practice', *Sociological Weekly*, vol. 39, pp. 351-359.

Sales, B., Manber, R. and Rohman, L. (1992), 'Social Science Research and Child Custody Decision Making', *Applied and Preventive Psychology*, vol. 1, pp. 23-40.

Salmon, P. (1989), 'Old Age and Storytelling', in *British Psychological Society, Psychotherapy Section Newsletter*, No 7, December 1989, pp.44-51.

Sanchez, L. and Thomson, E. (1997), 'Becoming Mothers and Fathers-Parenthood, Gender, and the Division of Labour', *Gender and Society*, vol. 11, pp.747-772.

Sandelowski, M. (1991), 'Telling Stories: Narrative Approaches in Qualitative Research', *Image: Journal of Nursing Scholarship*, vol. 23, pp. 161-166.

Saposnek, D. (1992), 'Clarifying Perspectives on Mandatory Mediation', *Family and Conciliation Courts Review*, vol. 30, pp. 490-506.

Sarat, A. and Felstiner, W.L.F. (1995), *Divorce Lawyers and their Clients: Power and Meaning in the Legal Process*, Oxford University Press, New York.

Sarbin, T. (ed) (1986), *Narrative Psychology: The Storied Nature of Human Conduct*, Praeger, New York.

Sarbin, T. and Kitsuse, J. (1994), *Constructing the Social*, Sage, London.

de Saussure, F. (1915), 'Nature of the Linguistic Sign', reprinted in D. Lodge (ed) *Modern Criticism and Theory: A Reader*, Longman, London, (1988).

Saxton, L. (1993), *The Individual, Marriage and the Family* (8th edn), Wadsworth, Belmont, California.

Scheff, T.J. (1990) *Microsociology: Discourse, Emotion and Social Structure*. University of Chicago Press, Chicago.

Schuz, R. (1996), 'Divorce and Ethnic Minorities', in M.D.A. Freeman (ed), *Divorce: Where Next?*, Dartmouth, Aldershot.

Scott, J. (1998), 'Changing Attitudes to Sexual Morality: A Cross-National Comparison', *Sociology*, vol. 32, pp. 815-845.

Scott, J., Braun, M. and Alwin, D. (1993), 'The Family Way', *International Social Attitudes*, vol.10, pp. 23-47.

Seligman, M. (1975), *Helplessness*, Freeman, San Fransisco.

Sellers, S. (1991), *Language and Sexual Difference: Feminist Writing in France*, Macmillan, London.

Seltzer, J.A. (1991), 'Relationships between Fathers and Children who Live Apart: The Fathers Role after Separation', *Journal of Marriage and the Family*, vol. 53, pp. 79-101.

Seltzer, J.A. (1994), 'The Consequences of Marital Dissolution for Children', *Annual Review of Sociology*, vol. 20, pp. 235-266.

Shafer, R. (1980), 'Narration in Psychoanalytic Dialogue', in W.J.T. Mitchell (ed), *On Narrative*, University of Chicago Press, London.

Shah-Kazemi, S. (1996), 'Family Mediation and the Dynamics of Culture', *Family Mediation*, vol. 6, pp. 5-7.

Sharp, D.J. (1988), 'Validation of the 30-Item General Health Questionnaire in Early Pregnancy', *Psychological Medicine*, vol. 18, pp. 503-507.

Sheridan, A. (1980), *Michel Foucault: The Will to Truth*, Tavistock, London.

Shildrick, M. (1997), *Leaky Bodies and Boundaries: Feminism, Postmodernism and (Bio)Ethics*, Routledge, London.

Shotter, J. and Gergen, K. (eds) (1989), *Texts of Identity*, Sage, London.

Siganporia, M. (1993), 'Indian Muslim Women: Post Divorce Problems and Social Support', *Indian Journal of Social Work*, vol. 54, pp. 355-363.

Silberman, L.J. (1982), 'Professional Responsibility Problems of Divorce Mediation', *Family Law Quarterly*, vol. 16, pp. 107-145.

Silverman, K. (1983), *The Subject of Semiotics*, Oxford University Press, Oxford.

Simon, R. (1992), 'Parental Role Strains, Salience of Parental Identity and Gender Differences in Psychological Distress', *Journal of Health and Social Behaviour*, vol. 33, pp. 25-35.

Simons, R.L., Beaman, J., Conger, R.D. and Chao, W. (1993), 'Stress, Support and Antisocial Behavior Trait as Determinants of Emotional Well-being and Parenting Practices among Single Mothers', *Journal of Marriage and the Family*, vol. 55, pp. 385-398.

Simpson, B., McCarthy, P. and Walker, J. (1995), *Being There: Fathers After Divorce*, Relate Centre for Family Studies, University of Newcastle upon Tyne.

Singer, D. (1992), 'Mediation: A Growing Means for Settling Divorce Conflicts', *Arbitration Journal*, vol. 47, pp. 21-25.

Singer, L.R. (1987), 'Divorce Mediation in the United States: An Overview', in Vermont Law School Dispute Resolution Project, *Divorce Mediation: A Comparative Perspective*, Vermont Law School, Vermont.

Smart, C. (1989a), *Feminism and the Power of Law*, Routledge, London.

Smart, C. (1989b), 'Power and the Politics of Child Custody', in C. Smart and S. Sevenhuijsen (eds), *Child Custody and the Politics of Gender*, Routledge, London.

Smart, C. (1995), *The Family and Social Change: Some Problems of Analysis and Intervention*, Research Working Paper No. 13, Gender Analysis and Policy Unit, University of Leeds.

Smart, C. (1997), 'Wishful Thinking and Harmful Tinkering: Sociological Reflections on Family Policy', *Journal of Social Policy*, vol. 26, pp. 301-321.

Smart, C. and Neale, B. (1997), 'Arguments Against Virtue: Must Contact be Enforced?', *Family Law*, vol. 27, pp. 332-336.

Smart, C. and Sevenhuijsen, S. (eds) (1989), *Child Custody and the Politics of Gender*, Routledge: London.

Smith, C. (1997), 'Children's Rights: Judicial Ambivalence and Social Resistance', *International Journal of Law, Policy and the Family*, vol. 11, pp. 103-139.

Smith, P. (1985), *Language and the Sexes*, Blackwell, Oxford.

Smith, S. (1993), *Subjectivity, Identity and the Body: Women's Autobiographical Practices in the 20th Century*, Indiana University Press, Bloomington, Ill.

Solomou, W., Richards, M., Huppert, F.A., Brayne, C. and Morgan, K. (1996), 'Divorce, Current Marital Status and Well-Being in an Elderly Population, unpublished paper, Centre for Family Research, University of Cambridge.

Solomou, W., Ely, M., Brayne, C. and Huppert, F. (1999), 'The Parent-Child Relationship in Later Life: The Longer Term Effects of Parental Divorce and Remarriage', in A. Bainham, S. Day Sclater and M. Richards (eds), *What is a Parent? A Socio-Legal Analysis*, Hart, Oxford (forthcoming).

Somary, K. and Emery, R.E. (1991), 'Emotional Anger and Grief in Divorce Mediation', *Mediation Quarterly*, vol. 8, pp. 185-197.

Spence, D.P. (1982), *Narrative Truth and Historical Truth: Meaning and Interpretation in Psychoanalysis*, Norton, New York.

Squire, C. (1989), *Significant Difference: Feminism in Psychology*, Routledge, London.

Stacey, J. (1996), *In the Name of the Family:Rethinking Family Values in the Postmodern Age*, Beacon Press, Boston, MA.

Stack, S. (1989), 'The Impact of Divorce on Suicide in Norway', *Journal of Marriage and the Family*, vol. 31, pp.229-238.

Stack, S. (1990), 'The Effect of Divorce on Suicide in Denmark', *Sociological Quarterly*, vol. 31, pp. 359-370.

Stack, S. and Wasserman, I. (1993), 'Marital Status, Alcohol Consumption and Suicide: An Analysis of National Data', *Journal of Marriage and the Family*, vol. 55(4), pp. 1018-1024.

Stanley, L. and Morgan, D. (eds) (1993), *Biography and Autobiography in Sociology*, Special Issue of Sociology, vol. 27(1).

Stanton, D.C. (ed) (1987), *The Female Autograph*, University of Chicago Press, London.

Steedman, C. (1986), *Landscape for a Good Woman*, Virago, London.

Steefel, N.M. (1992), 'A Divorce Transition Model', *Psychological Reports*, vol. 70, pp. 155-160.

Stewart, A.J. (1994), 'The Women's Movement and Women's Lives: Linking Individual Development and Social Events', In A.Lieblich and R .Josselson (eds), *The Narrative Study of Lives*, Volume 2, Exploring Identity and Gender, Sage, London.

Stewart, A., Franz, C. and Layton, L. (1988), 'The Changing Self: Using Personal Documents to Study Lives', *Journal of Personality*, vol. 56, pp.41-74, Special Issue on Psychobiography and Life Narratives.

Stivers, C. (1993), 'Reflections on the Role of Personal Narrative in the Social Sciences', *Signs*, vol. 18, pp. 408-425.

Stubbs, M. (1983), *Discourse Analysis*, Oxford, Blackwell.

Sudarkasa, N. (1993), 'Female-Headed African American Households: Some Neglected Dimensions', In H. McAdoo (ed), *Family Ethnicity*, Sage, CA..

Sugarman, S.D. and Kay, H.H. (eds) (1990), *Divorce Reform at the Crossroads*, Yale University Press, New Haven.

Sun, M. and Woods, L. (1990), *Mediation and Domestic Violence: A Practitioner's Guide*, National Center on Women and Family Law, New York.

Surtees, P.G. (1987), 'Psychiatric Disorder in the Community and the General Health Questionnaire', *British Journal of Psychiatry*, vol. 150, pp. 828-835.

Synge, J. (1994), 'Women and Divorce/Men and Divorce: Gender Differences in Separation, Divorce and Remarriage', *Journal of Comparative Family Studies*, vol. XXV, pp. 419-420.

Tambling, J. (1991), *Narrative and Ideology*, Open University Press, Milton Keynes.

Tannen, D. (1990), 'Ordinary Conversation and Literary Discourse: Coherence and the Poetics of Repetition', in E.H. Benclix, (ed), *The Uses of Linguistics*, New York Academy of Sciences, New York.

Tarnopolsky, A., Hand, D., McLean, E., Roberts, H. and Wiggins, R. (1979), 'Validity of Uses of a Screening Questionnaire (GHQ) in the Community', *British Journal of Psychiatry*, vol. 134, pp. 508-515.

220 *Divorce: A Psychosocial Study*

Tennant, C. (1977), 'The General Health Questionnaire: A Valid Index of Psychological Impairment in Australian Populations', *Medical Journal of Australia*, ii, 12, pp. 392-394.
Thiriot, T.L. and Buckner, E.T. (1991), 'Multiple Predictors of Satisfying Post-Divorce Adjustment of Single Custodial Parents', *Journal of Divorce and Remarriage*, vol. 17, pp. 27-48.
Thoennes, N., Salem, P. and Pearson, J. (1995), 'Mediation and Domestic Violence: Current Policies and Practices', *Family and Conciliation Courts Review*, vol. 33, pp. 6-29.
Todd, A.D. and Fisher, S. (eds) (1988), *Gender and Discourse: The Power of Talk*, Ablex Publishing Corporation, Norwood, New Jersey.
Tonkin, E. (1992), *Narrating Our Pasts: The Social Construction of Oral History*, Cambridge University Press, Cambridge.
Tonkmanian, S. and Rennie, D. (1992), *Psychotherapy Process Research: Paradigmatic and Narrative Approaches*, Sage, London.
Trovato, F. (1991), 'Sex, Marital Status, and Suicide in Canada 1951-1981', *Sociological Perspectives*, vol. 34, pp. 427-445.
Uhlenberg, P., Cooney, T. and Boyd, R. (1990), 'Divorce for Women after Midlife', *Journal of Gerontology, Social Sciences*, vol. 45, pp. S3-S11.
Umberson, D. and Williams, C.L. (1993), 'Divorced Fathers: Parental Role Strain and Psychological Distress', *Journal of Family Issues*, vol. 14, pp. 378-400.
Vaughan, D. (1987/1993), *Uncoupling: How and Why Relationships Come Apart*, Cedar/Mandarin, London.
Veevers, J.E. (1991), 'Traumas Versus Stress: Paradigms of Positive Versus Negative Divorce Outcomes', *Journal of Divorce and Remarriage*, vol. 15, pp. 99-126.
Vera, M.I. (1990), 'Effects of Divorce Groups on Individual Adjustment: A Multiple Methodology Approach', *Social Work Research and Abstracts*, vol. 26, pp. 11-20.
Vermont Law School Dispute Resolution Project (1987), *The Role of Mediation in Divorce Proceedings: A Comparative Perspective (United Stated, Canada and Great Britain)*, Vermont Law School, Vermont.
Vice, S. (ed) (1996), *Psychoanalytic Criticism: A Reader*, Polity, Cambridge.
Vitz, P.C. (1992), 'Narratives and Counselling, 1: From Analysis of the Past to Stories About It', *Journal of Psychology and Theology*, vol. 20, pp. 11-19.
Vitz, P.C. (1992), 'Narratives and Counselling, 2: From Stories of the Past to Stories of the Future', *Journal of Psychology and Theology*, vol. 20, pp. 20-27.
Volgy, S.S. (ed) (1991), *Women and Divorce/Men and Divorce: Gender Differences in Separation, Divorce and Remarriage*, Haworth, New York.
Wadsby, M. and Svedin, C.G. (1992), 'Divorce: Different Experiences of Men and Women', *Family Practice*, vol. 9, pp. 451-460.

Waggener, N.M. and Galassi, J.P. (1993), 'The Relation of Frequency, Satisfaction, and Type of Socially Supportive Behaviors to Psychological Adjustment in Marital Separation', *Journal of Divorce and Remarriage*, vol. 21, pp. 139-159.

Wallace, J.B. (1992), 'Reconsidering the Life Review: The Social Construction of Talk about the Past', *Gerontologist*, vol. 32, pp. 120-125.

Wallerstein, J.S. (1991), 'The Long-term Effects of Divorce on Children: A Review', *Journal of the American Academy of Child and Adolescent Psychiatry*, vol. 30, pp. 349-360.

Wallerstein, J.S. and Blakeslee, S. (1989), *Second Chances: Men, Women and Children, A Decade After Divorce*, Ticknor and Fields, N.Y.

Walker, J. (1993), 'Co-operative Parenting Post-Divorce: Possibility or Pipedream?', *Journal of Family Therapy*, vol. 15, pp. 273-293.

Walker, J. (1994), 'Dilemmas for Families Post-Divorce: Post-Divorce Transitions', Paper presented at the Successful Stepfamilies UK Conference, London, November 1994.

Walker, J., McCarthy, P. and Corlyon, J. (1994), *An Evaluation of Comprehensive Mediation for Divorcing Couples*, Relate Centre for Family Studies, University of Newcastle upon Tyne, Joseph Rowntree Social Policy Research Findings, No. 48.

Walker, J., McCarthy, P. and Corlyon, J. (1994), *Mediation: The Making and Remaking of Cooperative Relationships*, Research Report, Relate Centre for Family Studies, University of Newcastle upon Tyne.

Walters-Chapman, S.F., Price, S.J. and Serovich, J.M. (1995), 'The Effects of Guilt on Divorce Adjustment', *Journal of Divorce and Remarriage*, vol. 22, pp. 163-177.

Wasserman, I. (1990), 'The Impact of Divorce on Suicide in the United States, 1970-93', *Family Perspectives*, vol. 24, pp. 61-67.

Weedon, C. (1987), *Feminist Practice and Poststructuralist Theory*, Blackwell, Oxford.

Weintraub, K.J. (1978), *The Value of the Individual: Self and Circumstance in Autobiography*, University of Chicago Press, Chicago.

Weitzman, L. (1985), *The Divorce Revolution*, Free Press, New York.

Wetherell, M. (1986), 'Linguistic Repertoires and Literary Criticism: New Directions for the Social Psychology of Gender', in S. Wilkinson (ed), *Feminist Social Psychology*, Open University Press, Milton Keynes.

Wetherell, M. and Potter, J. (1992), *Mapping the Language of Racism*, Harvester/Wheatsheaf, London.

White, H. (1980), 'The Value of Narrativity in the Representation of Reality', in W.J.T. Mitchell (ed), *On Narrative*, University of Chicago Press, London.

White, L.K. and Booth, A. (1991), 'Divorce Over the Life Course: The Role of Marital Happiness', *Journal of Family Issues*, vol.12, pp. 5-21.

Widdershoven, G.A.M. (1993), 'The Story of Life: Hermeneutic Perspectives on the Relationship Between Narrative and Life History', In R. Josselson and A. Lieblich (eds), *The Narrative Study of Lives*, vol. 1, Sage, London.

Widdicombe, S. (1993), 'Autobiography and Change: Rhetoric and Authenticity of 'Gothic' Style', in E. Burman and I. Parker (eds), *Discourse Analytic Research*, Routledge, London.

Wiersma, J. (1988), 'The Press Release: Symbolic Communication in Life History Interviewing', *Journal of Personality*, vol. 56, pp. 205-238, Special Issue on Psychobiography and Life Narratives.

Wilkinson, S. (1988), 'The Role of Reflexivity in Feminist Psychology', *Women's Studies International Forum*, vol. 11, pp. 493-502.

Wilkinson, S. (ed.) (1996), *Feminist Social Psychologies*, Open University Press, Milton Keynes.

Williamson, J. (1978), *Decoding Advertisements: Ideology and Meaning in Advertising*, Marion Boyars, London.

Winnicott, D. (1953/1971), *Playing and Reality*, Routledge, London.

Witherspoon, S. (1985), 'Sex Roles and Gender Issues', *British Social Attitudes*, vol. 2, pp. 55-94.

Wood, L.A. (1981), 'Review of *Structured Mediation in Divorce Settlement* by O.J. Coogler', *Social Indicators Research*, vol. 9, pp. 243-245.

Wright, E. (1984), *Psychoanalytic Criticism: Theory in Practice*, Methuen, London.

Wynn, L.C., Shields, C.G. and Sirkin, M.I. (1992), 'Illness, Family Theory and Family Therapy', *Family Process*, vol. 31, pp. 3-18.

Zibbell, R.A. (1995), 'The Mental Health Professional as Arbitrator in Post-Divorce Child-Oriented Conflict', *Family and Conciliation Courts Review*, vol. 33, pp. 462-471.

Appendix 1   The General Health Questionnaire

The General Health Questionnaire (GHQ-28) was used in this study as a quantitative indicator of psychological well-being. The GHQ was designed as a self-administered screening test for assisting in the detection of minor psychiatric disorders in general practice and community settings. It is also a useful device for monitoring progress on a series of occasions (Globe *et al*, 1979). Over fifty validity studies have been published (Goldberg, 1985). The original version comprised 60 items. In our study, we used the 'scaled' 28 item version (GHQ-28), the development of which was based on a four factor solution of the original GHQ-60 (Goldberg and Hillier, 1979). It detects both the inability to carry out one's normal healthy functions and the appearance of new symptoms of a distressing nature. As a screening test, the GHQ-28 does not enable a clinical diagnosis to be made; rather it focuses on 'the hinterland between psychological sickness and health' (Goldberg and Hillier, 1979, p. 139) and assists in the detection of 'probable cases' which, if desired, can subsequently be checked by means of clinical interviews.

For each individual, the GHQ gives information about the present mental state rather than about personality traits, or the likelihood of falling ill in the future (Goldberg and Blackwell, 1970). The model of psychological impairment implicit in the GHQ is that of a continuum, with no sharp distinction being made between 'normals' and 'cases' (Farmer and Harvey, 1975). Corser and Philip (1978) agree that the GHQ is a useful screening device, but state that there are difficulties if it is used to predict outcome or future behaviour; 'one cannot determine for how long its classification of an individual holds good' (p. 175). The important point being made here is that the GHQ clearly identifies when psychological disturbance is present, but whether what it measures is best considered as psychiatric illness or as part of the normal range of emotional responses to life events remains to be clarified. Jones (1979) remarks that 'the type of illness measured by the GHQ is often quite fleeting' (p. 382), which invites the question as to whether what is measured by the GHQ should be referred to as 'illness' at all.

The GHQ-28 comprises four sub-scales: somatic symptoms, anxiety and insomnia, social dysfunction and severe depression. These scales are useful in studies in which the investigator requires more information than is provided by a single severity score, and therefore has applications in research (Banks *et al*, 1980). For research purposes, the GHQ-28 is useful in longitudinal studies, where it may be administered before and after a particular event. The ratio of the two sets of scaled scores can then reveal whether the external event had its greatest effect in a particular symptom area (Goldberg and Hillier, 1979). In addition, insofar as it detects recent changes in symptomatology, the GHQ-28 is useful in documenting individual changes in well-being over time.

Items in the GHQ consist of questions which ask whether the subject has recently experienced a particular symptom or item of behaviour, which is answered on a four-point scale: not at all, no more than usual, rather more than usual, much more than usual. There are two main scoring methods which can be used. First, the standard 'GHQ method', where subjects score '0' for endorsing either of the first two response categories, and '1' for endorsing either of the last two. Secondly, the 'Likert method', where responses are weighted 0, 1, 2 or 3.

Goldberg and Hillier (1979) report that, for the GHQ-28, the most effective scoring method is the simpler 'GHQ method', where a cut-off point for 'probable cases' of 4/5 is used. In general practice settings, using this cut-off score, the questionnaire has a sensitivity (the proportion of test positives to all positives) of 85.6% and a specificity (the proportion of test negatives to all negatives) of 86.8% (Goldberg, 1978). In a validation study of the GHQ-30 among women attending an ante-natal clinic, Sharp (1988) reports that using Goldberg's recommended cut-off point of 4/5 resulted in 43% of her sample being classified as 'probable cases', whereas raising it to 5/6 lowered the prevalence of higher scores to 35%. Raising the threshold further had little effect. Kumar and Robson (1984), in their study of postpartum women, reported a similar finding. Community samples show 15-30% of people having high GHQ scores (Tarnopolsky *et al.*, 1979). In clinical studies, the threshold is best set at the level where the probability of 'caseness' is 50% (Goldberg, 1985).

The GHQ has been extensively validated in community and general practice settings, but Goldberg (1985) recommends that where it is to be used for epidemiological research to estimate prevalence rates in a given population, a small validation study should be carried out, and the validity coefficients used to compare the predicted prevalence of illness in the entire population being screened. The percentage of patients with high scores must not be supposed to be the same as the probable prevalence of illness, as the predictive value of the test rises with increasing score (Goldberg, 1986). Validity has been established using a two stage design, where the GHQ is followed by a clinical interview to confirm the presence or otherwise of psychiatric disorder (Tarnopolsky *et al.*, 1979). In the present study, no separate validation was carried out, because we have used the GHQ as an indicator of individual well-being over time, and out sample is too small and heterogeneous for us to be able to make any overall assessment of the well-being of any population of divorcing people.

One criticism which has been voiced in relation to the use of the GHQ is the issue of whether it fails to detect chronic affective conditions. This problem can be addressed by using a revised scoring method but, as Surtees (1987) reports, the differences in sensitivity are not significant. The issue of chronicity is of greater relevance to screening studies and studies where the questionnaire is completed on only a single occasion. Tennant (1977) has also pointed out that the test may misclassify those who use 'denial' as a means of coping.

That separated people feature prominently among probable cases in community studies is a common, although not a consistent, finding. Banks *et al* (1980) found scores on the GHQ-12 to be unrelated to marital status. Boardman (1987) reports on a study which used the GHQ-28 for the detection of emotional disorders by General Practitioners in London; he found that GHQ scores were highest amongst those separated from their spouses and that these scores were significantly higher than those for people who were single, widowed, divorced and married. In Boardman's study, the GPs also attributed the highest rates of disorder to separated people.

The Health and Lifestyle Survey (Cox *et al.*, 1987), using the GHQ-30, considered GHQ score in relation to gender and marital status. The authors report gender differences in GHQ scores, with women having higher scores than men; 27% of men and 33% of women obtained scores at or above the threshold level. The authors remark that this is almost certainly an over-estimate of the true prevalence of psychiatric disorder, and highlights the problem that the threshold value which has been validated for general practice may be inappropriate for a community survey.

In an Australian community-based study (Finlay-Jones and Burvill, 1977), however, the gender differences were reported as not significant.

226 Divorce: A Psychosocial Study

The authors suggest that their findings invite the conclusion that gender interacts in complex ways with other demographic factors and that gender differences in scores cannot be explained on the basis of gender alone. Farmer and Harvey (1985) note that, as the menstrual cycle can affect psychological and other somatic symptoms, this could account, at least in part, for some of the gender differences that have been found.

On the question of the relationship between GHQ score and marital status, there have been contradictory reports. The findings of the *Health and Lifestyle Survey* (Cox *et al.*, 1987) for example, show that for men of all ages, the highest scores are obtained by those who are divorced and separated. It is unfortunate that this study included both divorced and separated people in a single category since, as Boardman's work suggested (Boardman, 1987), there is an indication that separated people score consistently higher than those who are divorced. In the *Health and Lifestyle Survey*, divorced and separated men of all age groups except 65+ have lower GHQ scores than divorced and separated women. The score for younger women (18-39) is particularly high, and the authors attribute this to the higher proportions of women in this age group who have sole responsibility for dependent children. Such an interpretation would be consistent with the findings of Brown and Harris (1978) as regards depression.

The Australian study (Finlay-Jones and Burvill, 1977) found the highest morbidity rate amongst separated and divorced people, as compared with those who were single, married and widowed, but the differences were not significant, possibly because of the small numbers of separated and divorced people included in the sample. Separated and divorced women had a slightly higher prevalence rate than did separated and divorced men, but again the difference was not significant. The authors report that other variables such as age, social class and place of birth need to be taken into account, and that the contradictory findings about the relations between GHQ score and marital status may be attributable to the complexities of these interrelationships.

Appendix 2   Data Tables

Table Appendix 2.1: GHQ scores at time 1, time 2 and time 3

Mediation

Subject Name	Time 1	Time 2	Time 3
James	12.0	19.0	19.0
Richard	2.0	17.0	0.0
Helen	18.0	12.0	24.0
Molly	18.0	16.0	25.0
Average Score	**12.5**	**16.0**	**17.0**

Non-Mediation

Fiona	10.0	10.0	9.0
Laura	5.0	1.0	0.0
Sheila	19.0	7.0	11.0
Alison	19.0	14.0	11.0
Gina	8.0	4.0	8.0
Jill	10.0	13.0	0.0
Alice	21.0	22.0	15.0
Average Score	**13.1**	**10.1**	**7.7**
Overall Average	**12.9**	**12.2**	**11.0**

Table Appendix 2.2   GHQ scores by sub-scales at time 1, time 2 and time 3

GHQ Sub-Scale	Somatic Symptoms			Anxiety/ Insomnia			Social Dysfunction			Severe Depression			Totals		
	T1	T2	T3	T1	T2	T3	T1	T2	T3	T1	T2	T3	T1	T2	T3
Mediation															
James	1	2	4	6	6	5	0	6	5	5	5	5	12	19	19
Richard	0	6	0	1	7	0	1	4	0	0	0	0	2	17	0
Helen	6	5	7	6	7	7	3	0	5	3	0	5	18	12	24
Molly	4	5	7	6	6	6	4	3	6	4	2	6	18	16	25
Non-Mediation															
Fiona	4	4	4	4	5	5	2	1	0	0	0	0	10	10	9
Laura	0	0	0	1	1	0	4	0	0	0	0	0	5	1	0
Sheila	5	2	4	7	3	5	2	0	2	5	2	0	19	7	11
Alison	3	2	2	7	6	5	5	4	3	4	2	1	19	14	11
Gina	0	2	4	6	1	3	2	1	1	0	0	0	8	4	8
Jill	2	3	0	3	3	0	3	3	0	2	4	0	10	13	0
Alice	4	5	1	7	5	6	6	7	7	4	5	1	21	22	15

Table Appendix 2.3   **Average GHQ scores by sub-scale at time 1, time 2 and time 3**

GHQ Sub-Scale	Somatic Symptoms	Anxiety/ Insomnia	Social Dysfunction	Severe Depression	Average
Mediation					
Time 1	2.75	4.75	2.00	3.00	3.12
Time 2	4.50	6.50	3.25	1.75	4.00
Time 3	4.50	4.50	4.00	4.00	4.25
Average	3.92	5.25	3.08	2.92	
Non- Mediation					
Time 1	2.57	5.0	3.42	2.14	3.28
Time 2	2.57	3.42	2.14	1.85	2.53
Time 3	2.14	3.42	1.85	0.28	1.92
Average	2.42	3.94	2.47	1.96	

Table Appendix 2.4   Semi-structured interview data on symptoms experienced

Symptom	James	Richard	Helen	Molly	Fiona	Laura
Tension	4	5	4	5	4	4
Anxiety	4	4	4	5	4	4
Panic	4	?	2	1	3	5
Sleep disturbance	0	4	5	3	5	0
Concentration problems	4	1	3	4	2	4
Decision-making problems	4	4	3	3	1	5
Restlessness	3	2	3	1	3	4
Loss of appetite	2	1	0	0	0	0
Over-eating	0	1	5	3	0	5
Irritability	5	5	4	5	1	4
Lose/gain weight	0	5	5	3	0	5
Totals	*30*	*(32)*	*38*	*33*	*23*	*40*

	Sheila	Alison	Gina	Jill	Alice	*Totals*
Tension	5	5	5	4	5	*50*
Anxiety	5	3	5	2	5	*45*
Panic	5	2	5	2	3	*(32)*
Sleep disturbance	5	5	2	5	5	*39*
Concentration problems	5	3	2	3	5	*36*
Decision-making problems	5	3	2	1	4	*35*
Restlessness	5	5	3	1	5	*30*
Loss of appetite	2	1	2	0	5	*13*
Over-eating	0	0	0	2	5	*21*
Irritability	4	5	3	2	5	*43*
Lose/gain weight	2	1	0	3	2	*26*
Totals	*43*	*33*	*29*	*25*	*49*	

(0 = not at all, 5 = strongly)

Table Appendix 2.5   **Semi-structured interview data on feelings experienced**

Symptom	James	Richard	Helen	Molly	Fiona	Laura
Loss	5	2	5	5	4	5
Confusion	4	3	5	1	1	5
Anger	3	5	4	5	1	5
Emptiness	5	0	4	0	4	4
Upset	4	4	4	5	4	4
Trauma	5	2	3	5	0	5
Numbness	4	0	3	5	1	5
Loneliness	4	0	5	3	4	5
Fear	4	3	5	3	2	5
Failure	5	0	5	3	0	4
Low self esteem	5	0	5	4	3	4
Sadness	5	1	5	5	4	4
Totals	*53*	*20*	*53*	*44*	*28*	*55*

Symptom	Sheila	Alison	Gina	Jill	Alice	*Totals*
Loss	5	4	3	5	5	*48*
Confusion	5	3	2	4	5	*38*
Anger	5	5	5	5	3	*46*
Emptiness	5	5	4	5	5	*41*
Upset	5	5	4	5	5	*49*
Trauma	5	4	3	5	5	*42*
Numbness	5	5	5	4	5	*42*
Loneliness	2	4	5	5	5	*42*
Fear	4	3	3	3	4	*39*
Failure	0	5	2	3	5	*32*
Low self esteem	5	5	2	5	5	*43*
Sadness	5	4	4	5	5	*48*
Totals	*51*	*52*	*42*	*54*	*57*	

(0 = not at all, 5 = strongly)

Index

233